Refugees in New Destinations and Small Cities

Pablo S. Bose

Refugees in New Destinations and Small Cities

Resettlement in Vermont

Pablo S. Bose
Department of Geography
University of Vermont
Burlington, VT, USA

ISBN 978-981-15-6385-0   ISBN 978-981-15-6386-7   (eBook)
https://doi.org/10.1007/978-981-15-6386-7

Cover credit: Rutland, Vermont, photo by Chris Booth/vibecommercialimaging.com

This Palgrave Macmillan imprint is published by the registered company Springer Nature Singapore
Pte Ltd.
The registered company address is: 152 Beach Road, #21-01/04 Gateway East, Singapore 189721,
Singapore

Acknowledgments

This book is made possible by the support, critiques, feedback, and labor of many. It is about a place that I scarcely knew when I moved here and that I have grown to love in the years since. And perhaps even more, it is about the people who have been so generous in sharing their experiences as newcomers in Vermont and elsewhere with me. It has been my very great privilege to work with, learn from, and learn about individuals, families, and communities that have been through unimaginable upheaval, loss, trauma, and change and yet remain so strong, resilient, and unbroken. The refugee communities and diverse individuals that I have had the honor to work with and meet during the course of my research have always been a profound inspiration to me and give me hope and guidance in my own times of personal or professional doubts and questions.

I am thus especially grateful to leaders within the refugee and resettlement communities in Vermont whom I have come to know over the years, especially Jacob Bogre, Thato Ratsebe, and Rita Neopaney along with many other wonderful staff at AALV. The VT State Refugee

Coordinator Denise Lamoreux has been a constant source of information and encouragement. The Refugee and Immigrant Service Provider Network (RISPNET) meetings she organizes and leads each month are an amazing resource not only for academics like myself but for the broader community as a whole. Amila Merdzanovic, Judy Scott, and numerous staff with VRRP/USCRI-VT have also lent considerable assistance to me. Jenelle Eli and Katy Jones were of exceptional assistance in making contacts in Washington and with resettlement agencies nationally. Vermont's congressional delegation and staff—especially Susan Sussman and Diane Derby with Senator Patrick Leahy's office—have also been strong supporters for this work in Washington and in Vermont.

The research on which the book is based has been funded at various times by the National Science Foundation, the US Department of Transportation, and the Office of Refugee Resettlement, as well as by the University of Vermont (more specifically by the College of Arts and Sciences, the Department of Geography, Food Systems and the office of the Vice President for Research). I am especially appreciative of the guidance and assistance that Antoinette Winklerprins at the NSF and Lisa Aultman-Hall with the Transportation Research Center at UVM provided as I completed grants focused on resettlement and mobility respectively, while Dean William Falls of the College of Arts and Sciences at UVM has been tremendously encouraging for many years. The Office of Undergraduate Research at UVM has provided material support for many of my students to undertake theses, internships, and independent research with my community partners.

Other colleagues at UVM, past and present, have likewise been central to this work. Glen Elder brought me to Vermont for what I thought would be a short two-year stint, now going on well over a decade. Reecia Orzeck, Matt Himley, Carlos Vargas-Silva, Susannah McCandless, and Clayton Rosati made my first few bewildering years in a new discipline and a new home much more manageable. Meghan Cope and Beverley Wemple have been simply the best mentors one could ever hope for. Rashad Shabazz's work on blackness and urban environments and Teresa Mares' fantastic research with migrant farmworkers have helped me to rethink relationships between race and space in particular. I have learned more from Cherie Morse's research on rural communities and global migration and Vermont in general than from almost anyone else. Karen Fondacaro and Andrea Green's (many) community-based interventions have been inspiring and thought-provoking. Harlan Morehouse, Shelly Rayback, Ingrid Nelson, Lesley-Ann Dupigny-Giroux, Jenny Baldwin, and Vibeke Burley have reminded me daily how lucky I am to be in the Geography Department. Other colleagues at UVM I would like to thank include Randall Harp, Alex Zakaras, David Massell, Paul Martin, Jinny Huh, Joel Goldberg, Alec Ewald, Richard Watts, Susan Munkres, Alan Rubin, Vicki Brennan, and Cynthia Reyes. Beyond UVM, I am appreciative of collaborations and feedback from Elizabeth Lunstrum, Denver Nixon, Margaret Walton-Roberts, Alison Mountz, Jennifer Hyndman, Elizabeth Chacko, Karin Jacobsen, and Peter Penz.

Jonah Steinberg's work on transnationalism, diaspora, and migration has complicated and broadened my understanding of all of these complex formations and processes. He has been a particularly helpful sounding board and critic for many of my ideas and the direction of my research. I am deeply grateful for his friendship and help over the years, as I am also for that of Emily Manetta and of Zaki, Amittai, and Ananya.

My students have been absolutely instrumental in the research that has gone into producing this book. Of particular note has been my main assistant and collaborator for the past several years, Lucas Grigri. Others I have worked with and learned from include Brenna Foley, Sammie Ibrahim, Tilden Remerleitch, Meraz Mostafa, Gillian Tiley, Kim Furtado, Elizabeth Wolfe, Erika Shepard, Emma Gianoplus, Annie Ryan, Emily Klofft, Alex Rosenberg, Sarah Barrett, Tony Hollop, Emma Tait, Tyler Wilkinson-Ray, Rachel Ocher, and Isabel Dunkley. I am very appreciative of the efficiency and efforts of Josh Pitt and Rachel Daniel at Palgrave Macmillan in getting this project to publication.

Perhaps no one has helped me understand Vermont more than the extended Laramee clan, especially the insights about places like Winooski given to me by Armand and Bernice Laramee. Monica and Bill Laramee have offered much support and many opportunities to learn about Vermont (especially outside of Burlington), while I gain so much each year from Collin, Sophie, Elliot, Jane, Wren, and Quinn. Billy and Wendy, Michael and Kathleen, and Jamie and Allison have introduced me to new and productive ways of thinking about what building a good life in a new place means.

I am as ever thankful to my sister Sarika Bose for her eternal love and support. My mother Mandakranta Bose continues to amaze me with her capacity to take on so many different projects and stay busy no matter what the world does around her. My father, Tirthankar Bose, as he seems to have been since I was in high school, provides the indispensable final word on so much that I write, offering critical commentary, sage advice, and careful editing suggestions.

And finally, this book would not be possible without the myriad contributions of my daughter Lily—from helping retake higher-resolution photographs, to paginating the index, to choosing a cover and so much more. Her boundless curiosity, intelligence, and patience impress me each day. And I thank my wife, Alisha Laramee, my partner in life and in my community-based research, who has taught me more about these topics, about thoughtful interventions, and how to critically interrogate my own assumptions and biases more than I could have imagined and thus made my work all the better for it.

Contents

Abbreviations

AALV	Association of Africans Living in Vermont
CSA	Community-Supported Agriculture
DACA	Deferred Action on Childhood Arrivals
DCF	Department of Children and Families (Vermont)
ELL	English Language Learning
ORR	Office of Refugee Resettlement
PRM	Bureau of Population, Refugees, and Migration
R & P	Reception and Placement
RAPP	Refugee Agricultural Partnership Project
SIV	Special Immigrant Visa
TPS	Temporary Protected Status
USCIS	United States Citizenship and Immigration Services
USCRI-VT	United States Committee for Refugees and Immigrants—Vermont
USRAP	United States Refugee Admissions Program
VOLAG	Voluntary Agency (resettlement agency)
VRRP	Vermont Refugee Resettlement Program

List of Figures

List of Tables

appropriate are existing services for helping refugees? How are social services affected by the influx of new clients? Have inter-ethnic tensions developed between refugees and other migrant or minority groups or with the society at large? In many mid-sized towns across the US, civic leaders, school officials, community organizers, and the population at large have been raising just such questions and concerns regarding their capacity to incorporate and acculturate refugee newcomers; in recent years, these questions have become increasingly contentious within the deeply divided political cultures of the country.

Refugees in an Age of Rising Xenophobia

It is not only in the US that we have witnessed a rise in controversies and subsequent backlash regarding refugees. A similar pattern of demonizing and mischaracterizing refugees (and immigrants more broadly) can be seen across the globe. One could argue that immigration is—along with climate change—one of the defining issues of the contemporary moment. This has in part to do with the sheer number of refugees and displaced persons in the world today, the largest since the end of the Second World War. And these numbers have been growing steadily over the last decade, from approximately 34 million in 2010 to over 70 million in 2019 (UNHCR 2019). While those who are foreign-born may still make up less than 5% of the world's population, the *sense* that so many people are on the move is more pervasive than ever, especially with images of migrants fleeing war, poverty, disease, natural disaster, and environmental degradation dominating our screens. This has in turn inflamed political debates and discussions and animated a resurgent set of nativist and populist sentiments worldwide, with immigrants and refugees often scapegoats for a wide-ranging set of fears regarding 'outsiders.' Xenophobic rhetoric, restrictive citizenship and immigration policies, the increased detention and deterrence of asylum seekers, protests against refugees, diminished capacity, and willingness to allow resettlements are all examples of this backlash against refugees.

In Europe, the drawn-out drama regarding the UK's withdrawal from the European Union plays against a backdrop of anti-immigrant sentiment and a desire among a share of the population to have greater control over national borders. Similar themes—as well as an explicit fear of refugees and asylum seekers—have fueled a rise in the popularity of right-wing and anti-immigrant political parties in France, Sweden, Finland, Germany, Hungary, Italy, Spain, Greece, Poland, and other countries in the EU. But it is not just in Europe that we see such trends. Australia has continued to use off-shore detention to try and discourage migrants from reaching its shores. In Myanmar and India, long-standing resentments against impoverished Muslim populations have led to the stripping of citizenship, forced expulsion, and in the worst cases genocidal attacks against those deemed to be 'illegal immigrants.' Migrant laborers find themselves demonized and attacked in South Africa, South Korea, and Brazil. Travel bans, border walls, visa restrictions, and cuts to refugee programs seem to be the order of the day.

The US is certainly not immune to such patterns; indeed, one might argue that the world's preeminent political power leads the way in its retreat from humanitarian obligations and multilateral protections for those in peril as well as in rising anti-immigrant policies. It is worth noting that while much of the Trump administration's rhetoric has focused on controlling or reducing unauthorized migration through border walls, enforcement, and deportation, at least as much effort has gone into slashing legal migration (Meissner and Gelatt 2019). This has included attempts to eliminate the Visa Diversity Lottery program (which allocates immigration approvals to applicants from underrepresented countries), reduce and restrict visa programs that bring students and highly skilled workers to the country (such as the H1-B and J-1 programs), and institute new restrictions on immigrants' use of social services, including housing, food assistance, and medical care (the so-called public charge rule). The Trump administration has also cut a number of other related programs for legal migration, including the Deferred Action for Childhood Arrivals (DACA) program which protected a select group of migrants who had been brought to the US as children and had since proven themselves to be 'worthy' of legitimization because of military service, education, or employment. The Trump administration has also proposed rolling back protections for some 97% of those granted Temporary Protected Status (TPS) due to unsafe conditions in their home countries because of natural disasters or conflict in places like El Salvador, Haiti, Honduras, and Yemen (Miyares et al. 2019). The elimination of the DACA and TPS programs alone affects between 1 and 1.5 million individuals. The closure of these programs has meant more than just a reduction in numbers; they have suggested a fundamental redefinition of the terms of protection—on what grounds will the US grant or even consider sanctuary? The very notion of safety and what constitutes harm has been transformed in recent years as factors such as domestic and gender- or sexuality-based violence become less accepted by immigration officials.

Refugee resettlement in the US has similarly been upended in recent years. The US Refugee Admissions Program (USRAP) has existed since 1980, with millions resettled especially from the former Soviet Union, Southeast Asia, and Cuba. The numbers who have been accepted into the US have always risen and fallen in accordance with US foreign policy objectives as much as any humanitarian objectives. But by the second Obama administration, these numbers had stabilized at roughly 75,000 approvals a year. In 2016, the US increased this capacity by 10,000 spaces allocated to Syrian refugees to deal with the exodus from that country's civil war and ongoing conflicts. The plan was to raise this limit to 110,000 individuals for 2017, with much of that increase again attributed to Syrian refugees. While the USRAP has seen cuts in the past—the years following 9/11 saw steep declines in the actual numbers of refugees admitted to the US, for example—it has been virtually gutted by the federal government since 2017. The Trump administration took aim at the USRAP at the same time as it attempted to institute a progressive set of so-called Muslim travel bans. While barring the entry of citizens of several Muslim-majority countries, these bans called for a moratorium on any new refugee resettlements until vague new 'extreme vetting' measures were in place (furthering the inaccurate assertion that adequate screenings of refugees were not already being undertaken).

While the travel bans were contested in the courts (as the termination of the DACA and TPS programs have been) before a modified version was allowed to stand, the cuts to the refugee program have increased

but as Vanderbeck (2006) suggests, a particular kind of rural whiteness has long been a tool used by the state to market itself to wealthy vacationers. What does it mean to be a newcomer—especially one who is marked by race, ethnicity, religion, language, or some other characteristic as 'other'—in this homogenous and apparently bucolic space? For many refugees from Somalia, Sudan, and other parts of Africa, they find their identity marked as both black and often Muslim and are thereby treated to the same forms of stereotypes prevalent in other parts of the US. On the other hand, Central European refugees such as Bosnians and Kosovars—while no less 'othered' initially by language or religion—may be able over time to 'whiten' in ways akin to the trajectory of working-class European immigrants in turn-of-the-century America. Yet others such as the Bhutanese refugees who constitute one of the largest recently resettled populations in the US and have achieved remarkable successes in terms of employment and education in a relatively short period may be viewed through the lens of the 'model minority' formation that has been deployed so perniciously within American racial politics.

What do such racial dynamics mean in the daily lives of refugees, and what implications do they hold for the towns in which they are placed? In this book, I look not only at the history of resettlement of refugees in Vermont, but the ways in which they have reshaped the landscapes of their new homes while simultaneously being transformed themselves. What does the story of resettlement in Vermont teach us about the placement of refugees in new destinations like Burlington? How are we to understand the ways in which a semi-rural state with a low-density population, a scattering of small towns, a dearth of economic opportunity, and a homogenous population has dealt with the influx of newcomers from all corners of the world? I argue in this book that examining the impacts of refugee resettlement on communities, towns, and individuals alike is crucial for understanding the changing demographics and cultural patterns in multiple locations, from Vermont to Iowa and Ohio, from the US to Norway and Germany, and to many others besides.

Methodology

The primary methodological tradition in which this book and the inquiry on which it is based are grounded is participatory, action-oriented research utilizing a mix of qualitative techniques—interviews, surveys, and community-mapping workshops. Its goals are to contribute to the scholarly understanding of the phenomenon of refugee resettlement in new destinations like Vermont, refine policymaking regarding these trends, and improve the outcomes and lived experiences of refugees and reception sites alike. Participatory research provides both the conceptual framework and the methodological tools to help produce such results. As Kindon and Elwood (2009: 21) describe in their overview of the research tradition:

> [its] goal is not just to describe or analyse social reality, but to change it…[commonly], research takes place within a group setting involving the academic researcher as a facilitator of focus-group discussions, interviews, diarying and participatory techniques such as community mapping and diagramming.

Participatory approaches have long been influential in a number of disciplines seeking to connect scholarly inquiry actively with the subjects of study, communities being investigated, and in service of broader goals to better the world. We see numerous examples of this orientation, from the participatory rural appraisal (PRA) strategies of international development work beginning in the 1960s (Chambers 1994) to the catalytic nature of community-based projects in social work (Rubin and Babbie 2011), from attempts to destabilize hierarchies between researcher and researched in education (Cammarota 2017) to the interventionist goals of Participatory Action Research (PAR) in a range of disciplines.

Within human geography, participatory research has had an equally long-standing and significant history (Kindon et al. 2007). Pain (2004: 652) describes it as a 'collaborative and nonhierarchical approach which overturns the usual ways in which academics work outside universities.' She highlights in particular the contributions that feminist and radical geographers have made in terms of making research more reflexive and self-critical, and as a result both insightful and more socially relevant. The lessons provided by participatory research have influenced the ways in which all of the research instruments I have utilized have been developed, with regular input and feedback from community partners in shaping these tools. I have thus often prioritized the objectives of my community partners and the need to respond to pressing and ongoing issues within which they operate over scholarly output. For example, I have participated in discussions and debate, provided media interviews, and produced reports meant to counteract xenophobic rhetoric and the mischaracterization of immigrants and refugees in public discourse both locally and nationally. I have also worked to provide community partners with data and analysis that will be helpful for their own advocacy efforts and to help strengthen their organizational capacity. In all of this work, I have had the luxury and privilege of a tenured academic appointment to support my own efforts.

My community partners—especially the Association of Africans Living in Vermont, the US Committee on Refugees and Immigrants—Vermont, and the Office of the Vermont State Refugee Coordinator—have been invaluable throughout the process. They have helped me to find participants, identify significant issues, and helped to shape and reshape the research project itself. Halfway through my work on these projects, my wife took up a new job working for AALV and directing their refugee agriculture project. She has provided insight and assistance into many of the dynamics I describe in this book and we have collaborated (especially working together supervising student internships), though we have tried to maintain some regular distance between our professional spheres. These connections have helped me to widen the scope of my inquiry beyond Vermont, providing leads and links to other organizations and examples in parallel and distinct cases. I have also provided regular presentations of my research findings in-progress at various meetings and venues and have received useful, constructive, and candid feedback. I have even had the opportunity to collaboratively analyze some of the data with my partners and embark on shorter projects that they have initiated, as detailed below. Projects utilizing such frameworks—often described also as 'community geography'—have been emphasized in recent years by work on healthcare inequality in low-income neighborhoods (Hawthorne and Kwan 2012), emergency food needs in underserved areas (Robinson 2011), citizen participation in urban planning (Wilson and Tewdwr-Jones 2019), and action-oriented research with 'hidden' or potentially marginalized communities (Browne 2005).

While participatory research is the overarching framework for this book, it also draws from several other traditions. Spatial demography—an approach usually associated with quantitative methods—has a long tradition of tracking the macro (national and international)-scale of migration patterns and in producing multiregional demographic models. It has seen a reemergence in recent years, connected to new technologies and new models such as fractal analysis and fuzzy models used to analyze population change in small areas (Akkerman 1992; Goodchild and Janelle 2004). Within the discipline of geography, spatial demography has begun to be taken up more recently by those interested in the patterns of migration to new destinations (Goodchild et al. 2011; Weeks et al. 2007; Weeks 2004) through its explicit linkage of demographic characteristics, spatial statistics, and GIS. Spatial demography makes clear the connection between where you live and who you are; approaches from this tradition help to situate the project's parallel interest in refugees and receiving locations alike.

Finally, since this book also utilizes refugees' and residents' perceptions of landscape change as a result of migration, it draws on the extensive discussions within cultural geography of a 'sense of place' (Massey 2005; Schein 1997). It takes up the debates regarding, for example, non-representational theory and the challenge to structuralist readings of specific locations (Lorimer 2008) to examine the ways that refugees and new destinations are made and remade through the resettlement process. In particular, it builds on work in mobilities research, especially mobile ethnographies (Sheller and Urry 2006; Cresswell 2012) to explore the ways that place may be understood by the actions taken by those within them. Or as Vannini (2012) has suggested in his study of island life on Canada's west coast, places are constituted by the dynamic interplay of its inhabitants, their 'taskscapes,' and a host of practices of creative incorporation. It is to discover the complex ways in which refugee and new destination landscapes are co-created, challenged, and redefined that this book turns to community visualization exercises—keeping this sense of the malleability of place in mind.

The emergent field of qualitative GIS (Cope and Elwood 2009) is of especial use therefore for this research. While GIS conceived of as a primarily quantitative field that is both technology-fixated and unyieldingly positivist in nature has long been critiqued by feminist and critical scholars (Hanson 2002; McLafferty 2002; Schuurman 2000; Kwan 2002), Pavlovskaya (2006) argues against a binary view of GIS and suggests instead that it has always been non-quantitative in origin. Knigge and Cope (2006) similarly reject a dichotomous view in their proposal of an integrated analytical method they call 'grounded visualization,' which combines rigorous qualitative data with quantitative, often technologically mediated forms of geographic visualization. For Wilson (2009), qualitative GIS represents a powerful and critical mode of inquiry, one that can help us answer important research questions while simultaneously engaging with the issues of positionality and power that go into both analyzing and representing spatial knowledge. Qualitative GIS is not simply another way to triangulate research; as Nightingale (2003) demonstrates in her work on community forestry in Nepal, it can be a vital way to uncover the silences and gaps that reveal the very partiality of knowledge that challenges positivist traditions. In this book, I have used qualitative GIS, drawing on multiple methods and data to visualize spatial relations. These include using community-mapping approaches with refugee communities and integrating ward and neighborhood maps with oral histories and photographs to examine diverse uses of public space in new destinations. I also combine ethnographic interviews with resettlement agency staff and with federal resettlement statistics to create a 'grounded visualization' of placement patterns at a number of different scales. I have also utilized web-based GIS applications in working with refugees and service providers to visualize mobility and access issues in terms of the key acculturation processes that are the focus of the study.

Methods and Sources

There are several forms of data that were collected and analyzed to form the basis of this book. The primary source data include interviews with key informants and stakeholders at the national and local levels, nearly 800 collected over a ten-year period, over half of which were conducted in the Vermont context. These interviews were with many stakeholders involved with refugee resettlement including politicians, refugees, resettlement workers, community leaders, social service providers, civic officials, and many others besides them. I have found such semi-structured interviews to be a particularly effective method for investigating my key research questions, following up on promising leads and exploring unexpected pathways and discovering new insights.

Fieldwork visits and participant observation were also important tools for my research. I have visited many neighborhoods within Vermont as well as other parallel sites to catalog the effect of the influx of refugees at a local scale. During the course of this form of fieldwork, I had the opportunity to speak with many people who were both in favor of and opposed to the resettlement of refugees, asylum seekers, and irregular migrants to better understand their perspectives. Specific towns in Vermont that feature in this book include the key resettlement communities of Burlington and Winooski, as well as the adjacent towns of Essex, Essex Junction, and South Burlington. I also spent some time in the city of Rutland, a town in the southern part of the state that had a short-lived and controversial experience with refugee resettlement. Some of the parallel case studies I also draw upon include fieldwork visits to resettlement sites in Kentucky, Arizona, and Iowa in the US, British Columbia, and Ontario, Canada, southern Germany, and southern France.

I have also collected other data including the results from two sets of indicator surveys with 100 recently resettled refugees in Vermont in 2015–2016. These participants were asked to fill out a 30-question survey within three months of arrival regarding their aspirations and hopes in six categories—education, employment, housing, transportation, health care, and civic involvement. I asked questions regarding the wages that refugees hoped to receive in jobs, the educational opportunities they might wish to pursue, the number of bedrooms in a home they might occupy, and the ways they might wish to participate in social organizations in their new homes. One year later, I re-surveyed the same 100 people and asked what the outcomes had been—how much pay they received, whether they had taken classes, how many bedrooms were in their home, whether they had participated in any social groups, and so on.

To get a better sense of the reception that refugees have received in Vermont in particular, I also added four questions to the annual Vermonter Poll conducted by the Center for Rural Studies at the University of Vermont. Between 2015 and 2019, I asked a representative sample of the state population about their level of support for refugee resettlement, who was most responsible for successful resettlement outcomes, what component of outcomes were the most important, and where in the state refugees should be placed. My research collected maps, diaries, photographs, and other materials produced by participants in workshops designed to understand landscape change as a result of resettlement. Most extensive among these methods was a series of Photovoice projects in which we recruited recent arrivals to take photographs of important locations and places within refugee neighborhoods and enclaves in Vermont (Image 1.1).

All of this information has been transcribed, categorized, and analyzed using qualitative software (NVivo), focusing in particular on themes regarding the suitability and desirability of the new destinations for refugee resettlement. The findings in this book are by no means comprehensive but they represent these multiple methods and indeed research projects that I have used to explore these issues at length. Among the projects that the data have been collected from are the following (Table 1.1).

Aside from two of the projects—which expanded the scope of my inquiry to look at the context of refugee resettlement, asylum, and irregular migration in the US and across much of the Global North over the past two decades—my research has focused on a series of in-depth case studies in Vermont. The work has involved multiple methods, locations, and examples throughout these various projects, with qualitative and mixed methods particularly prominent.

Image 1.1 Corner store and market serving new refugee populations

Plan of the Book

Refugees in the Green Mountain State comprises 10 chapters, divided into three sections. These sections focus on three scales of inquiry—national/international, the city, and the body. Section 1, 'Context,' gives the reader an overview of global migration and resettlement patterns and the particulars of refugees in the US and in Vermont. The introductory chapter with which this section begins offers a look at contemporary trends in forced migration and resettlement and the connections between what is taking place in Vermont and what is happening nationally and globally. Chapter 2 gives the reader a more specific and in-depth review of refugee resettlement in the US, beginning with the post-Second World War period but focusing mainly on the program as it has evolved since the mid-1970s, what its structure is and where refugees have been placed across the US. In Chapter 2, I draw in particular on data I have collected and analyzed regarding settlement trends across the US between 2012

Table 1.1 Selected research projects on refugees undertaken by the author

Project	Funding source or community partner	Time period	N	Method
Refugee mobilities and transportation equity	US Department of Transportation	2008–2010	300 50	Surveys Interviews
Refugees in US-Canada Border Regions	Government of Canada	2009–2010	20 5	Interviews Site visits
Refugees in Vermont	UVM College of Arts and Sciences	2010–2011	100	Interviews
Gender, Age, Transportation	US Department of Transportation	2011–2012	300 50	Surveys Interviews
Food and Migration	UVM Food Systems Program	2011–2012	50	Interviews
Refugee resettlement in non-traditional destinations	National Science Foundation	2014–2018	300 100 5 5 2	Interviews Surveys Polls Site visits Photovoice
Comparative global refugee resettlement policies	UVM REACH Program	2016–2018	5 100	Countries Interviews
Asylum and protection on the US-Canada Border	Social Sciences and Humanities Research Council of Canada	2018–2019	4 25 100	Sites Interviews Surveys
Refugee youth development	AALV	2018–2020	25 100	Interviews Surveys
Refugee employment	AALV and USCRI-VT	2019–2020	50	Interviews

and 2016. Chapter 3 examines Vermont's own immigration record and details the history of labor migration from Canada and Europe and the much more recent influx of refugees from Asia, Central Europe, and Africa. I also examine in this chapter attitudes toward refugee resettlement in Vermont, drawing on the results of opinion polls I have conducted with residents of the state from 2014 to 2019.

The second section of the book—'Places of Settlement'—focuses on the impacts of newcomers on communities in Vermont, looking particularly at the community and neighborhood level and three particular Vermont towns. Chapter 4 looks at the major site of resettlement, the city of Burlington and in particular its Old North End neighborhood, a long-standing immigrant and low-income area. Chapter 5 examines a smaller community across the river from Burlington, the town of Winooski which has a similarly long history of immigrant settlement and is generally poorer than its neighbor. Both of these have been the main areas into which refugees have been initially settled in Vermont, and in these two chapters, I look at some of the successes and failures in each, especially in terms of the impacts that refugees have had on local schools, employment, and housing. I draw on interviews with residents new and old as well as on the results of a Photovoice project with refugees reflecting on their perceptions of their new homes in these chapters. In the final chapter of this section, Chapter 6, I look at the failed attempt to bring refugees to the southern Vermont town of Rutland. This chapter explores the rationales behind the planned resettlement, the controversies that arose in 2016, and the ultimate result for the town as well as for the refugees, and connects this local context to the national debates on immigration and refugee resettlement.

Section 3 of the book—'Transforming Identities'—shifts the focus to the embodied experiences of refugees within their resettlement sites. In Chapter 7, I draw on surveys and interviews with refugees to look at the challenges of mobilities and transportation for newcomers, what encountering American car culture looks like, and what barriers and obstacles to integration constrained movement might bring. Chapter 8 focuses on the importance of food and migrant identities and explores the various ways in which refugees attempt to forge connections to old and new homes. These include starting new restaurants and ethnic grocery stores that

cater to multiple clientele and reproduce familiar cuisines, and participating in an innovative refugee agriculture program. Chapter 9 takes up
the complex questions of hybrid, contested, and complicated identities
and explores the ways that racialization, language politics, and cultural
transformation help to forge refugee identities. I draw in particular on
research with both youth and elder refugee communities in this chapter
to explore very different notions of heritage, culture, and obligation. The
book's concluding chapter draws some lessons from the story of refugees
in Vermont to outline some new directions for research, activism, and
policy regarding newcomers in non-traditional immigrant destinations.
As I suggested at the beginning of this introduction, the very fact that
Vermont is a small—indeed a tiny—state lends it validity as a micro-
cosmic site for the study of migration as a many-layered phenomenon
across the entire American nation, indeed across global humanity.

References

Akkerman, Abraham. 1992. Fuzzy targeting of population niches in urban
    planning and the fractal dimension of demographic change. *Urban Studies*
    29 (7): 1093–1113.
Browne, Katharine. 2005. Snowball sampling: Using social networks to
    research non-heterosexual women. *International Journal of Social Research
    Methodology* 1464–5300 (8): 47–60.
Cammarota, Julio. 2017. Youth participatory action research: A pedagogy of
    transformational resistance for Critical Youth Studies. *Journal for Critical
    Education Policy Studies* 15 (2): 190–213.
Chambers, Robert. 1994. The origins and practice of participatory rural
    appraisal. *World Development* 22 (7): 953–969.
Cope, Meghan, and Sarah Elwood (eds.). 2009. *Qualitative GIS: A mixed
    methods approach*. Thousand Oaks: Sage.
Cresswell, Tim. 2012. Mobilities II: Still. *Progress in Human Geography* 36 (5):
    645–653.
Goodchild, Michael, and Donald Janelle. 2004. Thinking spatially in the social
    sciences. In *Spatially integrated social science*, ed. Michael Goodchild and
    Donald Janelle. Oxford: Oxford University Press.

Goodchild, Michael, Donald Janelle, and Stephen Matthews. 2011. Future directions in spatial demography. *UC Santa Barbara: Center for Spatial Studies*. Santa Barbara: UCSB.

Hanson, Susan. 2002. Connections. *Gender, Place and Culture* 9 (3): 301–303.

Hawthorne, T., and M.-P. Kwan. 2012. Using GIS and perceived distance to understand the unequal geographies of healthcare in lower-income urban neighborhoods. *The Geographical Journal* 178 (1): 18–30.

Johnston, Ron, Michael Poulsen, and James Forrest. 2003. And did the walls come tumbling down? Ethnic residential segregation in four US metropolitan areas 1980–2000. *Urban Geography* 24 (7): 560–581.

Kindon, Sara, and Sarah Elwood. 2009. Introduction: More than methods—Reflections on participatory action research in geographic teaching, learning and research. *Journal of Geography in Higher Education* 33 (1): 19–32.

Kindon, Sara, Rachel Pain, and Mike Kesby (eds.). 2007. *Participatory action research and methods: Connecting people, participation and place*. New York: Routledge.

Knigge, LaDona, and Meghan Cope. 2006. Grounded visualization: Integrating the analysis of qualitative and quantitative data through grounded theory and visualization. *Environment and Planning a* 38 (11): 2021–2037.

Kwan, M.-P. 2002. Feminist visualization: Re-envisioning GIS as a method in feminist geographic research. *Annals of the Association of American Geographers* 92 (4): 645–661.

Lorimer, Hayden. 2008. Cultural geography: Non-representational conditions and concerns. *Progress in Human Geography* 32 (4): 551–559.

Massey, Doreen. 2005. *For space*. London: Sage.

Massey, Douglas, and Jonathan Tannen. 2018. Suburbanization and segregation in the United States: 1970–2010. *Ethnic and Racial Studies* 41 (9): 1594–1611.

Massey, Douglas, Jonathan Rothwell, and Thurston Domina. 2009. The changing bases of segregation in the United States. *The Annals of the American Academy of Political and Social Science* 626 (1): 74–90.

McLafferty, Sarah L. 2002. Mapping women's worlds: Knowledge, power and the bounds of GIS. *Gender, Place and Culture* 9 (3): 263–269.

Meissner, Doris, and Julia Gelatt. 2019. *Eight key US immigration policy issues: State of play and unanswered questions*. Washington, DC: Immigration Policy Institute.

Miyares, Ines, Richard Wright, Alison Mountz, and Adrian Bailey. 2019. Truncated transnationalism, the tenuousness of temporary protected status, and Trump. *Journal of Latin American Geography* 18 (1): 210–216.

Nightingale, Andrea. 2003. A feminist in the forest: Situated knowledges and mixing methods in natural resource management. *ACME: an International E-Journal for Critical Geographers* 2 (1): 77–90.

Omi, Michael, and Howard Winant. 1994. *Racial formation in the United States: From the 1960s to the 1990s*, 2nd ed. New York: Routledge.

Pain, Rachel. 2004. Social geography: Participatory research. *Progress in Human Geography* 28 (5): 652–663.

Pavlovskaya, Marianna. 2006. Theorizing with GIS: A tool for critical geographies? *Environment and Planning a* 38 (11): 2003–2020.

Portes, Alejandro, and Ruben Rumbaut. 2014. *Immigrant America: A portrait*. Oakland, CA: University of California Press.

Robinson, Jonnell. 2011. Points, lines and people: Plotting a course for community geography. Public presentation, October 15. University of Vermont.

Rubin, Allen, and Earl Babbie (eds.). 2011. *Research methods for social work*. Belmont, CA: Brooks/Cole.

Schein, Richard H. 1997. The place of landscape: A conceptual framework for interpreting an American Scene. *Annals of the Association of American Geographers* 87 (4): 660–680.

Schuurman, Nadine. 2000. Trouble in the heartland: GIS and its critics in the 1990s. *Progress in Human Geography* 24 (4): 569–590.

Sheller, Mimi, and John Urry. 2006. The new mobilities paradigm. *Environment and Planning a* 38 (2): 207–226.

UNHCR. 2019. Figures at a glance. Available from https://www.unhcr.org/en-us/figures-at-a-glance.html. Accessed January 26, 2020.

Vanderbeck, Robert. 2006. Vermont and the imaginative geographies of American whiteness. *Annals of the Association of American Geographers* 96 (3): 641–659.

Vannini, Phillip, and Jonathan Taggart. 2012. Doing islandness: A Non-representational approach to an island's sense of place. *Cultural Geographies* 20 (2): 225–242.

Weeks, John. 2004. The role of spatial analysis in demographic research. In *Spatially integrated social science: Examples in best practice*, ed. M. Goodchild and D. Janelle, 381–399. New York: Oxford University Press.

Weeks, Gregory, John Weeks, and Amy Weeks. 2007. Latino immigration to the U.S. South: 'Carolatinos' and public policy in Charlotte, North Carolina. *Latino(a) Research Review* 6 (1–2): 50–72.

Wilson, Matthew. 2009. Towards a genealogy of qualitative GIS. In *Qualitative GIS: A mixed methods approach*, ed. M. Cope and S. Elwood, 156–170. Los Angeles: Sage.

Wilson, Alexander, and Mark Tewdwr-Jones. 2019. Let's draw and talk about urban change: Deploying digital technology to encourage citizen participation in urban planning. *Environment and Planning B: Urban Analytics and City Science*: 2399808319831290.

2

The US and Refugee Resettlement

As I have argued in the previous chapter, the landscape of refugee resettlement in the US has changed dramatically since 2017. While the US was once one of the main third country resettlement locations in the global refugee system, its participation has dwindled significantly. The US Refugee Admissions Program (USRAP) is thus at a crossroads, threatened by a president and an administration that does not believe in its mission, its history, its importance, its future, or its very existence. In this first section of the book, I provide the background to better understand the current situation. I begin in these two chapters by focusing on the international and national scales, to examine the processes through which refugees end up in a place like Vermont. What are the politics and what is the history behind this process? What is the structure of the USRAP and how has it evolved over time? How has migration operated historically in Vermont and how has this too changed over time?

Since its inception in 1980, the USRAP has placed well over three million refugees across the US. In this chapter, I provide context and parallels for the arrivals in Vermont by looking at the evolution of the USRAP. I do so in four parts. In the first, I look briefly at the forces that push people out of their homes; in other words, the factors that create a

© The Author(s) 2020
P. S. Bose, *Refugees in New Destinations and Small Cities*,
https://doi.org/10.1007/978-981-15-6386-7_2

'migration crisis' in the first place. In the second, I examine the history of the USRAP—how many refugees have been accepted and from where, starting at the very beginning of the program. In the third, I describe the nature and structure of the refugee program in the US—what agencies are involved, what kinds of supports exist for refugees, and what some of the changes look like. In the fourth part, I look at the trends of refugee resettlement across the US in recent years to better situate the story in Vermont.

A World on the Move?

There are many reasons why people might leave their homes either voluntarily or under duress. In some cases, the migration is temporary—for seasonal or occasional labor, for education, to take care of a family member, to pursue a love, to try a new adventure, or even as a flight for short-term shelter. In others, the move is more permanent—for a job in another place, to reunite with family, in search of opportunity or freedom, to be safe from harm, or to reinvent oneself (de Haas et al. 2019). These so-called push and pull factors that drive migration are as varied (and yet as old) as human history itself, although the pace and scale of contemporary globalization often make it seem as though all the world is constantly and consistently on the move. When we actually look at the patterns of global migration, however, we see that despite our sense that populations are in constant motion, the opposite is in fact true. Even with a surge in global refugee populations due to instability and conflict in many parts of the world, the total number of migrants—that is people who lived outside of their country of origin and including economic, labor, and forced migrants—across the globe is estimated to be under 5% of the overall global population (UNHCR 2019).

When we examine the major drivers of migration across the world today, several particular themes stand out. One is the continued significance of economic motivations—both seasonal and more long term—in the movement of people for work. Particularly strong evidence of this trend can be seen in the enormous amounts of money that continue to be sent by overseas workers back to their countries of origin. Known as 'remittances,' such monies today rank second only to oil exports globally, reaching $689 billion in 2018 with $529 billion of that figure going from workers to the developing world and far outpacing both foreign direct investment and aid to developing countries (World Bank 2019). Much of this money has moved informally; those who have left home often send resources to assist their families in maintaining their lives or in building newer and better ones. This includes helping a parent to improve a house or purchase a larger plot of land, sending money to build a village hospital or a community school, or enabling distant relatives to live a more affluent lifestyle relative to their neighbors. The two main sets of flows of labor and capital we see in the world today in terms of remittances are from North America (primarily the US) to Latin America and the Caribbean (primarily Mexico) and from the Persian Gulf (especially the United Arab Emirates) to South Asia (primarily India).

Economics also drives other forms of migration—for example of skilled professionals and other transnational elites all across the world. These include doctors, engineers, and lawyers from both the developed and less-developed world to cities such as Dubai, Singapore, London, New York, and Tokyo. For many regions and countries, the movement of such people through so-called brain drain can be both a boon and a blessing—a benefit if such skilled people are coming into their cities or sending money home, but a significant burden if the loss of such talent diminishes one's home (Agrawal et al. 2011). The movement of professionals and other diasporic or transnational elites across the world has also played a significant role in a number of other processes including global gentrification, urbanization, and the development of new forms of ethnic enclaves (Bose 2015; King 2004).

Such movements of people, money, and skills have drawn the attention not only of scholars, but also of national governments and international organizations, especially as the importance of transnational networks in long-distance political conflicts remains as strong today in the 'global war on terror' as it was in previous decades with the involvement of expatriate Irish, Sri Lankan or Serbian and Croatian populations in the Balkans, South Asia, and the British Isles. Global conflicts also contribute to one of the largest contemporary population movements today that of refugees. Today, as discussed in the introduction, over 70 million people worldwide are considered to be forced migrants (UNHCR 2019); that is, people who have been forced to flee their homes and livelihoods due to persecution, civil war, or other forms of violence. These numbers include official refugees, asylum seekers, and internally displaced persons (those not forced across a border but still outside of their homes) but do not include groups displaced by development projects (such as the building of dams or roads) or by the potential effects of climate change. There is an ongoing debate as to whether 'environmental' or 'developmental' forced displacement should be recognized but it is currently outside of the scope of UNHCR or international legal protections which are focused mainly on conflict and persecution where victims and perpetrators are (somewhat) easier to identify (Penz et al. 2011; Bose and Lunstrum 2019). Ongoing conflicts in North and Central Africa, in the Middle East, and in parts of South Asia are particular sources of refugee flight today. Still, refugees remain a relatively small part of the overall immigrant population worldwide.

In the context of the US, the past three decades have been witness to the largest surge of immigration into the US since the late nineteenth century (Portes and Rumbaut 2014). But where a century ago the main immigrant sending countries to America were European ones, today they are primarily Latin American and Asian. And where in the late nineteenth century it was in New York, Chicago, and San Francisco that Irish, Italian, Polish, and other immigrants settled, today it is in the Midwest, the South, and all across rural regions and small towns (as well as the more traditional metropolitan areas) that we are seeing immigrants arrive in the US (Massey 2008; Smith and Furuseth 2006). The bulk of such activity comprises Latino labor migration, though the movement of other immigrant groups to new locations is increasingly becoming a topic of interest for scholars and local communities; it is to this burgeoning trend that refugee resettlement—especially in a place like Vermont—contributes.

History of the USRAP

While migrants may still constitute a small percentage of the world's overall population, their numbers have been growing. This is especially true for refugees and asylum seekers, who have always been a relatively small subset of the global migrant population. The rise in forced migrant populations has been a result of multiple factors—including ongoing political conflicts, economic uncertainties, and environmental change and vulnerabilities for many groups and individuals. Such 'push factors' have, however, been coupled with resurgent nationalist and xenophobic movements in various countries and called into question the multilateral systems of refugee protection that have evolved since the end of the Second World War.

Those systems are themselves complicated, both for the general public to understand and certainly for those in need of protection to navigate. If one is able to successfully flee one's home or homeland and seek shelter and security, there are many steps before one ends up resettled in another country—if this indeed occurs. After all, the main goal of international protection systems is to return people to their homes and livelihoods once conditions have improved. But there are many situations when this is not possible. Conflicts may rage on for years, decades, and generations, making it unsafe to ever return. A natural disaster or a changing climate might forever alter the environment, rendering it uninhabitable or incapable of sustaining cultivation. In a tiny minority of cases, those who have been displaced and have no hope of return might find themselves in the unusual circumstance of being resettled into a new and distant country. Those who have this opportunity are few—in 2019 less than 200,000 people were resettled worldwide out of a population of over 70 million who had been displaced (UNHCR 2019).

To become an officially recognized refugee therefore means overcoming many hurdles and winning what amounts to a lottery. One must be accepted into a camp run by the UNHCR or some other entity, be selected for resettlement by a third country, and endure a battery of tests, interviews, and screening procedures. During the 2016 US presidential election, Donald Trump repeatedly decried the lack of such screening and upon assuming office imposed what he called 'extreme vetting' measures (additional interviews and restrictions). Yet even prior to these new obstacles, on average it took over 1000 days from application to acceptance for refugees in the US. It can now take much longer to actually be resettled into a country like the US.

The program that exists in the US has developed as a private-public partnership between the federal government, individual states, and non-governmental agencies since 1980. We can look at resettlement in terms of six distinct periods (Table 2.1).

The USRAP's evolution can be seen as one that moved from an informal to a much more standardized structure. The US was itself not a signatory to the initial treaties and covenants that were created following

Table 2.1   US refugee resettlement eras

Period	Structure	Major populations
1948–1979	Ad hoc, led by private ethnic and religious organizations	Displaced Europeans (post-Second World War) Cold War refugees (Cuba, Soviet Union/Soviet bloc, Southeast Asia)
1980–1991	Refugee Resettlement Act establishes USRAP, a public-private partnership between the federal government and resettlement agencies	Cold War refugees (Cuba, Soviet Union/Soviet bloc) Southeast Asia
1992–2000	USRAP with some innovations (including limited private sponsorship models)	Balkans/Former Yugoslavia Former Soviet Union Africa
2001–2007	USRAP significantly curtailed following 9/11 attacks, special limitations on applicants from Muslim-majority countries	Africa Afghanistan Eastern Europe
2008–2016	USRAP in steady state (75,000/year), planned expansion to new locations and numbers 2017	Afghanistan Bhutan Burma Congo Iraq Syria
2017–	USRAP numbers cut dramatically each year to the lowest approvals since program inception	Bhutan DRC Syria

the end of the Second World War to address the millions of displaced Europeans across that devastated continent, but it soon became a destination both for those forced migrants and for many who sought to escape from behind the Iron Curtain throughout the Cold War. Through the 1950s and 1960s, many fled both specific conflicts (such as Hungary in 1956 or Czechoslovakia in 1968) and ongoing ones (such as Cuba following the overthrow of the US-supported Batista regime).

The most significant changes to the US refugee program occurred in the 1970s. In the aftermath of the Vietnam War, hundreds of thousands of Vietnamese, Cambodians, and other Southeast Asians were accepted into the country through direct presidential action between 1975 and 1979 (Miyares 1998; Hein 2006). Recognizing the need for a more standardized system instead of the ad hoc manner in which refugee resettlement had functioned since the end of the Second World War— especially since the US withdrawal from Vietnam in 1975—Congress passed the Refugee Act of 1980, with President Carter signing it into law in early 1980. Between 1975 and 1979, an ad hoc Refugee Task Force worked to try and assist the hundreds of thousands attempting to flee Southeast Asia and this legislation was designed to regularize resettlement (Pho et al. 2007). The Act amended the Immigration and Nationality Act and the Migration and Refugee Assistance Act, expanding asylum to all those fleeing their homes under 'a well-founded fear and persecution' as standardized by the 1951 UN Geneva Convention (Betts and Leoscher 2011). The system that developed as a result of this legislation—the US Refugee Admissions Program (USRAP)—was a public-private partnership, with the federal government primarily responsible for choosing and vetting prospective refugees and its partner resettlement agencies—a collection of faith-based, ethnic, and humanitarian organizations—tasked with helping newcomers make the transition to life in the US (Mott 2010). The large-scale resettlements of this period up to and including 1980 reflected what has arguably always been as central to US refugee policy as any humanitarian motive—geopolitical considerations (Haines 2010).

This is not to say that there were no altruistic motives behind US resettlement during this period. The protection of human rights and responding to atrocities overseas did influence at least some members of the public to support resettlement—though refugee programs have always been controversial and favored by only a minority of the general population in the US. Yet one might argue that a humanitarian agenda motivating refugee policy in the US was primarily driven by private actors—faith groups and ethnic communities—rather than by the US government, whose main goals were pursuing foreign policy objectives of destabilizing its international rivals and not antagonizing various allies and client states (Portes and Rumbaut 2014). This focus on US foreign policy interests became increasingly clear during the Reagan administration as the scope of who the US would allow—and in what numbers—began to narrow (RPC 2018). Indeed, even though the number of refugees worldwide grew by nearly 400% between 1975 and 1985, the US's annual ceiling steadily decreased until 1986, when it was capped at 67,000 (RPC 2018). For the Reagan administration, third-party resettlement to the US was not the ultimate goal in addressing displacement overseas. Instead, it repeatedly argued that resettlement was the least desirable option and instead advocated for repatriation in the home country and resettlement within the sending region as the better courses of action (Bloemraad 2006).

Of those who were granted refugee status in the US, admissions heavily favored those fleeing Communist countries, such as Cuba, the Soviet Union, and other countries of the Soviet bloc. At the same time, many forced migrants within the US regional sphere of influence—such as those from US-allied regimes in El Salvador, Guatemala, and Honduras and other conflicts in Central and South America—had little chance of being granted status in the US and were instead labeled as economic migrants rather than as refugees or asylees. President Reagan also launched the so-called Private Sector Initiative during his second term, which brought a limited number of refugees (primarily Soviet Jews and Cubans) through private sponsorship—a total of approximately 16,000 during the eight years of the program (Bloemraad 2006).

Several decades of the Cold War stalemate had led to relatively little population movement in Europe, but the collapse of the Soviet Union caused massive upheavals throughout the region. The Lautenberg Amendment of 1989 admitted Jews from the former Soviet Union without their having to demonstrate specific persecution (Bruno 2015).

This law was later expanded to apply to other religious minorities worldwide and altogether contributed to the resettlement of hundreds of thousands. Additionally, the breakup of Yugoslavia and the subsequent Balkan Wars resulted in a tremendous exodus of refugees from the area, with over 2.5 million people displaced in the region, the largest displacement in Europe at the time since the Second World War (Kandel 2014). This led to significant third-party resettlement in other countries, including the US, which was to eventually resettle tens of thousands of refugees from the region. In 1993, the US approved the acceptance of 142,000 refugees—the highest number since the program's first two years, even though the actual number admitted ended up being slightly higher in 1992 (RPC 2018). Toward the end of the 1990s, a second spike in resettlement approvals occurred, due to the conflict in Serbia over the struggle for independence in Kosovo. By the end of the decade, Balkan region refugees comprised the largest groups admitted into the US, with admissions for African refugees also rising in response to the Rwandan genocide and other regional African conflicts (RPC 2018).

During this period, the US increased its position as a global leader in third-party resettlement, certainly in absolute numbers if not in terms of per capita acceptance of refugees. In the 1980s, annual admission ceilings averaged 116,170—this includes 1980–1981 when the ceilings were greater than 200,000—while they averaged 110,400 throughout the 1990s. The actual number of refugees who were resettled in the US was slightly higher in the 1990s—1,009,885—compared to the 1980s—974,006 (RPC 2018). However, while those admitted during the 1980s were clearly related to US foreign policy objectives and conflicts overseas, during the 1990s the US increasingly became a key player in the global refugee regime and addressing international conflicts in which it did not have as direct or as obvious a stake, in both short-term and protracted situations. This role became especially important as the number of displaced persons worldwide grew due to a number of conflicts as well as expanding definitions for protection throughout the 1990s.

The shift in the US's role and its direct relation to (some) refugee-producing conflicts meant that as the waves of displacement from the Balkans, former Soviet Union, and Southeast Asia began to wind down, the US resettlement program correspondingly began approving fewer refugees. This did not mean that there were fewer refugees in the world—as mentioned previously, there continued to be many conflicts and expanding recognition of conditions for flight worldwide as the 2000s dawned (Betts and Leoscher 2011)—but rather than resettling large groups from just one or two countries, in the early 2000s, the USRAP began to adjust its scope by dividing the refugee intake among many smaller and more diverse cases. Refugees from nearly eighty countries were being resettled in the US by this time, some in large numbers and others in much smaller groups, with resettlement capacity dropping from an average of 90,000 individuals a year in 1990 to 80,000 in 2000, and actual resettlements averaging closer to 70,000 per year in both decades (RPC 2018). This led to a much more diverse refugee population and often considerable challenges in stretching resources across multiple locations and trying to address significantly different contexts—including languages, reasons for flight, security screenings, and integration capacities—for the various groups of refugees (Committee on Foreign Relations 2010; GAO 2012). By the beginning of 2001, African refugees surpassed Europeans as the largest forced migrant group being resettled in the US (RPC 2018).

The combination of shifting priorities and the challenge of resettling newer (and more diverse) groups meant that the number of admissions had slowed by the early 2000s, but the terrorist attacks of September 11, 2001, resulted in wholesale changes to the program—and indeed immigration itself—across the US and much of the Global North. Heightened screenings and the suspension of many visa programs—including a two-month freeze in the refugee resettlement program—meant a significant reduction in newcomers. Domestic fears that terrorist groups or dangerous individuals might exploit the USRAP to enter the US led to a close and lengthy review of vetting, resulting in additional measures to heighten the security of the program and ensure the overall thoroughness of the admissions process. As a result, instead of the nearly 70,000 spaces for refugees originally allocated in 2002, just over 27,000 individuals were actually allowed into the country, the lowest on record since the passing of the Refugee Act of 1980 (RPC 2018). The effects of 9/11 were felt around the world as global refugee acceptance numbers in third countries also fell sharply. Between 2001 and 2003, the USRAP was characterized by low resettlement numbers, reflecting these changes to the admissions process. Additionally, global instability in multiple regions meant that planned interviews were often put on hold and vetting of applicants in many places slowed significantly. By 2004, however, new screening mechanisms and the focus on different groups meant that admissions began to recover as they rose to above 50,000 for 2004–2005. As former US State Department official Arthur E. Dewey, Assistant Secretary for Population, Refugees, and Migration stated in 2003, '9/11 may have given us reason to be more vigilant about those who may threaten us, but it has not diminished our commitment to aiding and protecting the world's most vulnerable people' (Dewey 2003).

The USRAP slowly increased admissions over the next few years; by 2009, the number of refugees approved for resettlement reached 70,000 again for the first time since 2000 (RPC 2018). The annual ceiling never fell below 70,000 during the Obama administration, and each of the final four years saw admissions missing the ceiling by just about 100 persons annually. Admissions dipped in FY2011 and 2012, but asylum figures for those years were slightly higher than usual (RPC 2018). Between FY2012 and FY2014, the USRAP was approving close to 75,000 refugees each year for admission to the US. In response to the Syrian Civil War and resulting migration crisis—especially in the huge increase in asylum seekers from the Middle East and North Africa to Europe and other parts of the world—the Obama administration raised the annual ceiling in FY2016 to 85,000 (Federal Register 2016) and, unlike previous years, the actual number of refugees who arrived in the US came close to matching those approved. For FY2017, the Obama administration planned on an even greater expansion, with an approval ceiling of 110,000 refugees—somewhat closer to the numbers in the USRAP's peak periods during the early 1980s and mid-1990s and the highest in over twenty years (Federal Register 2017). For the Obama administration, this was a question of both need—by 2015, there were over 45 million refugees and displaced persons worldwide—and the US having the capacity to absorb more refugees.

Others, however, did not agree with this assessment. Refugee resettlement, which has always represented a fairly small part of the overall immigration landscape in the US, became especially politicized due to a number of reasons. European anxieties regarding an influx of migrants, growing Islamophobia, and mass terrorist attacks carried out by Islamic extremists across the globe—often blamed on refugees and asylum seekers but carried out for the most part by native-born or immigrant (but not refugee) individuals and groups—led to a significant backlash against refugees worldwide. In the US, many state governors and a smaller number of cities announced in November 2015 (following terrorist attacks in Paris) that they would no longer support refugee resettlement in their areas. The issue became a central feature of the Republican presidential primaries in 2015–2016, with eventual winning candidate Donald Trump taking a lead role in advocating against refugee resettlement, especially from Muslim-majority countries. In 2016, states like Texas and Maine officially withdrew from the USRAP, though refugees were still resettled in those states—especially Texas which has had the largest share of refugee arrivals in the US (Kennedy 2016). And following his election, the ascent of Trump to the US presidency ushered in an era of uncertainty and anxiety for the USRAP.

Such fears were not unfounded. In one of his first acts, President Trump instituted a ban on arrivals from several Muslim-majority nations as well as an immediate suspension and review of the USRAP, all in the name of national security. While these so-called travel bans were challenged successfully in court in the months to follow, the resettlement program in particular was deeply affected (Pierce and Meissner 2017). Where the USRAP and the many government and nonprofit agencies that make up the program had planned on expanding in 2017, the opposite was to actually come true. The program ended up settling little more than 50,000 people—less than half of what the Obama administration had planned, and more in line with what the original travel ban had threatened. In the first three years of the Trump administration, the refugee numbers have been successively lowered—45,000 in FY2018 (of whom just over 22,000 people were actually resettled), 30,000 in FY2019 (of whom approximately 28,000 people were approved), and a planned 18,000 in FY2020 (Federal Register 2018, 2019). This last represents the lowest number of refugees ever approved for entry into the US since the USRAP's founding. This, combined with the eventual approval of the travel ban by the US Supreme Court and an expansion to include other countries in 2020, has drastically curtailed the USRAP. Additionally, the FY2020 Presidential Determination was accompanied by a Presidential Order mandating the need for written approval by states and cities to accept refugees.

There are those who argue that cutting refugee numbers is just 'common sense' in terms of both security and focusing the US' humanitarian efforts on its own citizens. And it is true that both of these concerns are real ones—the US government has a duty to protect its people and to provide services to those who need them. It is also true that the threat of extremism has grown in recent years. But are refugees or the USRAP to blame for any of this? There is no evidence that they are. Indeed, contrary to the assertions of some politicians that refugees are not properly 'vetted' or that we do not know who they are or what they believe, refugees are among the most heavily screened groups in the US. As mentioned earlier, to be approved for resettlement in the US, one must go through an average of at least a thousand days of screenings. Of the over three million refugees resettled since the program's inception and nearly 900,000 since 9/11, only three have been convicted of terrorism-related charges, all of them for overseas activities (Newland 2015). Additionally, the argument that refugee resettlement is a drain on other programs has little evidence backing it; most serious scholarly research would suggest on the contrary that there is a substantial net economic benefit to refugee resettlement in the US (Evans and Fitzgerald 2017). Refugees have also been resettled in many places outside of the traditional metropolitan gateway cities of the US (Massey 2008; Singer and Wilson 2011). For many of these communities—often in the rust-belt or with declining or aging populations—refugees bring in much needed vitality, start new businesses, provide a more stable taxpayer base, and diversify schools and neighborhoods (Bose 2016).

While the US has played a historically significant role—especially in the past three decades—in global refugee resettlement, the trends set by the current administration move the country in the opposite direction. Where the US has at times accepted more than all other countries combined (though per capita the Scandinavian countries have historically taken in more refugees), drastically cutting the program imperils the very delicate systems of protection that have emerged to help those in the greatest need. Moreover, by shrinking the USRAP and limiting the scope of its protections, the US undermines its own moral leadership in the area of human rights, as well as weakens its geopolitical importance with allies and neighbors.

Structure of the USRAP

Despite the ups and downs of the program, many individuals still arrive in the US. But what is the process through which they actually arrive? Who supports them upon arrival? What does it mean to arrive in the US as a refugee? It is important to begin by noting that refugee resettlement in the US is a fragmented, convoluted, and semi-privatized process. Those one thousand days that take individuals and groups from refugee camps to the US begin with a battery of interviews and tests overseas with refugees navigating both international (UNHCR) and state bureaucracies—in the case of the US this includes US Citizenship and Immigration Services (USCIS, in the Department of Homeland Security) and the Bureau of Population, Refugees and Migration (or PRM, in the Department of State)—during the international phase of determination.

PRM staff continue to assist in the selection of the specific locations to which refugees will be sent, working with officials in the Office of Refugee Resettlement (or ORR, in the Department of Health and Human Services) to provide services and support for the placements. These federal entities must also collaborate with state-level officials in this process. In Vermont, this means a State Refugee Coordinator whose office was created at the same point that the state was designated as an official resettlement site in 1987. There is often little to no official role played throughout the resettlement process by either the cities that host refugees or the refugees themselves—a long-standing point of contention that the Trump administration has sought to clumsily address by giving local and state officials essentially a veto power over arrivals in their communities.

While helping to assign refugees to their new homes, this assemblage of federal and state authorities in the US is only partially involved in the actual resettlement process. The work of finding refugees a place to live, a job, food and clothing, counseling, connections within their new community, language classes, transportation to destinations, and all the myriad other elements of acculturation is contracted out to what used to be known in the US as VOLAGs (voluntary agencies) or more recently as resettlement agencies (though I will use both terms interchangeably here). There are currently nine federal resettlement agencies that work to place refugees either through field offices or local affiliated organizations—which might mean a state or municipal agency, an ethnic association, or a community organization.

The nine resettlement agencies include five faith-based (Church World Service, Episcopal Migration Ministries, Lutheran Immigration and Refugee Services, United States Conference of Catholic Bishops, World Relief), two ethnicity-based (Ethiopian Community Development Council, Hebrew Immigrant Aid Society), and two secular (International Rescue Committee, US Committee for Refugees and Immigrants) organizations, though each works with refugees regardless of their creed, ethnicity, politics, or geographic background (ORR 2020a). Most resettlement sites have two or more resettlement agencies operating in them. In Vermont, there is just one, the US Committee on Refugees and Immigrants VT (USCRI-VT), which is primarily responsible for the first year after arrival (though for some services it can work with refugees for up to an additional four years). Much of the support provided for refugees beyond the first year is taken up in Vermont by another organization, a mutual aid association, the Association of Africans Living in Vermont (AALV).

The US federal government provides up to eight months of direct financial assistance to refugees, paid through the resettlement agency responsible for the resettlement. Some refugees who are deemed strong candidates for transition due to language skills, previous training and experience or aptitude, can also participate in accelerated programs that provide more financial support over a shorter time period such as the federal Matching Grant Program (ORR 2020b). Additionally, refugees may access a range of employment and other social services from federal, state, and local programs. Mutual aid associations like AALV do not provide initial financial assistance but may participate in many of the other supports in concert with or instead of the VOLAGs.

As several scholars have noted, the role of the state and private agencies is central to understanding how resettlement operates—and whether it is successful or not—in the US. Mott (2010), for example, discusses in detail the 'scattering' of recent refugees through official resettlement all across the US (rather than being clustered together as seen in previous practice with Cubans in Florida or Southeast Asians in California). She argues that VOLAGs and their relationships with local reception sites play a large part in determining where refugees end up going. Nawyn (2010) argues that the NGOs carrying out resettlement are in effect extensions of state policy and social control, reifying the compliance-driven model of welfare that characterizes the neoliberal state. She writes (2010: 163–164) that:

> Because much of their service provision was geared toward quick employment, most VOLAGs provided an opportunity structure that reproduced gender and racial/ethnic hierarchies in the job market…Refugees certainly have agency independent of refugee NGOs. But because these NGOs are among the first institutions with which refugees interact after arriving in the U.S., the particular ways in which they structure opportunities for refugees is relevant to their later adaptation experiences.

Such a context leads to a situation where mutual hostility may emerge between the refugees and the agencies most directly involved in their resettlement. In Caron et al. (2013) study of lead poisoning among children in the refugee community in Manchester, NH, and the attempts to address the situation by the local VOLAG, what becomes abundantly clear from the interviews conducted with the service providers is a high level of paternalism in their attitudes toward their clients while from the refugees there appears to be a significant level of distrust. For the authors, such a strained relationship emerges at least in part from the stress that the need to find employment for refugees—currently the only real measure for successful resettlement mandated by the US state—places on refugees and VOLAGs alike.

This dynamic is not a new one; it was recognized early on that for Southeast Asians arriving in the US the resettlement process itself could be an alienating experience. Writing at the height of these resettlements, Timberlake and Oahn Cooke (1984) note the deeply traumatic process not only of being violently uprooted from one's home and social network but also of trying to adjust to the expectations of the new place. The authors note, for example, that social work's standards of professionalism can appear to be expressions of disinterest or aloofness to the refugee themselves. For such reasons, it has become increasingly commonplace for VOLAGs to employ former refugees themselves as caseworkers where they can act as more than language interpreters but also as cultural brokers and advocates. Shaw (2014: 292–293) points out, however, that the insider/outsider dynamic can lead to significant problems for those in these positions, including exploitation and questions regarding one's allegiances:

> Speaking about the challenges of being in the casework position as a community member, caseworkers said it can be difficult to differentiate roles, and the expectations of the community are high…When resettlement agencies do not have adequate resources, caseworkers may feel caught between following agency protocols and meeting the unstated assumption of the agency that they will address the client's needs.

I will return to these particular dynamics in my examination of particular cases in Vermont in later chapters, as the majority of both USCRI-VT and AALV staff are former refugees themselves and occupy such hybrid positions.

VOLAGs are, of course, not the only ones involved in resettlement besides the refugees themselves. Barneche and Joe (2014) suggest that in the case of asylum seekers faith-based communities that are not constrained by the rules of funders and the state are able to assist those in need more readily, helping to access basic needs such as transportation, shelter, and food, as well as companionship and support. Sawtell et al. (2010) argue that in the case of refugee resettlement in rural Australia, volunteers have increasingly been filling the gap between under-resourced government and community service workers, and like faith-based communities, volunteers are not hamstrung by the rules and regulations that proscribe agencies. Yet there are serious questions regarding the lack of training and support for these informal (though clearly important) networks. So too is their ongoing status as peer/support/outsider organizations.

And beyond these other actors, the role of cities, counties, and other jurisdictions remains opaque and complicated within the USRAP. Some (especially larger) cities have departments and staff dedicated to supporting refugee arrivals, or a historical experience and infrastructure meant to address immigrant needs. In newer destinations, such resources may be lacking. Indeed, this last has been a long-standing concern for scholars and policymakers regarding the placement of refugees in non-traditional metropolitan locations. Is there the knowledge in such spaces for effective integration efforts? Are there the resources necessary to support the success of new arrivals? Such resources might include language training, workforce development, sensitivity to cultural differences, the distinctions within as well as between different refugee groups, and access to housing, transportation, educational, and other supports that are often crucial to the first weeks, months, and even years of settlement into a new community. Such concerns have for many years been a part of the discussion within the US refugee regime, among resettlement agencies and federal, state, and local authorities (as well as refugee advocates and communities) well before the current controversies.

In Vermont, we see too that the environment of refugee resettlement extends well beyond the official organizations that are tapped to work with newcomers—city officials, banks, libraries, youth organizations, healthcare providers, schools, and many others besides are part of the broader constellation of those who work with refugees. The structure of the USRAP encourages this kind of networked approach to resettlement. Beyond the resettlement agencies, the role of mutual aid associations (or ethnically based community organizations as they are also called) like AALV has become increasingly prominent. While Nawyn (2010) lumps them together with VOLAGs as part of a broader parastatal assemblage—both receiving governmental funding and both employing resettlement professionals and former refugees alike—the genesis of these groups is markedly different. MAAs—at least in their formation—often constitute an insider group. They are formed most often within ethnic or subnational communities and are united by a set of common cultural beliefs and interests. Their founding is often related to a perceived gap or lack within their resettlement site.

In Hume and Hardwick's (2005) study of African and Eastern European refugees in Portland, Oregon, for example, the growing belief that VOLAGs were not able to meet the specialized needs of a wide range of refugees from different African countries led to the formation of the African Refugee and Immigrant Network of Oregon (ARINO) in 2000. Modeled on existing pan-ethnic coalitions in the Asian and Latino communities, ARINO was meant to assess community needs and develop plans to address them. Yet Hume and Hardwick argue that while on the surface the notion of pan-African solidarities makes sense, in practice refugees still primarily preferred to turn to people from their own countries to assist them. Additionally, this mutual assistance association was dominated by members of the larger and longer-established groups (Hume and Hardwick 2005). As the story of refugees in Vermont will suggest, such dynamics are not unique to Portland.

Resettlement in the US 2012–2016

In the final section of this chapter, I turn from looking at the history and structure of the USRAP and return to the question of migration and settlement geographically. How exactly do refugees end up in a place like Vermont? What are the processes by which these groups are placed in a semi-rural state with low levels of diversity? What are the patterns of refugee resettlement in the US in recent years? Over the past three decades, immigrants as a whole in the US have been settling outside of traditional 'gateway cities' like New York, Chicago, and San Francisco and moving instead to the Southern, Midwestern, and Northwestern regions of the country and to smaller cities and rural areas as well. If we were to look at the first decade of the 2000s and contrasted some of the largest 'immigrant' cities in the US with a number of smaller, less traditional destinations, this pattern becomes quite clear (Table 2.2).

Table 2.2 Refugee resettlement in selected US cities 2000–2010

Resettlement site	2010 census	Refugee placements	% of overall population
Chicago, IL	9,461,105	9320	0.09
New York, NY	18,897,109	8000	0.04
Los Angeles, CA	12,828,837	2653	0.02
Miami, FL	5,547,051	200	0.003
Utica, NY	62,235	4384	7.04
Bowling Green, KY	58,067	2742	4.72
Burlington, VT	49,684	2170	4.37
Turlock, CA	68,549	1678	2.45

Source US Department of State Population, Refugees and Migration Admissions—Refugee Processing Center, Refugee Arrivals as of 18 January 2012

By the period of main focus in this book—2012–2016—we see that such patterns had intensified. While just under 20% of refugees accepted into the US were settled in large gateway metropolitan areas of over 1 million people, nearly the same numbers were settled in small towns of less than 100 thousand inhabitants and a further 35% in small cities of between one hundred and four hundred thousand residents. Some of these smaller urban areas fall within the orbit of a much larger city or are part of a larger metropolitan statistical area—yet there are many smaller resettlement sites that are not particularly close to large cities all across the US (Table 2.3).

Table 2.3 Refugee resettlement sites in US 2012–2016 by city population

Resettlement site population	Number of participating cities	Resettlement site population	Number of participating cities
2 million +	5	80k–89k	5
1–1.9 million	5	70k–79k	6
800k–999k	6	60k–69k	17
600k–799k	11	50k–59k	13
500k–599k	7	40k–49k	17
400k–499k	7	30k–39k	9
300k–399k	16	20k–29k	9
200k–299k	24	10k–19k	9
100k–199k	53	Less than 10k	4
90k–99k	7		

Source ACS 2013 and RPC 2019

Overall, the picture of refugee resettlement in the US between 2012 and 2016 looks like this in absolute numbers (Fig. 2.1).

There are some caveats and some trends that we can see across the US in terms of resettlement during this period. Refugees continue to make up a very small percentage of both the overall *and* the immigrant populations in most states. Additionally, the states currently resettling the most refugees in absolute numbers are some of the same states that immigrants have historically settled in, especially those with 'gateway cities' like New York, San Francisco, Houston, and Miami. As a percentage of both the overall and foreign-born population, however, refugee resettlement is proportionately much higher in so-called non-traditional immigrant-destination states such as Vermont, Idaho, and North Dakota and also in states where Latino labor migration is relatively recent, such as Kentucky and Tennessee (Fig. 2.2).

During my study period, a total of 231 sites were approved as official resettlement locations across the US. It should be noted that there may be some slight variation in the actual cities identified because the federal government uses the head offices of resettlement agencies to identify placements rather than the specific city in which refugees end up. For these reasons, I am using state rather than municipal location data to illustrate trends in US resettlement. In Vermont, for example, the national data use Colchester as the resettlement site (because that is where USCRI-VT's office is located) rather than Burlington and or Winooski which are the actual towns of resettlement I discuss in this book. The main refugee populations resettled in the US during FY2012–2016 came from Burma, Iraq, Bhutan, the Democratic Republic of Congo, Syria, Somalia, and Ukraine. Individuals from all but the last are present in significant numbers in Vermont.

The most popular destinations for refugees, as noted previously, are some of those states that have been traditionally popular with immigrants and that usually also contain large gateway cities: New York, California, Texas, Florida, Illinois, and New Jersey. Texas and California in addition have been the two most active refugee resettlement states—though their future is now up in the air as Texas in 2020 used the Trump administration's new rules to decline further refugee placements. Beyond these, many of the most active refugee states are located on the East Coast

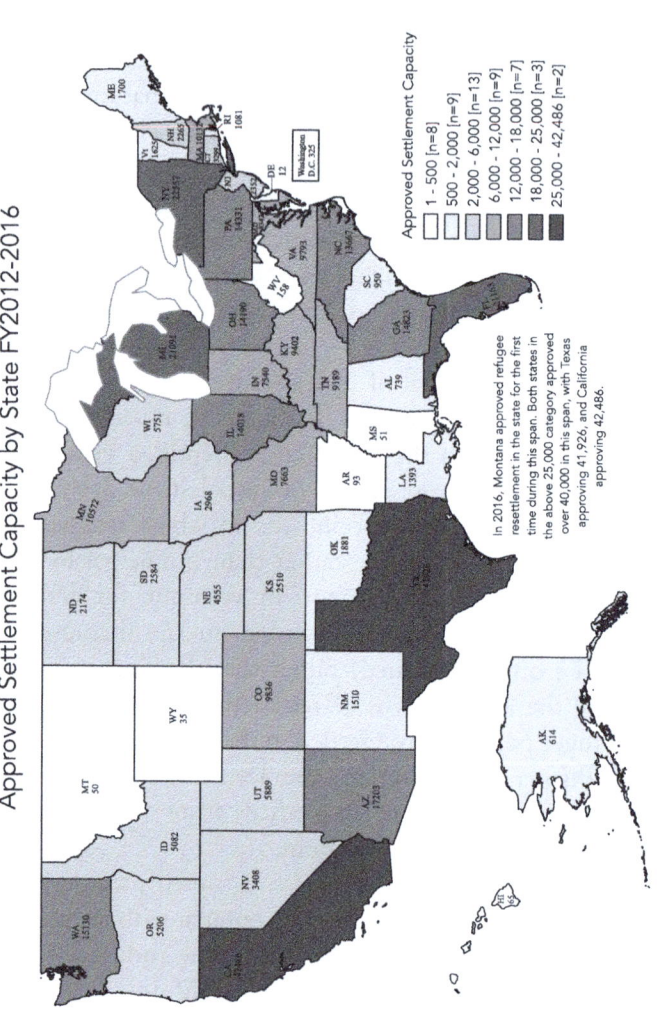

Fig. 2.1 Approved refugee numbers in US 2012–2016 by state (*Source* WRAPS Data on Refugee Placement, Bureau of Population, Refugees and Migration 2012–2015, Migration Policy Institute and 2010 US Census. Authorship: Lucas Grigri, Refugees in Vermont Project, NSF Award#1359895, December 30, 2016)

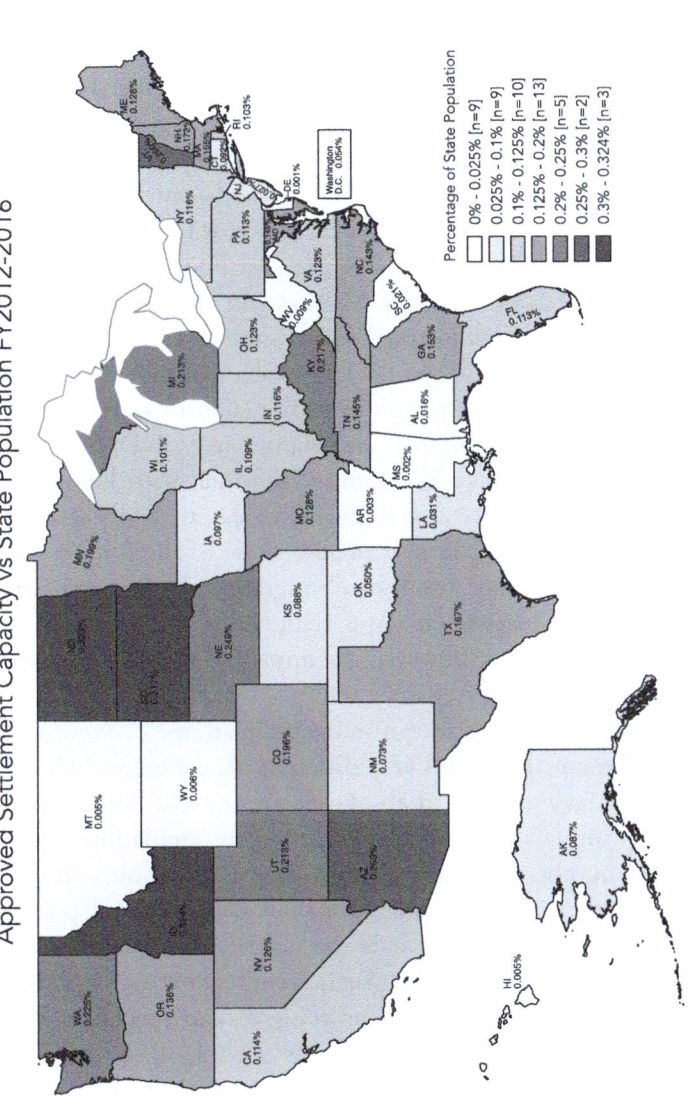

Fig. 2.2 Approved refugee numbers in US 2012–2016 by population (*Source* WRAPS Data on Refugee Placement, Bureau of Population, Refugees and Migration 2012–2015, Migration Policy Institute and 2010 US Census. Authorship: Lucas Grigri, Refugees in Vermont Project, NSF Award#1359895, January 4, 2017)

and along the Great Lakes. Refugees were accepted in every single state during my study period, though the numbers of those approved for resettlement varied from a high of 42,486 (CA) to a low of 35 (WY).

So, while looking at absolute numbers of refugees tends to reinforce our perception of refugee settlement patterns mirroring traditional migration flows to the US, when we look at refugees as a percentage of the population of the states in which they are settling, a very different picture emerges. It is a picture that—as I have said—mirrors what has been happening in immigration and settlement across the US for at least two decades. Immigrants have been increasingly settling in so-called non-traditional sites in the South and the Midwest, in rural and suburban areas, and in rustbelts and deindustrialized communities as well. Some of the states in which refugees make up the largest share of the foreign-born population are among the least populous in the country, often without a significant history as an immigrant destination (e.g., ND, SD, KY). Southwestern border states like Texas and California, with long histories of migration from Mexico and Latin America, are both active in resettlement and feature refugees as a smaller share of the foreign-born population. States that are not 'traditional' migration destinations (such as VT and Idaho) may resettle far fewer refugees in absolute numbers than their larger counterparts; however, the impact of such resettlements is potentially considerably greater since refugees make up a significantly larger share of their overall and foreign-born populations.

Refugee resettlement thus looks very different depending on whether we think about the new arrivals in absolute terms or as a percentage of overall population or as a share of the foreign-born population in each state. In absolute numbers, traditional immigrant-destination states still dominate the resettlement landscape. As a share of the overall population and foreign-born population, it is the new destinations that take on a much more significant profile. Such trends allow us to rethink which states are most active in resettling refugees and speculate about what resettlement would look like in states such as California and New York if they resettled refugees as a proportion of their population in a similar ration to states like Vermont and North Dakota. It is important to examine more closely those states such as Arizona, Washington, Michigan, North Carolina, and Georgia which have been resettling refugees in larger numbers *and* where refugees represent a higher percentage of their overall and foreign-born populations. What have been the experiences for such states in resettlement and what lessons might others learn from them?

Looking at resettlement as it compares to the foreign-born population of these states speaks to how different refugee resettlement experiences can be depending on a state's history of migration. While states such as California, Florida, and Illinois may be more accustomed to integrating people of different cultures and backgrounds, states like Vermont, Kentucky, and North Dakota are significantly changing their demographics through refugee resettlement. This is not only shifting for state and city governments, but also for individual interactions within these communities. The personal experience for individual refugees may also vary greatly depending upon the location's history of migration and integrating foreign-born residents as later chapters in this book will examine in greater detail.

References

Agrawal, Ajay, Devesh Kapur, John McHale, and Alexander Oettl. 2011. Brain drain or brain bank? The impact of skilled emigration on poor-country innovation. *Journal of Urban Economics* 69: 43–55.

Barneche, Kelly, and Joe. 2014. Faith and responses to displacement. *Forced Migration Review* 48 (November): 9.

Betts, Alexander, and Gil Leoscher. 2011. *Refugees in international relations.* Oxford: Oxford University Press.

Bloemraad, Irene. 2006. *Becoming a citizen: Incorporating immigrants and refugees in the United States and Canada.* Berkeley: University of California Press.

Bose, Pablo S. 2015. New Vermonters and perspectives on Vermont migration. *Northeastern Geographer* 7: 89–101.

Bose, Pablo S. 2016. Challenging homogeneity: Refugees in a changing Vermont. In *After the flight: The dynamics of refugee settlement and integration,* ed. M. Poteet and S. Nourpanah, 228–253. Newcastle-upon-Tyne: Cambridge Scholars Publishing.

Bose, Pablo S., and Elizabeth Lunstrum. 2019. What constitutes environmental displacement? Challenges and opportunities of exploring connections across thematically diverse areas. In *The refugee research network*, ed. Susan McGrath and Julie Young, 23–252. Calgary: University of Calgary Press.

Bruno, Andorra. 2015. Refugee admissions and resettlement policy. *Current Politics and Economics of the United States, Canada and Mexico* 17 (3): 485–500.

Caron, Rosemary, Thandi Tshabangu-Soko, and Krysten Finefrock. 2013. Childhood lead poisoning in a Somali refugee community in New Hampshire. *Journal of Community Health* 38 (4): 660–669.

Committee on Foreign Relations. 2010. *Abandoned upon arrival: Implications for refugees and local communities burdened by a U.S. resettlement system that is not working* (No. 9780160862458 0160862450). Washington: US Government Printing Office.

de Haas, Hein, Stephen Castles, and Mark Miller. 2019. *The age of migration: International population movements in the modern world*. New York: Guilford Press.

Dewey, Arthur. 2003. Immigration after 9/11: The view from the United States. Remarks to the American Society for International Law, Washington DC, April 3. Available from https://2001-2009.state.gov/g/prm/rls/2003/37906.htm.

Evans, William, and Daniel Fitzgerald. 2017. The economic and social outcomes of refugees in the United States: Evidence from the ACS. National Bureau of Economic Research Working Paper No. 23498, June.

Federal Register. 2016. Presidential determination on refugee admissions for fiscal year 2017. 81 FR 70315. Executive office of the President. No. 2016-13. September 28.

Federal Register. 2017. Presidential determination on refugee admissions for fiscal year 2018. 82 FR 49083. Executive office of the President. No. 2017-23140. September 29.

Federal Register. 2018. Presidential determination on refugee admissions for fiscal year 2019. 83 FR 55091. Executive office of the President. No. 2018-24135. October 4.

Federal Register. 2019. Presidential determination on refugee admissions for fiscal year 2020. 83 FR 55091. Executive office of the President. No. 2018-24135. November 1.

GAO. 2012. Refugee resettlement: Greater consultation with community stakeholders could strengthen the program. GAO-12-729. Washington: US Government Printing Office.

Haines, David W. 2010. *Safe Haven? A history of refugees in America.* Sterling, VA: Kumarian Press.

Hein, Jeremy. 2006. *Ethnic origins: The adaptation of Cambodian and Hmong refugees in four American cities.* New York: Russell Sage.

Hume, Susan, and Susan Hardwick. 2005. African, Russian and Ukrainian refugee resettlement in Portland, Oregon. *The Geographical Review* 95 (2): 189–209.

Kandel, William A. 2014 Permanent legal immigration to the United States: Policy overview. Congressional Research Service 7-5700.

Kennedy, Merrit. 2016. Texas pulls out of federal refugee resettlement program. *NPR.* September 30. Retrieved from http://www.npr.org/sections/thetwo-way/2016/09/30/496098507/texas-pulls-out-of-federal-refugee-res ettlement-program.

King, Anthony. 2004. *Spaces of global cultures: Architecture, urbanism, identity.* London: Routledge.

Massey, Douglas S. 2008. *New faces in new places: The changing geography of American immigration.* New York: Russell Sage Foundation.

Miyares, Ines. 1998. *The Hmong refugees experience in America: Crossing the river.* New York: Routledge.

Mott, Tamar E. 2010. African refugee resettlement in the US: The role and significance of voluntary agencies. *Journal of Cultural Geography* 27 (1): 1–31.

Nawyn, Stephanie. 2010. Institutional structures of opportunity in refugee resettlement: Gender, race/ethnicity, and refugee NGOs. *Journal of Sociology and Social Welfare* 37 (1): 149–167.

Newland, Kathleen. 2015. The US record shows that refugees are not a threat. Migration Policy Institute. Available from https://www.migrationpolicy.org/news/us-record-shows-refugees-are-not-threat.

ORR. 2020a. Resettlement agencies. Office of Refugee Resettlement. Available from https://www.acf.hhs.gov/orr/resource/resettlement-agencies. Accessed February 1, 2020.

ORR. 2020b. Voluntary Agencies Matching Grant Program. Office of Refugee Resettlement. Available from https://www.acf.hhs.gov/orr/programs/mat ching-grants. Accessed February 1, 2020.

Penz, Peter, Jay Drydyk, and Pablo Bose. 2011. *Displaced by development: Ethics, rights and responsibilities.* Cambridge: Cambridge University Press.

Pho, Tuyet-Lan, Jeffrey Gerson, and Sylvia Cowan. 2007. *Southeast Asian refugees and immigrants in the mill city: Changing families, communities, institutions—Thirty years afterward*. Burlington: University Press of New England.

Pierce, Sarah, and Doris Meissner. 2017. *Revised Trump executive order and guidance on refugee resettlement and travel ban*. Washington, DC: Migration Policy Institute.

Portes, Alejandro, and Rubén Rumbaut. 2014. *Immigrant America: A portrait*. Berkeley: University of California Press.

RPC. 2018. Admissions and arrivals. Available from http://www.wrapsnet.org/admissions-and-arrivals/.

Sawtell, John, Virginia Dickson-Swift, and Glenda Verrinder. 2010. It's not all tied up with bureaucrats and funding: Autonomous volunteer participation in the rural resettlement of refugees. *Australian Journal of Social Issues* 45: 543–558.

Shaw, Stacey. 2014. Bridge builders: A qualitative study exploring the experiences of former refugees working as caseworkers in the United States. *Journal of Social Service Research* 40 (3): 284–296.

Singer, Audrey, and Jill H. Wilson. 2011. From 'there to here': Refugee resettlement in metropolitan America. In *Race, ethnicity, and place in a changing America*, 2nd ed, ed. J. Frazier, E. Tettey-Fio, and N. Henry, 364–388. Albany: State University of New York Press.

Smith, H., and O. Furuseth. 2006. *Latinos in the New South: The transformation of place*. London: Ashgate Press.

Timberlake, Elizabeth, and Kim Oahn Cook. 1984 *Social work* (March–April): 108–113.

UNHCR. 2019. Figures at a glance. Available from http://www.unhcr.org/figures-at-a-glance.html.

World Bank. 2019. Record high remittances sent in 2018. Available from https://www.worldbank.org/en/news/press-release/2019/04/08/record-high-remittances-sent-globally-in-2018. Accessed January 26, 2020.

3

Immigration, Refugees, and Vermont

The story of migration into and out of Vermont is a complex one. For urban geographers or migration studies specialists, the state would not seem like an obvious place to situate one's work. Instead, as I have highlighted in earlier chapters, the bulk of such scholarship has focused on large-scale immigration and gateway cities—the primary destination of most newcomers in many countries. Yet the emerging dynamics of migration in Vermont today demonstrate that the state is a microcosm—albeit with its own peculiarities and uniqueness—of many of the same processes, motivations, and dynamics that have driven people in and out of place in the US as well as internationally. In this chapter, I explore the patterns of migration into Vermont both historically and in the present moment.

I do so in four parts. I begin by looking at Vermont's longer history with migration since its modern history as a settler state. I focus in particular on the impact of European and especially French-Canadian movement into the region. I include as well a look at the much more recent history of international immigration—primarily Latinx labor and refugee resettlement—in the state. In the second part of this chapter, I turn to refugee resettlement and offer an overview of how and where

© The Author(s) 2020
P. S. Bose, *Refugees in New Destinations and Small Cities*,
https://doi.org/10.1007/978-981-15-6386-7_3

in the state of Vermont refugee resettlement has been attempted. Next, I describe the backgrounds and contexts of the various refugee groups in the state and how these particularities have shaped their outcomes. In the final part of the chapter, I explore attitudes toward refugees in Vermont as revealed through a set of opinion polls I have conducted over the past five years with the general public across the state. What do Vermont locals feel about the latest arrivals and about having them as neighbors?

Migration and Vermont

That Vermont does not appear in the American imaginary as a recent migration destination is not surprising. Its demographics suggest that many of those newcomer groups that have come to dominate recent immigration to the US are present in much smaller numbers, if they are present at all. In the early 1970s, immigration into the US was just picking up again after an especially restrictive period between 1924 and 1965 when federal policies severely limited entries. In the late nineteenth and early twentieth centuries, most immigrant origins in the US were European. But labor migration and the opening up of the US immigration system in 1965 had changed the demographic mix of immigrants considerably. By the 1970s, the most recent arrivals to the US were from Mexico, the Philippines, and Canada (Portes and Rumbaut 2014). Over the succeeding decades, things have shifted again, so that in 2020 the three most common immigrant groups in the US are from Mexico, India, and China (US Census Bureau 2020). Within Vermont, the most common immigrant origins today are from Canada (especially Quebec), Northern Europe, and more recently (and in smaller proportions) Asia and Africa. What are the roots of the changes in these patterns?

The land that has today come to be known as Vermont is the ancestral territory of the Abenaki, an indigenous group that was part of a confederation of linguistically and culturally connected First Nations communities in Northeastern North America (Calloway 1994; Manore 2011). Over centuries of colonial conquest and discrimination, the Abenaki were dispossessed of their land and livelihoods and Vermont emerged as a European colony, claimed first by the French, then by the British, and finally by Americans—originally as a republic and then as the fourteenth state to join the US. Its modern history is as a rural state with its economy based upon resource extraction and small-scale agriculture.

Migration into Vermont—one of the smallest and least populous states in the US—has traditionally come from other parts of the country, from Canada, and from Europe. It has also experienced considerable out-migration, losing significant numbers of inhabitants. This is a long and rich history; I would argue that while it may not conjure visions of an immigrant destination in the minds of most, Vermont has been both a source of emigrants and a destination for in-migrants for generations. Most of this influx has been related to the aforementioned resource industries and small-scale agriculture. Marble quarries drew in skilled workers from Europe while the lumber industry and later textile mills recruited labor from Quebec. Today, while less than 5% of its approximately 650,000 people are foreign-born, a majority of Vermonters have Quebecois or European heritage (US Census Bureau 2020). Yet even by the late nineteenth century, Vermont was losing people—so much so that state officials attempted to recruit immigrants from Sweden to try and compensate for the family farms disappearing as a result of the departures from the state (Searls 2019). The decline especially affected rural populations, as young men left homes to find work and access to land by moving to the few relatively urban areas (like Burlington) or out of the state entirely (Mudgett and Morse 2017).

Compounding the challenge of ongoing population decline was the politics of race in the US as it was emerging by the late nineteenth and early twentieth centuries, especially in relation to immigration. A new 'white' identity was being actively forged during this period, cobbling together disparate pseudo-sciences and mythologized histories to produce new typologies of race and biology (Roediger 2005). In Vermont, new racial imaginaries were used to explain population decline and the supposed 'weaknesses' of its genetic stock, as evidenced by a high rate of rejections of its men from the First World War draft. The nineteenth-century appeal to Swedish farmers to repopulate abandoned farms in Vermont is similar in this sense to the Canadian government's attempt to find the 'right' kind of immigrants to work its lands, what Day (2000) has referred to as a 'great chain of race' that placed Northern Europeans at the top of that list and made strong attempts to entice them to Canada. Many of the immigrants entering Vermont at this time were thus unwelcome, accused of 'diluting' the supposedly 'pure' Yankee origins of earlier settlers. For such reasons, the eugenics movement sweeping Europe and the US, especially in the early part of the twentieth century, found fertile ground in Vermont (Vanderbeck 2006). The Vermont Commission on Country Life and the Vermont Eugenics Survey targeted poor French-Canadian women, people with Abenaki ancestry, and Italian and Irish immigrants as undesirable. At its worst extremes, the eugenics movement in Vermont resulted in over two hundred and fifty forced sterilizations, involuntary commitments to mental institutions, and discrimination against racialized others (Gallagher 1999).

By the early twentieth century then, Vermont was in decline. Eugenics as public policy did not leave the state until the 1950s—well after it had been mostly discredited in other parts of the country. There was little industry to draw in workers either; Vermont's main attraction was for elites in neighboring states looking for a vacation or second home. When in-migration really began in the 1960s and 1970s, it took the form of so-called back-to-the-landers—members of the counter-culture, urbanites, and environmentalists seeking a bucolic landscape and a (re)turn to a more natural landscape (Wilbur 2013; Brown 2011). The decade between 1970 and 1980 saw the addition of an estimated 40,000 back-to-the-landers in Vermont, helping both to offset to some degree the ongoing population loss and to significantly alter the local culture and politics, turning what was once a reliably conservative-voting state into a far more libertarian and in some places liberal one (Kelley 2016).

But the arrival of so many 'back-to-the-landers'—sometimes also called 'flatlanders' as a synonym for their urban or supposedly non-mountainous origins—has done little to stem the overall trend of gradual population decline and especially the loss of youth and of rural identity. Geller et al. (2015) argue that this has been a long-standing concern of politicians and community leaders in Vermont for some time, relating to fears of both demographic shrinkage and cultural erosion. In more recent years, however, the majority of narratives regarding migration and Vermont has centered on the perceived loss of skilled young people from the state, moving abroad or to other parts of the US to pursue education or for work.

Vermont is certainly not alone in such fears—the so-called brain drain has occupied the attention of policymakers and community members at multiple scales, from rural villages and farms to cities of the Global South to developing nations. This is not simply a case of circumstances diminishing the population of certain areas but eroding their capacities for growth and resilience. If the best and brightest are to leave a given place, what opportunities does it have to thrive—or at least survive? The issue of brain drain also raises questions regarding the investments that places make in developing their communities, not least through public education. In the case of India, for example, critics have long decried state investments in science and technology education when the recipients of such training are then recruited to jobs overseas to places like Silicon Valley (Varma and Kapur 2013), while the loss of publicly trained medical professionals from Africa to Western industrialized countries has been a similar source of consternation in many parts of that continent (Mills et al. 2011).

For Vermont, the fact that nearly two-thirds of young people attending college do so out of their home state and that the age 19–34 population has shrunk by close to 20% in the past twenty-five years has contributed to a similar perception. Yet as Geller et al. (2015) argue in their analysis of the positions taken by politicians as well as through media discourse on the topic, the rural youth out-migration narrative has become a broadly accepted, internalized, and somewhat reductionist one that often functions as a given truth rather than as a trend which requires careful unpacking and examination. Indeed, Morse and Mudgett's (2018) study of long-term attachments and return migration via the Vermont Roots Migration Project takes a fascinating look at the reasons that some have chosen to leave the state, why some have stayed, and why yet others have chosen to return. Attachment to specific places, traditions, livelihoods, and family connections all play a major role in these decisions in Vermont as they do in other places across the world.

Coupled with the fact that out-migration flows are greater than those of in-migration flows, the difference between 'new' and 'true' Vermonters becomes potentially more magnified—at least in the perceptions of quality of life, political representation, ideological affiliations, and commitments to variously defined 'traditional values' (Bolduc and Kessel 2015). Such differences and potential conflicts between newer and more established communities are of course not a new phenomenon and indeed has become increasingly common in the world due to the influx of wealthier, more educated populations seeking rural or small-town experiences in multiple sites from Canada's eastern shores (Grant and Mittelsteadt 2004) to the American South and Pacific Northwest (Nelson et al. 2014) and in the Chinese countryside (Salazar and Zhang 2013) and Swedish coastal communities (Tjørve et al. 2013) among many others.

In most of these examples, however, the influx of newcomers is as international as it is internal. That has not been the case for the most part for Vermont until relatively recently. 'Back-to-the-landers' from other parts of the US may have started arriving in Vermont during the 1970s, but international migration was not increasing in the ways that were apparent for large states on the coasts in the US during the same period. The restrictionist immigration policies enacted by the US implicitly in the early twentieth century and explicitly from 1924 onward had effectively closed the country off for decades, but when the immigration system was overhauled in 1965, the influx of newcomers to the US was not replicated in Vermont. Successive waves of immigrants—especially from Latin America, Africa, and Asia—began to change the demography of the US, but there was scant evidence of this in Vermont until the 1990s. And unlike other parts of the country, immigration to Vermont was rarely about the entry of people seeking jobs, education, or to be reunited with their families and leaving directly from their homes overseas. There are certainly some—those who come to train as doctors at the University of Vermont, for example, or those who come to work in the semiconductor manufacturing facility that is one of the largest private employers in the state, as well as some other professionals.

But in terms of larger numbers, there have been mainly two major forms of immigration coming into Vermont over the past three decades, even as international migrants comprise nearly half of the movement into the state during this period (US Census Bureau 2020). Both of these sets of newcomers have been concentrated in the northern part of the state—one in rural areas and the other in a select number of towns. The first of these migration patterns is that of Latinx labor migrants—relatively small in scale and linked primarily to the dairy industry. They are not the first to come in the recent period—a small number of primarily Jamaican fruit pickers have been coming for decades to help with the apple harvest in orchards in the northern Vermont (Stechschulte 2017)—but because dairy is a year-round industry, the migrant farmworkers who sustain it are not eligible for such authorized jobs. Instead, Latinx workers—many of them displaced from small-scale agriculture in southern Mexican states by the dynamics of transnational agribusiness and free trade agreements—come undocumented and toil on Vermont dairy farms (Radel et al. 2010). Their presence has had a significant impact on these farms.

The dairy industry in Vermont has long been central to local identity and a source of anxiety and distress as family farms close. Latinx workers have been crucial to the existence of those that have survived, with anywhere between 1500 and 3000 mostly young men working grueling hours to sustain local dairy production (Mares 2019; Baker and Chappelle 2012). They have in turn helped to transform local politics in their own right, launching their own activist organizations to advocate for their rights even as increasingly xenophobic rhetoric and immigration crackdowns have led to more targeting, detentions, and deportations (Hewitt 2019). In Vermont, as in other parts of the US, greater efforts to securitize the border have changed what used to be circular patterns of labor migration that have traditionally drawn young men away from home for temporary periods of work rather than as part of a longer-term resettlement (Mares 2019). In the case of many Mexican households, such work abroad was traditionally as much a part of a kind of male coming-of-age process as an economic necessity (Terrazas et al. 2011); today, Latinx farmworkers take more perilous journeys to come to Vermont and stay longer in the state when they do arrive (Mares 2018) though they do not stay as refugees. It is the other category of newcomers—immigrants formally recognized as refugees and resettled as such by official agencies—that is the subject of this book.

Refugees Resettled in Vermont

Since the late 1980s, there has been a marked increase in the foreign-born population, at least in the northern part of the state. The bulk of this growth consists of official refugees resettled in the main metropolitan area surrounding the city of Burlington, including newcomers who hail from diverse locations in Southeast Asia, Eastern and Central Europe, Africa, and South Asia. The arrival of so many newcomers into such a putatively homogenous community raises many questions about their integration as well as the impact on their new homes, as I explore in the next two sections of the book. As I have detailed in previous chapters, such trends are not unique to Vermont—as migrants arrive in more new or unfamiliar destinations similar questions are being asked across the world (Massey 2008; Singer and Wilson 2011; Eastmond 2011).

Unlike other areas, however, in Vermont refugees are overwhelmingly the main source of immigrants. Since 1987, nearly 7500 refugees have been resettled in Vermont as compared to approximately 1500–3000 migrant farmworkers and a relatively negligible population of other immigrants. And refugees are unlike other immigrant groups in the fact that they (a) receive state support for the first year of their transition to new homes and (b) have little or no say on where they will be placed in that initial year. Unlike almost any other immigrant group in the US (or globally for that matter), refugees are resettled at the behest and direction of the state.

I should also note here that Vermont is unlike some other US states in that it sees a relatively small number of asylum seekers—those who may have equally compelling cases as official refugees, but who make a claim for sanctuary upon arriving in the US rather than from a refugee camp overseas (Bose 2019). The reasons for the lack of this particular population is geographic and political—geographic because Vermont is a landlocked state not proximate to Central America, the Caribbean or Asian and African countries that have become a major source for asylum claimants worldwide, and political because the existence of the Safe Third Country Agreement between the US and Canada makes it virtually impossible for migrants to transit to Vermont via its northern neighbor to make claims (Gilbert 2019).

Prior to 1980, when the USRAP was formalized, a small number of refugees had come to Vermont. Mostly these had been Southeast Asians and some Tibetans who had been sponsored by faith-based organizations and individuals through the ad hoc systems of protection that existed during that time. Following the creation of the USRAP, the process in Vermont for bringing refugees became somewhat muddled. Some informal or privately sponsored arrivals still occurred, but few accurate records exist from that period. The state began to formally track arrivals starting in 1987, during the period of peak resettlements of Southeast Asian refugees in the US (RPC 2020). Since then, the arrivals in Vermont have mirrored the national resettlement patterns seen across the US, with some obvious exceptions related primarily to geography. Vermont is underrepresented as far as Cubans and Ukrainians are concerned, for example, and there are few Central American asylum seekers or Temporary Protected Status recipients from countries like Honduras, El Salvador, or Haiti in the state.

But as far as other refugee groups—especially those accepted for official resettlement through the USRAP—are concerned, Vermont is representative of the program as a whole. This has meant successive waves of resettlement including Southeast Asians during the late 1980s, Central Europeans during the 1990s, and African groups from approximately 2000 onward (Portes and Rumbaut 2014) and South Asian groups from 2008 onward (RPC 2020). The largest refugee populations currently in Vermont are Bosnians, Vietnamese, and Nepali-speaking Bhutanese with significant numbers of Somali Bantu, Congolese, Sudanese, Burundians, Meskhetian Turks, Iraqis, and Burmese also present (RPC 2020). Many of these groups have arrived in large numbers over a relatively short time—for example roughly 1700 Bosnians were resettled between 1994 and 1997 and nearly 2400 Bhutanese were resettled between 2008 and 2014 (Table 3.1).

While the absolute numbers of refugees in Vermont are small compared to states such as California, Texas, or New York, the program has had a successful history, with nearly 7500 refugees settled since 1987. It is the specificity of this placement that is important to note— while Vermont's roughly 300 refugees per year between 2012 and 2016 seem small compared to the annual US resettlements of nearly 75,000

Table 3.1 Refugee arrivals in Vermont

Countries of origin	Time period	Approximate numbers
Vietnam	1980s	1100
Bosnia, Kosovo, ex-USSR	Mid-late 1990s	2000
Sudan, Rwanda, Burundi	Early 2000s	300
Somalia, Congo	Early 2000s–present	1200
Iraq	Mid-1990s; mid-2000s	250
Syria	2016–2017	14
Bhutan, Burma	2008–present	2400
DRC	2016–present	300

during the second Obama administration, yet when put into the context that all are placed within a metropolitan area of approximately 200,000 people, there is a disproportionate impact compared to the less than 1000 who were sent annually to New York City over the same period. While the resettlement program was headed by an organization called the Vermont Refugee Resettlement Program (and later the US Committee for Refugees and Immigrants-Vermont), a more accurate description might be the Greater Burlington or Chittenden County Refugee Resettlement Program—because all but a handful of those who have been settled in Vermont have ended up in one county and within that county only in two or three towns (Fig. 3.1).

There are many reasons that refugees end up in such a small area. It is the largest urban agglomeration, and therefore, housing—expensive as it is—is more readily available, especially for larger families. The services that refugees rely on upon arrival—job training, employment assistance, English language and citizenship classes, and a whole raft of other supports—are more easily accessible here as well. The Burlington metro area has an excellent school system and many social services have offices and affiliates located near refugee neighborhoods in the region. While the public transportation systems are challenging, as Chapter 7 explores in considerable depth, the most extensive of these are also concentrated within this area. Both of the main organizations that help to resettle refugees—USCRI-VT and the Association of Africans Living in Vermont (AALV)—are also located in the Greater Burlington region. As Chapter 6 examines in greater detail, few other locations have been tried as resettlement sites in Vermont and those that have been were

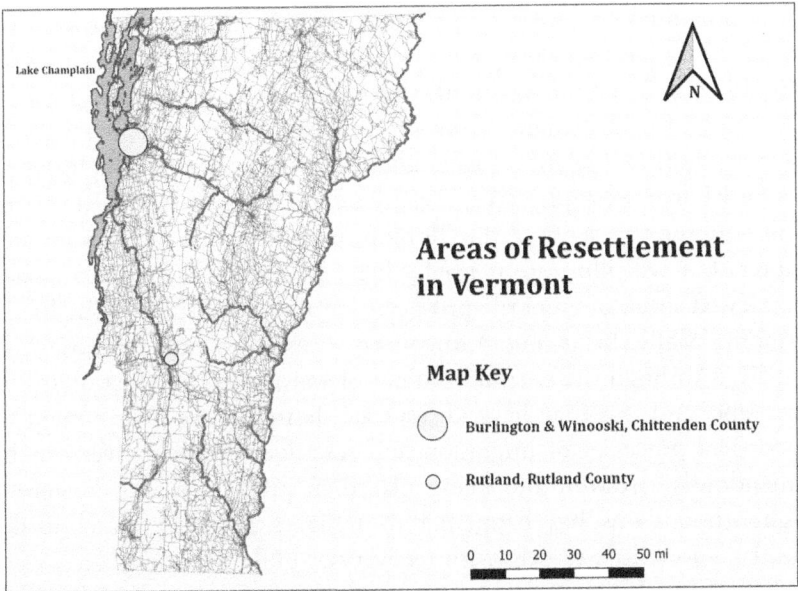

Fig. 3.1 Refugee settlement sites in Vermont (*Source* All basemap data comes from the Vermont Center for Geographic Information. Authorship: Refugee Resettlement in Small Cities, Lucas Grigri, March 24, 2020)

unsuccessful. For all of these reasons, refugees have been placed almost entirely in Burlington and its surrounding towns, and for the majority of the history of the program, few of them have either left the state or moved elsewhere within Vermont.

This last has changed, however, with some of the more recent arrivals. A number of individuals and families in the Bhutanese community have left for other locations since 2015, especially for cities in Ohio like Dayton and Columbus which have become hubs of Bhutanese culture in the US. While this trend is a source of great anxiety for local lawmakers, it may have less to do with a general dissatisfaction regarding life in Vermont and more to do with a desire to reunite with families, the availability of more affordable housing, and the lower living costs in the Midwest than in the Northeast (Walsh 2020). For refugees, there is a disincentive to move in the first years after arrival since benefits and supports are tied to one's resettlement location rather than carried by an individual or family. Some studies have suggested, however, that secondary migration picks up considerably for refugees after this first year (Mossad et al. 2019); in Vermont, this is a relatively new development.

Despite such challenges, Vermont and Burlington remain relatively attractive destinations for refugees and the program is often highlighted by USCRI as an example of a successful resettlement site (USCRI 2016). I will examine this sense of the Vermont experience for refugees in later chapters but will illustrate it briefly here. Many of the refugees I have interviewed speak often of the prospects for a peaceful and healthy life in Vermont. While this is not an uncommon desire for anyone, those who have lived through the horrific traumas of war, violent conflict, persecution, rape, and loss may have an especial desire for an environment of peace. The processes of migration and resettlement themselves can be tremendously stressful, and being placed in precarious and dangerous neighborhoods—as has happened to refugees in other parts of the country—does little to help with recovery or building a new life.

One refugee I interviewed who arrived with her family from Burundi echoed an unfamiliarity that many refugees I spoke with had regarding the place she was about to arrive in:

To tell you the truth, I had never heard of Vermont before. After all the interviews when they told me in the camps that we were going there we thought it was a mistake and they were sending us to Canada. But it is very nice. The people are friendly and helpful.

Another interviewee arrived in Vermont from the Democratic Republic of Congo. He too had little knowledge of the state, though like many others in the US, had heard of one of its more famous representatives:

Vermont? No, I didn't know it. Someone told me 'oh that's where Bernie Sanders lives.' I don't really know Bernie Sanders either but I had seen his picture. When I first came here then someone told me he owns the ice cream store. Then someone told me that was Ben and Jerry. But a lot of people here in downtown Burlington look like Bernie Sanders so who knows? They're nice, they like us, they like refugees, they want to help us. Maybe they are all Bernie Sanders? Or Ben and Jerry?

Another refugee, a Bhutanese man, also expressed positive sentiments about the nature of the Vermonters:

> They are very willing to help you, you just need to know how to ask. If you work hard and are willing to listen they will help you.

Yet another refugee originally from Somalia actually did have prior knowledge of Vermont. He and his family were initially placed in Georgia and moved to Vermont having heard of its reputation:

> We were originally located in Atlanta but it was in a housing project. It was very dangerous. There were gangs. We were concerned for our children and their future. Now we are in Vermont and we are much happier.

Others also spoke of moving, but out of the state, for the reasons discussed earlier. Another Bhutanese refugee said:

> I really like it here. The people are friendly and the place is quiet. I don't mind the snow or the cold. But the houses are terrible and I can't save up enough to buy a better one. If I move to Columbus or St. Louis I can buy a house so quickly. This is why we are talking about leaving.

These are just some of the perspectives—and mostly positive ones—that have been revealed in the decade-long research on which this book is based. I have been ascribing these views to refugee informants from particular backgrounds, yet it is important not to treat refugees as a homogenous or monolithic group. Even within different communities, all kinds of differences have helped to structure the varied experiences of individuals and families. The perception of refugee groups has also been distinguished by markedly different responses from receiving communities, with race, religion, and national origin playing particularly important roles as I have pointed out in previous chapters. Here I will briefly describe why the different major refugee populations in Vermont had to flee in the first place and how their diverse experiences give insight into some of the challenges and opportunities they have faced in their new homes.

Diverse Backgrounds

One of the largest refugee populations (and the earliest resettled) in Vermont is the Vietnamese who arrived beginning in the late 1980s. These are primarily those who fled Southeast Asia as a result of the Vietnam War and the US involvement in the region as part of its anti-Communist politics during the Cold War. Many millions were displaced either directly by the war or by the chaos that ensued once the US pulled out. In the case of Vermont, there are few Cambodians, Laotians, or Hmong who were originally placed in the state. Instead, it received mostly South Vietnamese individuals and families, some of whom had worked with the US as contractors or were the children of US soldiers, one of the largest groups to be resettled in the 1980s from the region. Most of the Vietnamese who have come to Vermont had at least a decade to wait before being resettled, though most did not spend the interim in a camp. The stories of Southeast Asian refugees in other parts of the country—especially in southern California, Louisiana, and Massachusetts—have been well documented, with notable successes in business, education, and politics tempered by enduring issues with poverty, education gaps, and literacy (Pho et al. 2007; Nguyen 2017). In Vermont, the Vietnamese community has been relatively successful, with a number of those in the second generation following traditional immigrant trajectories of upward mobility through education. Later in this book, Chapter 8 notes that the number of successful Vietnamese restaurants in the greater Burlington area is testament to the community's impact on the local landscape.

The next large group to be resettled in Vermont were Bosnians, who arrived beginning in the mid-to-late 1990s. Their flight was the result of the breakup of the former Yugoslavia following the collapse of the Soviet Union in 1991. In Yugoslavia, existing tensions between the different constituent parts of the country resulted in a civil war, the targeting of civilians by all sides, and the persecution of Bosnian Muslims, mainly by ethnic Serbs (Mertus 1997). A years-long siege of the city of Sarajevo and massacres of civilians throughout the region led to an exodus of refugees by the late 1990s. Unlike some of the other crises faced by other groups in Vermont, the Bosnian context is a relatively short one—a brief and brutal set of events, followed—for some—by a relatively quick resettlement in a third country. Some spent a significant period in a transitional area—usually another European country like Germany—before eventually coming to the US. The Bosnian refugee diaspora today is well-established across much of Europe and North America (Karabegović 2017). Like the earlier Vietnamese refugees, Bosnians and their children have become successful and integrated members of their Vermont communities. The current director of USCRI-VT is herself a former refugee from Bosnia and thus has lived experience with multiple facets of the resettlement experience.

From the early 2000s onward, African refugees began to arrive and today make up another significant refugee population in Vermont. They constitute one of the most diverse sets of communities, with members from multiple different countries and contexts. The largest group are Somali Bantu, an ethnic minority originally brought through the East African slave trade over centuries from sub-Saharan Africa to the northeast of the continent (Besteman 2012). Targeted by many sides in Somalia's civil wars, the Somali Bantu are an example of the victims of so-called protracted conflicts in which the displaced end up indefinitely stranded in refugee camps and quite often unable to return to their former homes (Smith 2013; Lindley 2011). Many of the Somali Bantu in Vermont spent years if not decades in camps in Uganda and Kenya before resettlement. A much smaller African community includes former child soldiers from Sudan who were resettled in Vermont. The conflicts in Sudan and South Sudan stemmed from political conflicts and civil wars as the latter emerged from the former as the world's newest sovereign state in 2011. The forcible recruitment of child soldiers is an especially terrible feature of these conflicts, as they are in other parts of the world as well and a number of these victims have come to Vermont (Bixler 2005).

Another large African community in the state comprises refugees who have fled different conflicts in and around the Lake Victoria Region, mostly from the so-called Great African or First and Second Congo Wars. Since the early 1990s and stretching over the past two decades, these conflicts have gripped much of the continental region, eventually involving nine African countries and at least two dozen armed forces (paramilitaries, rebel groups, and transnational organizations among them). Often described as the deadliest war in modern African history, between 3 and 8 million people are estimated to have died due to violence, disease, and starvation, while a further 2 million have been forced to flee to neighboring countries and another 3 million are thought to be internally displaced in the Democratic Republic of Congo alone. The Rwandan Genocide was part of this conflict and several of the refugees in Vermont trace their original displacements to this horrific moment and both the preceding and the resulting conflicts it spawned (Prunier 2009). The length and breadth of these conflicts have meant that a number of the refugees who have emerged from them and arrived in Vermont have also spent a significant period of time in camps before resettlement.

Such a long period of transitional stays is not as common with the next large refugee population: Iraqis. They arrived in Vermont in two waves—a smaller group in the mid-1990s following the first Gulf War, and from the mid-2000s onward following the invasion of Iraq by the US. Many of the latter came through the Special Immigrant Visa (SIV) program meant to support Iraqi and Afghan interpreters and translators who worked with the US military in each of those countries. A number has been displaced multiple times, usually internally within Iraq as a result of sectarian strife as well as foreign invasion, though they have not had the same experience of a prolonged stay in camps in third countries. The expectations of Iraqi refugees in the US and Vermont and especially of SIVs are often different than those of other groups like African or Bosnian refugees. Because the US has had a direct impact on their country of origin, and because for SIVs it was working with the US that made remaining in their country dangerous for them, Iraqi refugees have a different set of expectations and assumptions than other groups for whom resettlement is more of an explicitly humanitarian act. For these Iraqis, their resettlement is seen as an obligation on the part of the US. Iraqis are in this way more akin to Hmong refugees who had been recruited and trained by the CIA to fight a proxy war yet were essentially abandoned when the US withdrew from the conflict (Millsap 2016; Benson 2015). The refugees from Iraq that I interviewed in Vermont

were among the most vocal and the most critical of the failures of resettlement, critiques that are quite common among these communities across
the US (Yako and Biswas 2014).

The largest group of refugees in Vermont today were originally
displaced from Bhutan. They are a Nepali-speaking minority known
as the Lhotshampa (a large number of whom are also Hindu). Perse-
cuted by the Buddhist majority, especially from the 1950s onward, they
endured restrictions on their language, education, culture, and politics
(Evans 2010). By 1992, tensions and violence led to the departure of
over 100,000 Lhotshampa from Bhutan, some who left of their own
volition but most who were forcibly evicted by the military (Hutt 2003).
The majority of these individuals settled in camps in Nepal, while some
were placed in camps in India. The situation became a protracted one.
While living in the camps in Nepal, the Lhotshampa refugees lived under
severe restrictions on movement, ability to work, and general rights. In
the end, the situation was resolved through significant third-party resettlement—since 2008 nearly all of the camp population has been resettled
in a number of Western countries, with the vast majority (over 75,000)
placed in the US and smaller numbers in Canada, Australia, Denmark,
New Zealand, and Norway (Dhungana 2010). Bhutanese refugees thus
represent a significant forced migration population being addressed by
the global refugee regime today, though their circumstances and experience are markedly different from those of other groups—including their
potentially successful resettlement elsewhere, a 'solution'" that seems
lacking for others.

Another group of refugees from South Asia has also arrived in Vermont
over the past two decades. Beginning in 2008, Burmese Karen have been
resettled in the state. The Karen are a heterogeneous group of tribal
communities that have been waging an insurgent campaign in search
of sovereignty and rights against the military juntas in Burma/Myanmar
(Ertorer 2016; Bartholomew et al. 2015). Like other ethnic groups in
Myanmar (notably the Rohingya), the Karen accuse the military and
Buddhist majority of waging a campaign of ethnic cleansing against
them, including torture, rape, theft of land, and eradication of culture
(Sharples 2017). The Karen have been resettled especially in the US,
Canada, and Australia since the early 2000s (Lee et al. 2015). Many have

spent considerable time in camps along the Thailand-Myanmar border. Unlike some of the other groups resettled in Vermont, they are from primarily rural backgrounds. Most have limited English skills.

The remaining refugee communities in Vermont are relatively small. They include individuals and families from central Europe (Kosovars and Meskhetian Turks) who found themselves displaced due to the turmoil following the dissolution of the Soviet Union and Eastern Bloc countries in their own turn. A very different group of refugees consists of those who were supposed to come in larger numbers but did not, as in the case of Syrians detailed in Chapter 6 (Bose 2018). These, like the central European groups, do comprise a distinct community but one too small for their resettlement to be as noteworthy as that of the refugee communities so far mentioned.

There are thus both commonality and diversity in the refugee communities in Vermont, within and between various groups. That may seem like an obvious point, but it bears keeping in mind as I go on to discuss the places where refugees have settled and the impacts that resettlement has had upon individuals and communities. Most refugees have had similar experiences of displacement, often including torture, trauma, the loss of family and friends, livelihoods, homes, and cultural connections. Yet the particularities of the forced migration experiences themselves might lead to different outcomes during and after resettlement. The experience of living for months, years, or decades in a refugee camp may be quite different from a short and violent flight through neighboring countries to a new home—both of these experiences may be sharp and painful, but they remain different. Among the refugee groups in Vermont, time spent in camps between initial displacement and eventual resettlement—from shorter periods for Iraqis, Bosnians, and Syrians to much longer periods for Congolese, Somali, Bhutanese, Burmese, and Vietnamese—has led to many differences, for example, in education, work experience, and health care.

Even a prolonged stay in a refugee camp might be quite different depending on one's context. Children living in vast camps like Kakuma or Dadaab in Kenya often have had inconsistent schooling at best (Wright and Plasterer 2010). In many of the refugee camps in Nepal, on the other hand, a more organized English-based curriculum was offered to many students (Brown 2001). But the differences extend beyond particular conflicts or countries. The actual resources one might have at one's disposal—access to education and work, for example—might have much to do with the rules regarding refugee camps not only in different countries but in different regions. The Bhutanese in camps nearer Kathmandu, the capital of Nepal, were often able to work and become educated in ways that those in more rural camps did not. Caste and class also played important roles—in the case of Bhutanese refugees again, the US and other resettlement nations explicitly chose more educated, English-proficient, and skilled families to settle initially, as a former State Department official told me:

> The idea was to create a beachhead, to bring in the best and brightest from the refugee camps in Nepal and to create a leadership structure within the community. That would prepare the way for later refugees; they'd have their own leaders and own supports rather than having to rely on us. Of course, we didn't really understand some of the ways that caste would play out, recreating a lot of the inequalities from back home.

Rural versus urban backgrounds also play an important part in determining integration outcomes. One resettlement staff member told me that while Iraqis and Bosnians he had worked with came from urban areas and had demands related to public transportation, housing and business opportunities, for other groups, their expectations were different:

> They come from such backgrounds in the small area, rural area. So they feel more secure here and more, how do you say, it's not very congested, there's more freedom, they can move around and go to like—for example, a lot of family that I work with in the Burmese and Bhutanese community, they like to be outside in the country. Fishing, hunting, those kinds of things remind them that their culture is still there. It's not like going into the city and feeling like no one really knows you or you just have to go to work and come back and things like that—for them it's a little bit harder.

There are many other forms of identity and background that mark distinctions between the refugee experience in Vermont, as the next two sections of this book highlight. The main thing to keep in mind here is that there is no one monolithic set of similarities, but rather overlapping concerns, commonalities, and differences that structure a variety of outcomes. All of these provide a glimpse into the experience of refugees resettled in Vermont. But what about the flip side—what has been the attitude and experience of the non-immigrant populations already in Vermont to the influx of newcomers? The following chapters will explore such dynamics in greater detail but in this last section of this chapter on Vermont and immigration, I will set the stage by examining some of these perspectives as revealed through a series of public opinion polls I commissioned between 2015 and 2019.

Vermonter Attitudes Toward Newcomers

In the chapters that follow, I explore the experience for refugees of settling in Vermont and in three specific towns. But what has the attitude been of those already living in the state toward these newcomers. As I embarked upon my broader projects, it became clear that I needed to learn more about such attitudes. Accordingly, I added four specific questions related to this dynamic to the annual Vermonter Poll conducted by the Center for Rural Studies at the University of Vermont. Since 1990, this state-wide poll has explored public policy issues of contemporary significance, with researchers like myself able to commission questions to be asked of a representative set of Vermont households selected randomly via both landlines and mobile telephones.

The survey collected data for me between 2015 and 2019, in February and March of each year, using computer-aided telephone interviewing and a random sample of Vermont residents over the age of 18. The questions that I offered were among a much broader list of subject areas of significance to the Center for Rural Studies (conducting the survey) and of other researchers who had similarly added their own queries. In the five years that I asked my questions, between 650 and 680 households were surveyed, with the results having a margin of error of plus or minus

3.8% with a confidence level of 95%. This means that if this study were replicated 100 times, 95 of those times the results would fall within ±3.8% of the results found in this effort. The four questions I added to the poll each year were as follows:

1. Are you in favor of Vermont resettling refugees in the state?

    a. Yes, at the current rate of approximately 300 per year
    b. Yes, but at a lower rate per year
    c. Yes, but at a higher rate per year
    d. Yes, but not every year
    e. No

2. Where should refugees be settled in Vermont?

    a. Burlington metropolitan area
    b. Chittenden county
    c. In other counties outside of Chittenden County
    d. Evenly across the state

3. Who should be most responsible for helping refugees adjust to life in Vermont?

    a. City or town government
    b. State government
    c. Federal government
    d. Nonprofit organizations
    e. Religious organizations
    f. Local communities
    g. Themselves

4. What do you believe is the most important factor in successful integration of refugees into Vermont?

    a. Learning English
    b. Learning local customs
    c. Getting an education
    d. Getting a job
    e. Other, please explain.

The responses that I received were fascinating and speak to a number of themes throughout this book—about acceptance, tolerance, and xenophobia, about assumptions regarding integration and acculturation, and about the actual settlement sites for newcomers. For the first question, I found that despite the controversies, heated rhetoric, and rise in xenophobic discourse regarding immigration, within Vermont support for refugee resettlement remained high and in fact grew over the course of five years (Fig. 3.2).

In 2015, a solid 21.3% of respondents did not agree with settling refugees in the state at all, while over 20% suggested that they should arrive in either lower numbers or not on an annual basis. Over 57% of respondents suggested that refugees should come either at the same rate or at a higher rate than 300–350 people per year in 2015. These numbers have increased at the same time that refugee resettlement has been slashed and refugees themselves demonized in the US. The number of respondents saying that refugee arrivals should increase grew from 13.9% in 2015 to 29.10% in 2019. Those who believe the program should be cut entirely dropped from 21.3% in 2015 to 7.5% in 2019 (Fig. 3.3).

Unlike the question on program support, Question 2 on geographic location elicited fairly consistent responses. The options of resettlement in Burlington, in Chittenden County, and in counties other than and excluding those two places received few positive responses. On the other

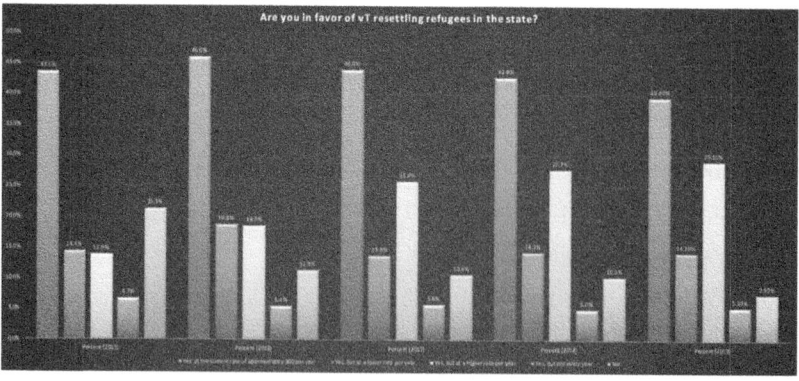

Fig. 3.2 Question 1—Views on resettlement

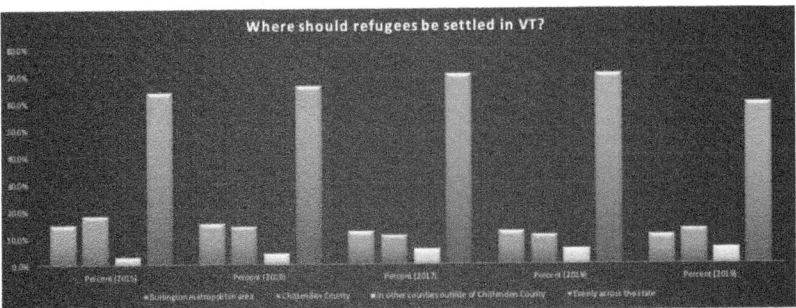

Fig. 3.3 Question 2—Settlement locations

hand, the idea of resettlement evenly across the state received between 60 and 70% of peoples' votes across all five years of the poll. Such a view does not take into account the particular challenges that exist with establishing resettlement sites in new locations, as described earlier and as we will see in the case of Rutland. But it does reflect a sense of 'burden-sharing' and collective responsibility that were also articulated by survey respondents (Fig. 3.4).

When asked who was most responsible for successful integration, the two most popular answers across each of the years focused on state and federal governments. This was in many ways the most distributed set of responses as nonprofit organizations and local communities were also seen as important participants in the process, as were refugees themselves. The only response that was of less significance was religious organizations, which is interesting given the important role that faith-based

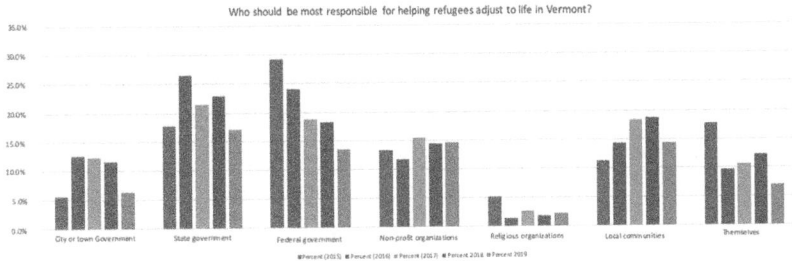

Fig. 3.4 Question 3: Integration supports

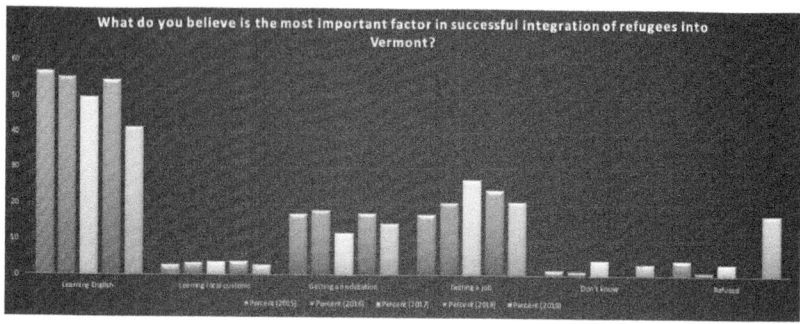

Fig. 3.5 Question 4—Important aspects of integration

groups played in the past in direct resettlement and how many local churches and synagogues are active in supporting refugees (Fig. 3.5).

The last question, which asked what respondents felt, was the most important part of a successful resettlement experience. Again, the focus here is on the general public rather than on refugees themselves. Later chapters will examine their perspectives on such success. Here the overwhelming number of responses focused on learning English—already a core component of what refugees are asked to do upon arrival. Employment and education also were significant for respondents. The first, like English language classes, is a major part of the refugee experience since 'self-sufficiency' (usually defined in economic terms) is a core tenet of the USRAP. Education is a regularly expressed desire of refugees in Vermont, though as we will see later in this book, it is often an unfulfilled one. Interestingly, learning local customs seems to play very little part in the general public's view of what would help newcomers adjust to Vermont. For a state whose history has often struggled with the 'authenticity' of its residents, this is a significant development.

What to make of such public opinion polls, of the seeming embrace of refugees by Vermonters? The impression one gets is that Vermont is indeed a place for such newcomers, even while doors are seemingly shut in other parts of the country (or to the country itself). But exploring this dynamic more closely requires looking at a different scale, not just of national borders and international flows, but at the level of the cities and towns into which they have been settled. I turn in the next three chapters to such an examination.

References

Baker, Dan, and Dave Chappelle. 2012. Health status and needs of Latino dairy farmworkers in Vermont. *Journal of Agromedicine* 17 (3): 277–287.

Bartholomew, Theodore, Brittany Gundel, and Neeta Kantamneni. 2015. A dream best forgotten: The phenomenology of Karen refugees' pre-resettlement stressors. *The Counseling Psychologist* 43 (8): 1114–1134.

Benson, Frederic. 2015. Genesis of the Hmong-American alliance 1949–1962: Aspirations, expectations and commitments during an era of uncertainty. *Hmong Studies Journal* 16 (2015): 1–62.

Besteman, Catherine. 2012. Translating race across time and space: The creation of Somali Bantu ethnicity. *Identities* 19 (3): 285–302.

Bixler, Mark. 2005. *The Lost Boys of Sudan: An American story of the refugee experience*. Athens, GA: University of Georgia Press.

Bolduc, Vince, and Herb Kessel. 2015. Vermont's domestic migration patterns: A cause of social and economic differences. *Northeastern Geographer* 7: 7–35.

Bose, Pablo. 2018. Welcome and hope, fear, and loathing: The politics of refugee resettlement in Vermont. *Peace and Conflict: Journal of Peace Psychology* 24 (3): 320–329.

Bose, Pablo. 2019. US policies and migration crises. In *The Oxford handbook of migration crises*, ed. Cecilia Menjivar, Marie Ruiz, and Immanuel Ness. Oxford: Oxford University Press.

Brown, Timothy. 2001. Improving quality and attainment in refugee schools: The case of the Bhutanese refugees in Nepal. In *Education in emergencies*, ed. Jeff Crisp, Christopher Talbot, and Anna Cipollone, 109–162. Lausanne: UNHCR.

Brown, Dona. 2011. *Back to the land: The enduring dream of self-sufficiency in modern America*. Madison: University of Wisconsin Press.

Calloway, Colin. 1994. *The Western Abenakis of Vermont, 1600–1800: War, migration, and the survival of an Indian people*. Norman, OK: University of Oklahoma Press.

Day, Richard. 2000. *Multiculturalism and the history of Canadian diversity*. Toronto: University of Toronto Press.

Dhungana, Shiva. 2010. Third country resettlement and the Bhutanese refugee crisis: A critical reflection. *Refugee Watch* 35: 14–36.

Eastmond, Marita. 2011. Egalitarian ambitions, constructions of difference: The paradoxes of refugee integration in Sweden. *Journal of Ethnic & Migration Studies* 37 (2): 277–295.

Ertorer, Secil. 2016. Acculturating into the Canadian society: A case of Karen refugees. *Journal of Ethnic and Migration Studies* 42 (11): 1864–1884.

Evans, Rosalind. 2010. The perils of being a borderland people: On the Lhotshampas of Bhutan. *Contemporary South Asia: Creating, Changing, and Recovering Community* 18 (1): 25–42.

Gallagher, Nancy. 1999. *Breeding better Vermonters: The eugenics project in the Green Mountain State*. Burlington: University Press of New England.

Geller, Wendy, Seth Marineau, and Richard Watts. 2015. Discourses of departure? Examining the 'Rural as Deficit' and 'No Jobs' narratives in Vermont. *The Northeastern Geographer* 7: 53–71.

Gilbert, Emily. 2019. Elasticity at the Canada–US border: Jurisdiction, rights, accountability. *Environment and Planning C: Politics and Space* 37 (3): 424–441.

Grant, Jill, and Lindsey Mittelsteadt. 2004. Types of gated communities. *Environment and Planning B* 31: 913–930.

Hewitt, Elizabeth. 2019. Police investigate harassment of migrant workers. *Seven Days*. August 27. Available from https://vtdigger.org/2019/08/27/police-investigate-harassment-of-migrant-workers/.

Hutt, Michael. 2003. *Unbecoming citizens: Culture, nationhood, and the flight of refugees from Bhutan*. Oxford and New York: Oxford University Press.

Karabegović, Dzeneta. 2017. Aiming for transitional justice? Diaspora mobilization for youth and education in Bosnia and Herzegovina. *Journal of Ethnic and Migration Studies* 44 (8): 1374–1389.

Kelley, Kevin. 2016. Historical society explores impact of Back-to-the-Landers on Vermont. *Seven Days*. August 31. Available from https://www.sevendaysvt.com/vermont/historical-society-explores-impact-of-back-to-the-landers-on-vermont/Content?oid=3632371.

Lee, Sungkyu, Sunha Choi, Laurel Proulx, and Jennifer Cornwell. 2015. Community integration of Burmese refugees in the United States. *Asian American Journal of Psychology* 6 (4): 333.

Lindley, Anna. 2011. Between a protracted and a crisis situation: Policy responses to Somali refugees in Kenya. *Refugee Survey Quarterly* 30 (4): 14–49.

Manore, Jean L. 2011. The historical erasure of an indigenous identity in the borderlands: The western Abenaki of Vermont, New Hampshire, and Quebec. *Journal of Borderlands Studies* 26 (2): 179–196.

Mares, Teresa. 2018. Farmworker gardens and food sovereignty in the northern borderlands. *Journal of Agriculture, Food Systems and Community Development* 8 (1): 1–4.

Mares, Teresa. 2019. *Life on the other border: Farmworkers and food justice in Vermont*. Berkeley: University of California Press.

Massey, Douglas. 2008. *New faces in new places: The changing geography of American immigration*. New York: Russell Sage Foundation.

Mertus, Julie (ed.). 1997. *The suitcase: Refugee voices from Bosnia and Croatia*. Berkeley: University of California Press.

Mills, E.J., S. Kanters, A. Hagopian, N. Bansback, J. Nachega, M. Alberton, and C.G. Au-Yeung. 2011. The financial cost of doctors emigrating from sub-Saharan Africa: Human capital analysis. *BMJ* 343: d7301.

Millsap, Chase. 2016. America's Ronin refugees: Forgotten allies of the wars in Iraq and Afghanistan. *Journal of International Affairs* 69 (2): 151–168.

Morse, Cheryl, and Jill Mudgett. 2018. Happy to be home: Place-based attachments, family ties, and mobility among rural stayers. *The Professional Geographer* 70 (2): 261–269.

Mossad, Nadwa, Jeremy Ferwerda, Duncan Lawrence, Jeremy M. Weinstein, and Jens Hainmueller. 2019. In search of opportunity and community: The secondary migration of refugees in the United States, September 24. Available at SSRN: https://ssrn.com/abstract=3458711 or http://dx.doi.org/10.2139/ssrn.3458711.

Mudgett, Jill, and Cheryl Morse. 2017. Longing for landscape: Homesickness and place attachment among rural out-migrants in the 19th and 21st centuries. *Journal of Rural Studies* 50: 95–103.

Nelson, Peter B., Lise Nelson, and Laurie Trautman. 2014. Linked migration and labor market flexibility in the rural amenity destinations in the United States. *Journal of Rural Studies* 36: 121–136.

Nguyen, Viet Thanh. 2017. *The refugees*. New York: Grove Press.

Pho, Tuyet-Lan, Jeffrey Gerson, and Sylvia Cowan (eds.). 2007. *Southeast Asian immigrants in the Mill City: Changing families, communities, institutions—Thirty years afterward*. Burlington: University of Vermont Press.

Portes, Alejandro, and Rubén Rumbaut. 2014. *Immigrant America: A portrait*, 4th ed. Berkeley: University of California Press.

Prunier, Gérard. 2009. *Africa's World War: Congo, the Rwandan Genocide, and the making of a continental catastrophe*. Oxford and New York: Oxford University Press.

Radel, Claudia, Birgit Schmook, and Susannah McCandless. 2010. Environment, transnational labor migration, and gender: Case studies from southern Yucatan, Mexico and Vermont, USA. *Population and Environment* 32 (2–3): 177–197.

Roediger, David. 2005. *Working toward Whiteness: How America's immigrants became White—the strange journey from Ellis Island to the suburbs*. New York: Basic Books.

Salazar, Noel B., and Yang Zhang. 2013. Seasonal lifestyle tourism: The case of Chinese elites. *Annals of Tourism Research* 43: 81–99.

Searls, Paul. 2019. *Repeopling Vermont: The paradox of development in the 20th century*. Montpelier: Vermont Historical Society.

Sharples, Rachel. 2017. To be Karen in the Thai-Burma borderlands: Identity formation through the prism of a human rights discourse. *Asian Ethnicity* 18 (1): 74–94.

Singer, Audrey, and Jill Wilson. 2011. From 'there to here': Refugee resettlement in metropolitan America. In *Race, ethnicity, and place in a changing America*, ed. J. Frazier, E. Tettey-Fio, and N. Henry, 364–388. Albany: State University of New York Press.

Smith, Yda. 2013. Resettlement of Somali Bantu refugees in an era of economic globalization. *Journal of Refugee Studies* 26 (3): 477–494.

Stechschulte, Ben. 2017. North Country at work: From Jamaica to Peru—Migrant apple pickers in the North Country. North Country Public Radio. October 25. Available from https://www.northcountrypublicradio.org/news/story/34928/20171025/north-country-at-work-from-jamaica-to-peru-migrant-apple-pickers-in-the-north-country.

Terrazas, Aaron, Demitriou Papademetriou, and Marc R. Rosenblum. 2011. *Evolving demographic and human-capital trends in Mexico and Central America and their implications for regional migration*. Washington, DC: Migration Policy Institute.

Tjørve, Even, Thor Flognfeldt, and Kathleen M.Calf Tjørve. 2013. The effects of distance and belonging on second-home markets. *Tourism Geographies* 15 (2): 268–291.

US Census Bureau. 2020. Vermont QuickFacts. Available from http://www.census.gov/quickfacts/VT. Accessed September 2, 2020.

US Committee for Refugees and Immigrants (USCRI). 2016. USCRI Vermont. http://refugees.org/field-office/vermont/. Accessed January 29, 2016.

Vanderbeck, Robert. 2006. Vermont and the imaginative geographies of American whiteness. *Annals of the Association of American Geographers* 96 (3): 641–659.

Varma, Roli, and Deepak Kapur. 2013. Comparative analysis of brain drain, brain circulation and brain retain: A case study of Indian Institutes of Technology. *Journal of Comparative Policy Analysis: Research and Practice* 15 (4): 315–330.

Walsh, Molly. 2020. As New Americans Leave Vermont, state seeks ways to be more hospitable. *Seven Days.* January 15. Available from https://www.sev endaysvt.com/vermont/as-new-americans-leave-vermont-state-seeks-ways-to-be-more-hospitable/Content?oid=29415645.

Wilbur, Andrew. 2013. Growing a radical ruralism: Back-to-the-land as practice and ideal. *Geography Compass* 7 (2): 149–160.

Wright, Laura-Ashley, and Robyn Plasterer. 2010. Beyond basic education: Exploring opportunities for higher learning in Kenyan refugee camps. *Refuge: Canada's Journal on Refugees* 27 (2): 42–56.

Yako, Rihab Mousa, and Bipasha Biswas. 2014. We came to this country for the future of our children: We have no future—Acculturative stress among Iraqi refugees in the United States. *Journal of Intercultural Relations* 38: 133–141.

4

Burlington

The last section began at the national and international scales, giving an overview of resettlement from a birds-eye view. In this three-chapter section, I examine what resettlement looks like at the level of the city. I present three case studies—the development of enclaves and refugee neighborhoods in the northwestern Vermont cities of Burlington and Winooski and a failed resettlement bid in the south-central city of Rutland. These three cases taken together offer many insights into the dynamics, practices, and outcomes of refugee resettlement in contemporary America in three related yet distinct instances. While all of these sites are located within the Northeastern US and in the state of Vermont and thus share certain similarities, they are also notably different from one another and in their own right representative of other resettlement sites across the US.

Burlington is a city of just over 40,000 residents that dominates a metropolitan area of just over 200,000 people (US Census Bureau 2020). Winooski falls within that area and Burlington's orbit, yet it is its own municipal entity (characteristic of the decentralized nature of towns within Vermont and of the strong streak of local autonomy

© The Author(s) 2020
P. S. Bose, *Refugees in New Destinations and Small Cities*,
https://doi.org/10.1007/978-981-15-6386-7_4

cherished in the state). It is a small community of just over 7000 residents. Roughly seventy miles to the south of these two towns, Rutland is the third largest city in Vermont, at just over 15,000 people. Unlike both Burlington and Winooski, which have been growing at close to the national average over the past decade, Rutland has been losing population at a prodigious rate—it is the town that has lost the most population in Vermont during the same period (Petenko 2019). These three sites thus allow me to examine resettlement (or aborted resettlement) in a small city, in a small suburb, and in a rustbelt city—representing three of the types of sites that have become increasingly common for the placement of refugees across the US. The first two are the most common resettlement sites in Vermont, the last an unsuccessful attempt to create a new site—also therefore mirroring national patterns of resettlement in existing sites as well as detailing the outcomes in an ill-fated expansion effort. In each case, I draw on interviews with residents both old and new about the history and perceptions of change in each community—actual for Burlington and Winooski, planned for Rutland. In the first two cases, I also present the results of my attempts to catalog some of these impacts by examining landscape changes within some of the main neighborhoods of resettlement. For Burlington and Winooski, I also explore perceptions of place from the perspectives of refugees themselves by presenting results from a Photovoice project analyzing their views on their new homes and communities.

This chapter therefore proceeds in four parts. In the first, I discuss the context of refugee resettlement outside of the large metropolitan areas that have traditionally been the destination of immigrants in the US, with particular attention to refugee resettlement in the US over the 2012–2016 period. In the second, I provide some background on the context of the city of Burlington. In the third section of this chapter, I look specifically at the neighborhood known as the Old North End within Burlington, one of the main refugee enclaves within both the city and the state. I close the chapter with a discussion of Burlington from the perspective of some of the refugee-background residents themselves, using the results from a Photovoice project I have conducted with community organizations in order to gain greater insights into the neighborhoods that newcomers live in and their relationships with of these places.

Refugees and Smaller Cities

As I argue in Chapter 1, it is important to look at the reasons why refugees have been placed outside of so-called gateway cities for the simple fact that so many have been located there in recent years, not only in the US but across the Global North in those countries that participate in refugee resettlement. During my study period of 2012–2016, the trend of refugees being settled in smaller cities across the US is clearly apparent. While several traditional large metropolitan gateway cities like New York, Chicago, and Los Angeles did participate in the USRAP, they did so at a much lower rate per capita than did many smaller communities. In Table 4.1, we can see, for example, while 10 of the 231 resettlement sites across the US were cities with populations of 1 million or more inhabitants, a far larger number of resettlement sites were in much smaller cities.

There are several clusters discernible in the resettlement numbers during this period (Table 4.2).

Table 4.1 Refugee resettlement sites in the US 2012–2016 by city population

Resettlement site population	Number of participating cities	Resettlement site population	Number of participating cities
2 million+	5	80k–89k	5
1–1.9 million	5	70k–79k	6
800k–999k	6	60k–69k	17
600k–799k	11	50k–59k	13
500k–599k	7	40k–49k	17
400k–499k	7	30k–39k	9
300k–399k	16	20k–29k	9
200k–299k	24	10k–19k	9
100k–199k	53	Less than 10k	4
90k–99k	7		

Source ACS (2013) and RPC (2018)

Table 4.2   Approved resettlements by site size and population 2012–2016

Resettlement site population range	Number of participating cities	Total approved refugees	% of Overall Approvals
1–2 million+	10	72,964	18.45
400k–999k	31	116,925	29.57
100k–399k	93	138,030	34.91
70k–99k	18	15,608	3.98
40k–69k	47	31,322	7.92
>10k–39k	31	20,392	5.16
		395,391	

Source ACS (2013) and RPC (2018)

What we can see here is that while just over 18% of refugees were approved for resettlement in the largest metropolitan areas in the US, nearly the same number was approved for placement in cities ranging from ten thousand to just under one hundred thousand inhabitants. In the smaller locations, the impact of newcomers would be disproportionately greater. An important caveat to remember when looking at these groupings is that there are two distinct kinds of newer locations visible in these groupings. There are some smaller locations—especially in the Northeast, where metropolitan clustering is often much denser than in other parts of the country—that fall within the orbit of a much larger city or are part of a larger metropolitan statistical area.

A very different kind of smaller city participates in the USRAP as well, however—these are smaller cities that are not particularly close to large metropolitan locations. In Massachusetts and Pennsylvania, for example, while significant resettlement occurs in the Boston and Philadelphia areas, many refugees are placed in smaller cities at some distance, such as Lowell and Springfield or Harrisburg and Lancaster. Similarly, in New York state, far more refugees are placed in Utica, Syracuse, and Buffalo than in New York City. We can see similar patterns in most other regions in the US, with resettlement in large cities, in smaller cities in their orbit, and in smaller cities well outside of their metropolitan area.

But why is this happening? What are the reasons that refugees are being placed in smaller cities like Burlington? A vibrant body of literature on migration and urbanization has asked similar questions (though about immigrants and cities more broadly) in geography, sociology, economics, anthropology, and migration studies, among other disciplines for many years. Such research has explored themes of community activism and the struggle for immigrant rights (Voss and Bloemraad 2011; Ramakrishnan and Bloemraad 2008), hybrid identities (Johnson 2006), acculturation in gateway cities (Khandelwal 2002), and segregation and social exclusion in new (metropolitan) destinations (Park and Iceland 2011), among a myriad of other topics. The broader question of the movement of immigrants to urban sites in multicultural countries such as the US has also had a long history and a significant geographic scope (Teixeira et al. 2011). The majority of such research, as noted previously, has tended to focus on traditional resettlement sites. Within the US, this has primarily meant metropolitan areas and states such as California, Texas, New York, Illinois, and Florida.

Over the past two decades, there has been an increasing focus on two groups in particular—professional and elite migrants in gateway cities and Latinx labor migrants in regions all across the US (Ley 2007; Li and Teixeira 2007; Ewers 2007). Since the 1990s, immigrants have not been coming as much to the traditional destination states. While the US foreign-born population grew by almost 60% in the 1990s, nearly one-third of these immigrants settled outside of the states listed above. The attention of many scholars in recent years has correspondingly begun to turn to new and emerging destinations (Lichter and Johnson 2009; McGrath 2009; Okamoto and Ebert 2010). These include the southwestern, northwestern, midwestern, and southeastern regions of the US (Massey 2008). Thirteen states primarily in the west and southeast (including several that had not been destinations previously) saw foreign-born growth rates that were more than double the national average between 2000 and 2010 (US Census Bureau 2020). Singer et al. (2008) have classified six different immigrant gateway types to suggest that we see newcomers settling in several different types of cities today including former destinations (e.g., Cleveland and Buffalo), continuous gateways (e.g., New York and Chicago), post-Second World War gateways (e.g., Los Angeles and Miami), emerging gateways (e.g., Dallas and Atlanta), re-emerging gateways (e.g., Seattle and Minneapolis), and pre-emerging gateways (e.g., Salt Lake City and Raleigh-Durham). My own research seeks to add empirical data on refugee placements to such studies of immigration and urban spaces more broadly.

In particular, I began with a curiosity as to what if any policy goal the USRAP was pursuing by placing refugees outside of traditional gateway cities. Other immigrant groups might be 'pulled' to particular places by the lure of jobs, of education, of reuniting with family members, or by other factors. Refugees do not have such choice; the USRAP and its constituent parts select locations on the basis of their own priorities. What might those be? I put the question to a number of officials with resettlement agencies and heard similar responses:

> No, there's no actual policy. If there's a number of job openings or available housing, that's what helps make our decisions.
>
> There's pros and cons to putting refugees in small towns. Con is that in a large city you can be kind of anonymous if you want to. But the flip side is that you can get more direct support in a small town. Either way, we don't actively promote one over the other.
>
> I don't know, I feel like we get a lot of requests from mayors and affiliates to think about smaller towns because they need people. But it's not something that we actively promote and after 2016 definitely not.

One resettlement agency official did say that they had participated in 2015 and 2016 in discussions to have a more intentional strategy:

> It's not a new idea. I remember us talking about this in 2013 too and it was not really going anywhere. Then when we were talking about expanding the program for the Syrians and opening up new sites we definitely talked about it – it was supposed to be a win-win: small towns needed people and refugees needed homes. Then the election happened and you know what happened next.

Over the course of my research, I asked this question regarding rationales of many key informants involved with refugee resettlement in the US. None of them spoke of a single vision, but instead of several overlapping reasons why refugees were being placed in smaller cities (Table 4.3).

For those intimately involved with the USRAP then, the rationale for putting refugees in newer locations did not represent a unified, coherent

Table 4.3 Most common themes by interviewee

	State refugee coordinator	State health coordinator	Federal agency	Resettlement agency	Municipal government	Community organization	Total
Total # of interviewees	50	50	15	30	50	40	250
Theme							
Revitalization	50	50	14	29	49	38	230
Diversity	50	50	13	29	39	29	212
Survival	43	42	14	24	48	32	202
Housing	36	32	10	21	26	30	155
Economic	32	30	8	26	30	28	154

strategy, but rather one that cobbled together existing conditions—available jobs, available housing, clustering of ethnic groups—and particular opportunities (like the expansion of the USRAP due to the Syrian crisis). What this also suggests, however, is that the USRAP's lack of intentional focus on the patterns of resettlement in new destinations meant that it did not necessarily put resources into those same locations—receiving communities that might have less experience than a traditional gateway in dealing with an influx of newcomers. Additional funds, grants, and expertise might indeed arrive in new destinations, but in a reactive fashion—in order to address a problem that had arisen, rather than proactively to prepare for newcomers.

Little surprise then that the trend of resettlement in new destinations has been raising concerns for many years now. Such concerns are not directly linked to the current controversies, though they often use similar language regarding capacity and ability to absorb newcomers. But whereas the antipathy toward refugee resettlement voiced by members of the Trump administration like immigration advisor Stephen Miller and many right-wing conservative commentators is grounded in xenophobic, racist and classist rhetoric, there have been longstanding concerns voiced by local governments, states and community leaders about their lack of agency and involvement in planning for resettlement. In many smaller cities across the US, civic leaders, school officials, community organizers, and the population at large have raised questions and concerns regarding their capacity to accept and integrate refugees for more than a decade (Committee on Foreign Relations 2010; Haines and Rosenblum 2010). For at least as long, refugee groups themselves—who often have little initial say in where they will be placed—have long challenged service providers and resettlement agencies to ensure that their needs are properly met (GAO 2012).

It behooves us therefore to critically examine the experience of towns receiving refugees and the experience of refugees settling in new destinations in order to gain more insight into these processes. With this context of small cities, refugee resettlement and a lack of planning or perhaps a unity of purpose driving the USRAP in mind, I turn to the case of Burlington.

Burlington the City

Vermont's major city Burlington has become increasingly recognizable as its former-mayor Bernie Sanders has garnered national attention during two political campaigns to become US president in 2016 and 2020. The city is one of a number that are often grouped together—along with places like Asheville, North Carolina, Boulder, Colorado, or Austin, Texas. These are smaller cities, often university towns, with vibrant arts scenes, often hoping to attract innovative industries and start-up companies, and a commitment to alternative energies and transportation. Burlington is often featured high on lists of 'livable' or desirable cities to live in within the US (City of Burlington 2020). Its civic boosters advertise a healthy lifestyle, outdoorsy culture, a vibrant local foods scene, a progressive politics, an excellent education system, and low levels of crime and pollution as reasons for newcomers—in this case young, educated families and professionals, not refugees—to settle in the city. Within Vermont, Burlington and its surrounding areas are sometimes referred to as a separate entity unto itself, so different as it is politically, socially, and economically from the mainly rural, agricultural, and libertarian-leaning rest of the state (Image 4.1).

Burlington's history is as a resource-town, dependent in particular on the lumber industry in the eighteenth and nineteenth centuries. Approximately 75 miles from the Canadian border, it has long drawn in migrant labor from Quebec, especially during its heyday as an entrepot for the lumber and textile trades, helping to facilitate trade via canal systems linking other centers north and west. By the twentieth century, Burlington had grown smaller in stature if not in size, as its industrial and manufacturing significance subsided. Its waterfront and industrial areas were in decline and as the urban hub of a state that relied heavily on tourism in its more rural and picturesque areas, Burlington's future seemed uncertain. But the 1970s and 1980s brought a new energy and vitality to the city, due in no small part to the surprise election of a socialist mayor—Bernie Sanders—and a cadre of progressive activists who helped to remake the city. He, like many of his peers, was not originally from Vermont, but part of the wave of counter-culture outsiders who flocked to the state in the 1970s, drawn by its

Image 4.1 Downtown Burlington

size, scale, and culture. But it was a culture that they were to transform, as the state—and especially the city of Burlington—shifted from
a relatively conservative, traditional New England society to one that (in
the imaginary of the broader US public at least) embraces all manner
of ultra-liberal views and beliefs. As I have pointed out previously, such
stereotypes are largely fictions in most of Vermont (which is far more
libertarian than it is liberal); but in Burlington, many of these myths
hold somewhat true.

Burlington in 2020 bears little resemblance to the resource city of its
past. Much of its current economic activity is based not on manufacturing but on jobs in technology, medicine, and higher education, with
Vermont's flagship university and its affiliated medical center located
in town along with a number of high-tech firms and startups. It is in
some sense a college town, with multiple institutions of higher education
nearby and a considerable white-collar workforce. The most common
industries are educational services (16%) followed by retail (15%),
hospitality services (15%), manufacturing (9%), professional, scientific
and technical services (8%), healthcare and social assistance (7%), and

Table 4.4 Selected characteristics of Burlington, Vermont and the US

Demographic measure	Burlington	Vermont	US
Per capita annual income	$27,105	$33,238	$32,621
Poverty rate (%)	24.7	11.0	11.8
Median house/condo value	$279,000	$223,700	$204,900
Median gross rent	$1177/month	$972/month	$1023/month
Foreign-born population (%)	12.7	4.6	13.5
Language other than English (%)	14.5	5.7	21.5
Unemployment rate (%)	3.0	3.1	4.8
White population (%)	85.0	94.2	76.5
Asian population (%)	6.3	2.0	5.9
Hispanic population (%)	2.8	2.0	17.6
Black population (%)	5.3	1.4	13.3

Source US Census Bureau (2020)

construction (6%) (US Census Bureau 2020). Unemployment is low as are crime rates. Yet income and wealth inequality are rampant within Burlington, as seen here (Table 4.4).

Such statistics make clear that Burlington is not an easy place when it comes to the cost of living, with a per capita income well below the national (and even state) average, and a significantly higher poverty rate than in the US overall. The single greatest cost to Burlingtonians is housing, with an exceptionally tight rental market, in addition to its housing market. Burlington is still a majority white place—though less so than Vermont overall. Its foreign-born population is close to the national average, making clear that refugees and other immigrants constitute a much greater share of the minority population in Burlington than in the rest of the US.

Refugees in Burlington

What has been the history and rationale for placing refugees in such a city, especially one that has become arguably more unaffordable during the same time that the resettlement program has grown? One might argue that Burlington does not 'need' refugees in the way that many of the other sites participating in the USRAP do. If we think about the top five reasons—diversity, revitalization, survival of cities, jobs, and housing—that those I interviewed within USRAP participant organizations suggested for placing refugees outside of traditional locations, only one (diversity) seems applicable to the case of Burlington. Burlington does not need refugees to survive and most arrived after the city's revitalization was well under way in the early 1980s. They are not drawn to address job shortages and certainly not to fill available and affordable housing—since there is little to be found and finding adequate housing is one of the chief concerns of the resettlement agencies operating in Burlington. Instead, I believe that increasing diversity and a commitment to progressive, pro-immigrant policies are some of the chief reasons that refugees have been placed in Burlington, at first on an ad hoc basis, and later more intentionally.

Refugee arrivals in Burlington predate the USRAP by some years. As one local church leader who has worked with new arrivals for several decades told me:

> Well, there were the people coming from Europe back in the Sixties, from the Cold War and to escape communism. A few people here and there, through different connections, we would sponsor some, work with others. Nothing like now, mostly through word of mouth or through a congregation.

A state official also talked about those earlier groups of arrivals:

> There were small groups – mostly individuals, really. Some Tibetans, some people leaving Russia and Eastern Europe after the fall of the Soviet Union. Nothing as organized as the Vietnamese or the Bosnians and nothing like the Africans or the Bhutanese and Burmese today.

Another community leader who had been active during the 1970s talked about the context of Southeast Asian refugees:

> There was a lot of confusion about what was going to happen with the Vietnamese. Other places there were Laotians and Cambodians, especially in Western Mass. But here most of the people who came were from the South Vietnam government or army and Vermonters who had served

in the war had met them or had some personal connection. It's why a lot of the Vermont Vietnamese I've met are so anti-Communist I think. Anyway, it took a long time for them to get to come to the US. Some came earlier, but most came in the mid-1980s and when they came here they had friends waiting.

Even prior to 1987, when Vermont first began officially accepting refugees, Burlington was beginning to resettle some people. But it was in the mid-1980s as the USRAP became more formalized that arrivals became more consistent. And when refugees arrived in Vermont, they came to two of the most common immigrant destinations for past generations—Burlington and Winooski. Certainly, other immigrants had come to other parts of Vermont—Swedes recruited to farm, Italians drawn by the marble industry in central Vermont, others to the mills or agriculture from Europe as well. But the Burlington area had been a particular draw for French Canadian immigrants for much of the nine-teenth century—until latent but virulent racism manifested in federal policies of immigration restrictions and Vermont policies of eugenics, effectively closing down the state and the city to newcomers.

When newcomers began arriving in significant numbers in Burlington in the 1980s, therefore, the gap between periods of immigration was significant. Whereas in much of the rest of the US—especially gateway cities—the period of immigration restriction was especially intense between 1920 and 1965, in Vermont that time frame could be stretched to an entire century, from the late 1880s through the mid-1980s. When refugees began to arrive in significant numbers in Vermont and in the Burlington area in particular, they were placed in locations that were traditional immigrant neighborhoods—but ones that had not seen a significant influx in decades if not generations. The two main refugee neighborhoods are to be found in the cities of Burlington and its neighboring town/suburb Winooski (Table 4.5).

We can see here that the largest group of refugees placed in Burlington during the last two decades have been Bhutanese, followed by Burmese and a number of African and Iraqi groups. The Bosnian and Viet-namese resettled during this time are family reunification cases with earlier arrivals.

96   P. S. Bose

Table 4.5 Refugee resettlement in Burlington 2002–2020

Country of origin	Numbers settled
Azerbaijan	3
Bhutan	987
Bosnia and Herzegovina	10
Burma	69
Burundi	1
Congo	1
Dem. Republic of Congo	20
Eritrea	1
Ethiopia	2
Iraq	37
Liberia	1
Nepal	7
Serbia	2
Somalia	58
Sri Lanka	1
Sudan	9
Togo	1
Vietnam	5
Total	**1336**

Source WRAPS (2020)

Burlington, as I have said, is a relatively small town, just over ten square miles in size, bounded by Lake Champlain to its west. There are generally six recognized neighborhoods within the city, though these do not align exactly with voting districts and municipal wards; they are not given official recognition but are generally identified as neighborhoods by residents. These neighborhoods include:

Downtown—the main commercial hub that includes a pedestrian-only thoroughfare known as Church Street, which extends for four blocks through the heart of shops and restaurants popular with tourists. The downtown area also extends down to a waterfront area that includes parks and marinas.

Hill Section—traditionally the wealthiest neighborhood in the city is literally the highest point in Burlington, with some of the largest, grandest homes commanding sweeping views of the lake and surrounding areas.

University District—the flagship university in the state is a dominant part of not only the local economy, but of the physical landscape, perched beside the Hill Section and overlooking the city as it slopes down to the lake. The neighborhood is home to thousands of students in dormitories as well as a number of former single-family homes that have been converted as rental properties for students who have moved off-campus.

South End—located along the shores of Lake Champlain to the south of downtown, this neighborhood was once home to a number of factories and industries. Since the 1950s, it has been mostly converted to middle-class residential neighborhoods and along the shoreline an arts district as well as home to a number of craft breweries, and tech companies.

Old North End—Burlington's oldest and most densely populated neighborhood is one that has historically been home to immigrants and working classes. Located to the north of Downtown and west of the University District, this neighborhood is the main source of housing for newly arrived refugees. There is also a significant low-income and student population in this section of Burlington, with many multi-family and multi-resident homes. Many locals also see this as a site of gentrification, with new businesses and residential developments contested as a result.

New North End—located just to the north of the Old North End, this is Burlington's most populous neighborhood and has been described by many residents as an almost suburban extension of the city. There is a higher proportion of resident ownership in the New North End and housing prices are somewhat lower than in the South End. Of those refugees who have been able to afford homes, most have moved to this part of the city. There is also a concentration of lower-income New Americans in a public housing project known as Franklin Square (Image 4.2).

There are also other important parts of the city—the Intervale and Winooski Valley Park Districts farming and recreation areas that are the main sites of refugee agriculture described in Chapter 8, for example,

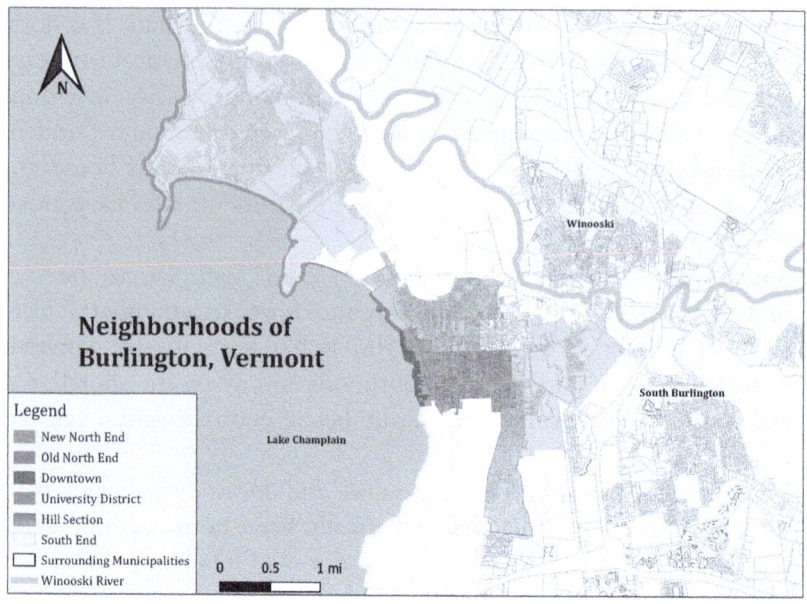

Image 4.2 Neighborhoods in Burlington (*Source* All basemap data comes from the Vermont Center for Geographic Information. Authorship: Refugee Resettlement in Small Cities, Lucas Grigri, March 24, 2020)

comprise a greater size than most of the neighborhoods described above—but they are not primarily residential.

It is the Old North End in which we find the majority of refugees placed in Burlington and as a result is the main focus of my inquiry in this chapter. Why this neighborhood? A local resettlement agency staff member suggests several reasons:

> We've worked with a number of landlords there over the years. We have a relationship and we don't have to explain who the refugees are or what their needs are. Also, because a lot of those landlords are used to shorter term rentals for students, they can be accommodating for our clients as well.

A local housing advocate, however, gave an opposite reading of the same dynamic:

> What's tough is to find adequate places to live for refugees. There's no pressure on a landlord to fix up their places because they'll fill them no matter what. The students will always come. So why bother investing in improvements? You can still charge whatever you want and you'll fill the space. In fact, it might be harder with refugees because they might want to stay longer and it doesn't make much sense to have to deal with that.

A community organizer was much blunter in their assessment:

> The resettlement agency calls them landlords. I call them slumlords. You wouldn't believe the conditions in those apartments. Broken windows during the winter. Inadequate heating. Multiple families crammed into an apartment. It's disgraceful.

Others were more measured in their criticism and their appreciation for the neighborhood, as this official with the city government:

> The Old North End gets a bad rap. It's not perfect, but for refugees I think it's pretty good transitional housing. At least it gives you a start.

During the earlier waves of resettlement—especially the Vietnamese in the late 1980s and early 1990s and the Bosnians in the mid-1990s—refugees were placed throughout the Burlington metropolitan area. But with the African and later Bhutanese arrivals in the 2000s, almost two-thirds have ended up in the Old North End, at least initially. This has meant over 1000 Bhutanese refugees between 2008 and 2016 being settled in a relatively compact neighborhood in the city. Those who have been able to secure steady, well-paying jobs, have moved elsewhere, notably the New North End and other cities in the metropolitan area. But a substantial number—estimated by some resettlement agency staff as at least 75% of who were initially placed there—have remained, calling into question the above city official's understanding of the Old North End as primarily transitional housing (Image 4.3).

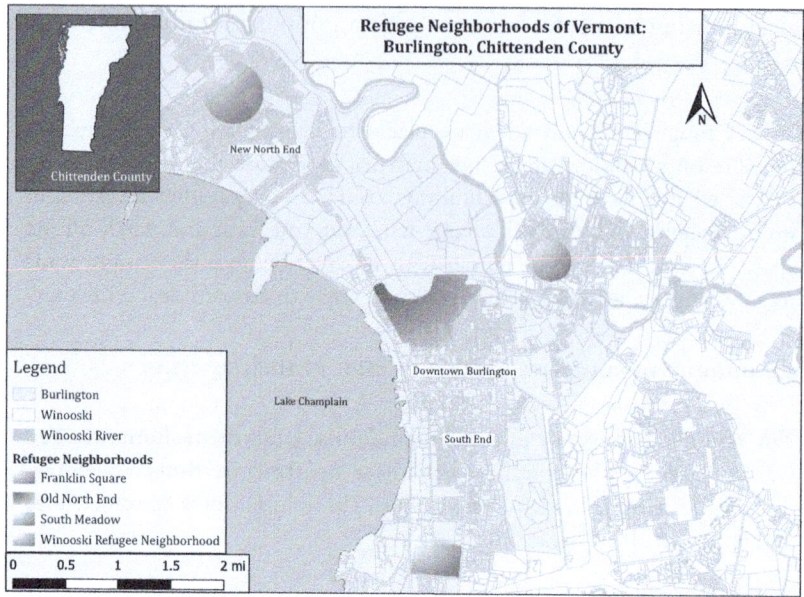

Image 4.3 Burlington Refugee Neighborhoods (*Source* All basemap data comes from the Vermont Center for Geographic Information. Authorship: Refugee Resettlement in Small Cities, Lucas Grigri, March 24, 2020)

Regardless of how permanent their stay, it is clear that the mark made by the newcomers on the landscape has been significant. As part of my research into the impact of refugees upon their communities of reception, I set about documenting the evidence of the presence of newcomers in the neighborhood and found many. Through interviews with residents (refugee and non-refugee alike) and other key informants, as well as through a careful, street-by-street documentation of spaces within the Old North End, I cataloged what uses and functions I saw in each.

I categorized these spaces in terms of those functions into eight broad groupings: community centers, food and drink, grocery markets, other businesses, public resources, public spaces, and religious institutions. Community centers could take many forms—an official space with a dedicated purpose, like a regular senior center or a more ad hoc youth program meeting area. Food and drink included restaurants, food trucks, and fast food outlets. Grocery markets—and increasingly ethnic grocery markets carrying goods popular with Bhutanese and African refugees—were especially visible along the main corridors of North Street, North Winooski, and North Avenue. Other businesses were varied—taxi companies employing refugee drivers, thrift stores, clothing shops, and equipment rental companies among them. Public resources mainly meant small offices maintained by local service providers that worked with refugee (and other) clients in the areas of mental health, or food pantries or tax services among others. Public spaces were mainly neighborhood parks and green areas. Religious institutions included formal churches and informal mosques and temples (Image 4.4).

One site of particular prominence within the Old North End is the Old North End Community Center (or O.N.E. Community Center). Formerly a Catholic school and located across from St. Joseph's Church it was once part of, the three-story building has become a prominent anchor for community activities for all residents in the neighborhood but

Legend

Type of Space
- ◎ Community Center [n=14]
- ◉ Food and Drink [n=9]
- ○ Grocery Market [n=14]
- ● Other Business [n=30]
- ○ Public Resource [n=12]
- ◎ Public Space [n=10]
- ● Religious Institution [n=4]

Image 4.4 Visualizing Burlington's Old North End (*Source* Vermont Center for Geographic Information [VCGI]. Authorship: Lucas Grigri, Alex Rosenberg, & Meraz Mostafa, Refugees in Vermont Project, NSF Award#1359895, August 14, 2015. This project also received support from the APLE Program)

particularly refugees. This is because the main offices of the Association of Africans Living in Vermont (AALV)—which works with refugees after the first year following arrival—is located in this building along with a number of other refugee-serving organizations. These include a mental health and psychological services clinic called Connecting Cultures, a Burlington Parks and Recreation Department-operated gym and a youth program co-facilitated with AALV, the Vermont Hindu Temple, a youth theater company, a community kitchen featuring an Eritrean and a Bhutanese chef, a senior center, two childcare facilities working with many refugee families, a pediatric health clinic for New Americans and other services (Image 4.5).

The value of this community center and of the Old North End neighborhood in general is that of accessibility. The main offices of the primary resettlement agency—USCRI-VT—are in Colchester, served by one bus line, and at significant distance from both the Burlington and Winooski refugee neighborhoods. The AALV (and other) offices, on the

Image 4.5   Old North End Community Center

other hand, are in walking distance for many refugees. Other health services and provider offices are also located within the Old North End. So, when we consider this neighborhood as a hub for refugee resettlement, we can see both the good and the bad. Sub-standard housing—widely acknowledged as a problem by many residents I interviewed as well as by housing and refugee advocates more broadly—is to some degree alleviated by the close reach of many services and supports that refugees need. This issue of mobility—discussed in Chapter 7 on refugee mobilities more extensively—should not be taken lightly, as integration outcomes are negatively affected by constraints on movement. And it is also true that the Old North End is not located particularly close to many of the large institutional employers—such as a few food and fragrance factories, the university, the hospital and hospitality industries—that employ many refugees. But that is also true of other clusters of refugee housing, including Franklin Square in the New North End and downtown Winooski, which are similarly disconnected from job locations (and opportunities) as well. And unlike those two locations, the Old North End offers many other necessary supports for those remaking their lives in a new home, putting important services within reach. While the Old North End Community Center was not planned by resettlement agencies but rather by municipal authorities, a county-led housing trust, and its resident organizations like AALV, it stands as an effective model for gathering and making more efficient such services at the neighborhood level.

Up to this point, I have been examining resettlement in this refugee neighborhood through the lens of key informants and outsiders like myself. But what do refugees think of their neighborhood? I turn in this last part of the chapter to their perspectives to examine this question more fully.

Photovoice: Refugee Images of Burlington

To understand better the responses of refugees to the neighborhoods in which they live, I utilized a method known as Photovoice in my research. The task was straightforward—recruit twenty individuals from refugee communities who lived in the towns with the greatest numbers of reset-tlements in Vermont and ask them to take photos of and discuss their views about their neighborhoods. The purpose was twofold; to help me understand the ways in which new arrivals might be reshaping the neigh-borhood, and to better incorporate the voices of residents into local planning processes. I had chosen to focus on Burlington and Winooski, the two towns with the greatest concentrations of refugees where, as I describe above, I had already begun to identify important locations according to our own observations and interviews. Yet my understanding of all of these was only ever going to be partial, given my lack of embed-dedness within the communities. I thus turned to residents to better understand their context.

In terms of the local planning process, the lack of involvement by new refugees had been identified by both them and neighborhood planning assemblies as serious and unaddressed problems. In recent redevelop-ment projects within both towns, very few refugee arrivals had taken part in public meetings and other outreach efforts designed to add resi-dent voices and priorities to the process. Adding translated materials and interpreters to meetings had done little to boost participation. Accord-ingly, I decided to use the tool of Photovoice—using prompts to have participants take pictures of a wide variety of neighborhood elements, provide an explanation and rationale for their choices, and have larger group discussions of the images to uncover the use, value and contested nature of various spaces—to better understand these neighborhoods.

Recruiting participants was not challenging at first. People within the communities I spoke with liked the visual aspect of the project and the promise that this might lead to actual changes that they desired. The project itself also seemed different from what they were used to—not the usual interview, focus group or survey, but the opportunity to be more creatively personal. It also seemed rather easy: walk around your neighborhood and take pictures. I offered the following four prompts to guide their activity:

a. Take 3 pictures of things you want to see changed in your neighbor-hood

b. Take 3 pictures of things you want to see stay the same in your neighborhood
c. Take 3 pictures of things that represent US/Vermont to you in your neighborhood
d. Take 3 pictures of things that represent home/community to you in your neighborhood

Participants then sent these pictures to me along with explanations of why they had chosen each image (interpreters were provided where necessary). A follow-up session was held consisting of each neighborhood group collectively meeting to discuss a selection of photos that I had curated. I focused on images and places that were common across multiple participants as well as those that revealed contested or multifaceted uses of particular spaces.

Such a research design has been used effectively in other instances as a community-based participatory research method to help intervene in specific issues or dynamics. Photovoice has been especially powerful in reimagining urban planning (Borowiak et al. 2018), immigration issues in Europe (Rania et al. 2014), children's perception of space (Burke et al. 2016; Greene et al. 2013; Fusco et al. 2012), gender and homelessness (Fotheringham et al. 2014), sexuality and space (Bain et al. 2014), racialization processes (Salazar Pérez et al. 2016; Goessling 2018) and public health (Sanon et al. 2014) among many others.

At its best, Photovoice is a method that can be used to reveal the narratives, logics, ideologies, and contested visions that lie hidden within and beneath places, processes, and people. My hope from the outset of this project has been to use Photovoice to identify changes that refugees wish to see in their communities in Vermont—what are the things, places and processes they value? How might they advocate for necessary changes and needs? How might they protect places that might not be seen as important by outsiders. My goal is to have the information gleaned from this process make its way into urban development and planning via neighborhood planning assemblies, city departments, municipal councils, and other local actors.

The results of the project were fascinating. The following were some of the most common responses grouped by theme (Table 4.6).

Table 4.6 Photovoice themes—Burlington

Category	Theme #1	Theme #2	Theme #3
Things to change	Potholes	Infrastructure	Graffiti
Things to stay	Community center	Green space/parks	Ethnic stores
US/Vermont	Flag	Convenience store	Own home
Home/Community	Community center	Religious building	Own home

The most commonly submitted images by participants of what they wanted to see changed in their neighborhoods were of things in need of repair. This very much supports the sense that the neighborhood of the Old North End is one that might be neglected either by city services—in terms of roads and sidewalks not cared for—or by residents themselves. Quite a few respondents talked about both (Image 4.6). One remarked:

> We live in America now. I thought this was a rich country. Why aren't these things fixed? It makes the neighborhood look poor.

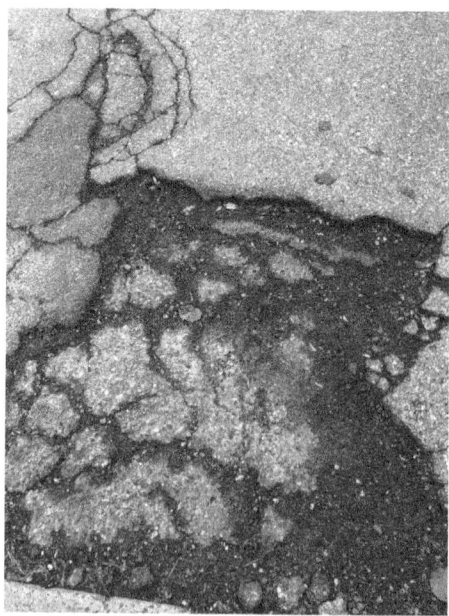

Image 4.6 Participant photo of cracked sidewalk

Another said:

> If I was able to fix something to benefit us I would fix the potholes because lots of people struggle to drive through them because there's so many huge ones.

Other infrastructure issues were mentioned. On participant said:

> I would like to change the number amount of sewer leaks that happen because it causes people to step in the water flowing out and it's an awful smell for the people in the neighborhood to be smelling which is also embarrassing to see.

Another said:

> Potholes everywhere are destroying our cars. Broken and weak electrical poles that breaks with the snowstorms and makes us lose power need to be fixed.

On the other hand, some participants drew attention to the role that local residents might play in a neighborhood in need of attention. One said

> Everywhere we go we see litter. For example, we would be walking around the neighborhood and there won't be a place that does not have a cigarette butt on the floor or just plastic waste. As you can see in the picture below, that there were lottery tickets, monster [drink] cans, carpet, and other types of litter just laying around the neighborhood. I think we should learn to pick our trash and throw it out in the right spot such as the trash can/recycle bin. I want to see changes happening such as a cleaner neighborhood.

Many participants mentioned graffiti in the Old North End. Said one:

> This graffiti everywhere is disrespectful. In my home country and even in the camp there was none of this. We should have architecture with a more beautiful design, not scribbling on the walls.

Another suggested that young people within their own community were responsible:

> Younger generation learns this at school in America. There is no need to dirty the walls of your own home or your neighbors. Here, this is what they learn.

On the other hand, those spaces that our participants valued showed much commonality. The O.N.E. Community Center was a top choice in both the categories for what people wanted to see stay the same and for what represented community to them (though admittedly, some participants may have taken the prompts quite literally, as is evident in the number of photos of American flags that were submitted as representative of the US). Some reasons that participants provided for choosing the O.N.E. Community Center included:

> We need community gathering places like this to relieve stress and mental health
>> I like having a place I can walk to so that I can enjoy activities
>> This place has many community leaders in it. Community leaders play a vital role in our community.

Religious spaces or ones in which cultural activities and gatherings could be held—mosques, temples, synagogues, and churches, for example—all featured prominently among participant photos. Within the Old North End, several of these can be found. A strong interfaith tradition within Burlington means that most of these places extend hosting to members of the refugee community regardless of the group's professed religious beliefs (Image 4.7).

Other spaces mentioned as significant were personal homes (again, the prompt to take photos of 'home' may have been taken quite literally here), and we also received many photos of homes when asked to provide images of the US/Vermont. Two other sets of common images of places residents valued within the Old North End were ethnic grocery stores and green spaces:

Image 4.7   Vermont Hindu Temple, located within the Old North End Community Center

All people should respect nature and beautiful trees like these ones.

This picture represents joy and celebration of freedom on this new land. We should protect our environment and ecosystem. Be cautious on what we dump in our lakes and rivers!

Vegetable gardens are important.

It is interesting that participants should highlight the importance of nature as the Old North End is one of the more urban neighborhoods within the city and does not have the same number of parks and recreational areas found in other ones. Even the refugee farms are not close to the neighborhood and the refugee agricultural program must often organize transport to and from them. Finally, ethnic grocery stores were photographed by many participants as well (Image 4.8):

Image 4.8   Ethnic grocery stores in the Old North End, Burlington

The African market represents my community to me.
Small stores such as these represent my Burlington to me.
The store across from my neighborhood because I shop there once a day so I already feel at home when I walk in.
I love to see markets like this. We need more beautiful markets like this.

Burlington's Old North End is thus a complicated landscape for refugees to enter into. Its old history as an immigrant enclave, its status as one of the poorest, mixed-population neighborhoods in the city, with a sometimes-crumbling infrastructure belie the significant marks that the most recent newcomers have made on its landscape.

This strategy of reaching into the resettlement experience has thus yielded data of considerable value in mapping the refugee presence as a reality that is at once objective and subjective. As this chapter has attempted to demonstrate, the evolving historical reality of the influx of refugees into American life must be understood as much from the refugee's point of view as from those of resettlement facilitators and the receiving communities. That understanding is essential to sharpen the perception of refugee resettlement as a comprehensive social, administrative and above all a political phenomenon.

References

ACS. 2013. United States community facts. *American Community Survey 2013 ACS 5-Year Population Estimate*. Available from https://factfinder.census. gov/faces/nav/jsf/pages/community_facts.xhtml?src=bkmk.

Bain, Alison, William Payne, and Jaclyn Isen. 2014. Rendering a neighbourhood queer. *Social and Cultural Geography* 16 (4): 1–20.

Borowiak, Craig, Maliha Safri, Stephen Healy, and Marianna Pavlovskaya. 2018. Navigating the fault lines: Race and class in Philadelphia's solidarity economy. *Antipode* 50 (3): 577–603.

Burke, Kevin, Stuart Greene, and Maria McKenna. 2016. A critical geographic approach to youth civic engagement: Reframing educational opportunity zones and the use of public spaces. *Urban Education* 51 (2): 143–169.

City of Burlington. 2020. Burlington accolades. Available from https://www. burlingtonvt.gov/Mayor/Burlington-Accolades.

Committee on Foreign Relations. 2010. *Abandoned upon arrival: Implications for refugees and local communities burdened by a U.S. resettlement system that is not working* (No. 9780160862458 0160862450). Washington: US Government Printing Office.

Ewers, Michael. 2007. Migrants, markets and multinationals: Competition among world cities for the highly skilled. *GeoJournal* 68 (2–3): 119–130.

Fotheringham, Sarah, Christine Walsh, and A. Burrowes. 2014. 'A place to rest': The role of transitional housing in ending homelessness for women in Calgary, Canada. *Gender, Place and Culture* 21 (7): 834–853.

Fusco, Caroline, Fiona Moola, Guy Faulkner, Ron Buliung, and Vanessa Richichi. 2012. Toward an understanding of children's perceptions of their transport geographies: (Non)active school travel and visual Representations of the Built Environment. *Journal of Transport Geography* 20 (1): 62–70.

GAO. 2012. Refugee resettlement: Greater consultation with community stakeholders could strengthen the program. GAO-12-729. Washington: US Government Printing Office.

Goessling, Kristen. 2018. Increasing the depth of field: Critical race theory and Photovoice as counter storytelling praxis. *Urban Review: Issues and Ideas in Public Education* 50 (4): 648–674.

Greene, Stuart, Kevin Burke, and Maria McKenna. 2013. Forms of voice: Exploring the empowerment of youth at the intersection of art and action. *The Urban Review* 45 (3): 311–334.

Haines, David W., and Karen Rosenblum. 2010. Perfectly American: Constructing the refugee experience. *Journal of Ethnic & Migration Studies* 36 (3): 391–406.

Johnson, Louise. 2006. Hybrid and global kitchens—First and Third World intersections (Part 2). *Gender, Place and Culture* 13 (6): 647–652.

Khandelwal, Madhulika S. 2002. *Becoming American, being Indian: An immigrant community in New York City*. Ithaca: Cornell University Press.

Ley, David. 2007. Countervailing immigration and domestic migration in gateway cities: Australian and Canadian variations on an American theme. *Economic Geography.* 83 (3): 231–254.

Li, Wei, and Carlos Teixeira. 2007. Introduction: Immigrants and transnational experiences in world cities. *GeoJournal* 68 (2–3): 93–102.

Lichter, Daniel, and Kenneth Johnson. 2009. Immigrant gateways and Hispanic migration to new destinations. *International Migration Review* 43 (3): 496–518.

Massey, Douglas S. 2008. *New faces in new places: The changing geography of American immigration.* New York: Russell Sage Foundation.

McGrath, Michael. 2009. The new gateways: Immigrant integration in unexpected places. *National Civic Review* 98 (1): 6–13.

Okamoto, Dina, and Kim Ebert. 2010. Beyond the ballot: Immigrant collective action in gateways and new destinations in the United States. *Social Problems* 57: 529–558.

Park, Julie, and John Iceland. 2011. Residential segregation in metropolitan established immigrant gateways and new destinations, 1990–2000. *Social Science Research* 40 (3): 811–821.

Petenko, Erin. 2019. As Vermonters leave small towns, Burlington region grows. *VT Digger.* October 3. Available from https://vtdigger.org/2019/10/03/as-vermonters-leave-small-towns-they-flock-to-burlington-region/.

Ramakrishnan, S. Karthick, and Irene Bloemraad. 2008. *Civic hopes and political realities: Immigrants, community organizations, and political engagement.* New York: Russell Sage Foundation.

Rania, Nadia, Laura Migliorini, Stefania Rebora, and Paola Cardinali. 2014. Enhancing critical dialogue about intercultural integration: The Photovoice technique. *International Journal of Intercultural Relations* 41 (2014): 17–31.

RPC. 2018. Admissions and arrivals. Available from http://www.wrapsnet.org/admissions-and-arrivals/.

Salazar Pérez, Michelle, M. Ruiz Guerrero, and E. Mora. 2016. Black feminist photovoice: Fostering critical awareness of diverse families and communities in early childhood teacher education. *Journal of Early Childhood Teacher Education* 37 (1): 41–60.

Sanon, Marie-Anne, Robin Evans-Agnew, and Doris Boutain. 2014. An exploration of social justice intent in Photovoice research studies from 2008 to 2013. *Nursing Inquiry* 21 (3): 212–226.

Singer, Audrey, Susan Hardwick, and Caroline Brettell. 2008. *Twenty-first-century gateways: Immigrant incorporation in suburban America*. Washington, DC: Brookings Institution Press.

Teixeira, Carlos, Wei Li, and Audrey Kobayashi. 2011. *Immigrant geographies of North American cities*. Toronto: University of Oxford Press.

US Census Bureau. 2020. Burlington, Vermont Quickfacts. Available from https://www.census.gov/quickfacts/burlingtoncityvermont. Accessed September 2, 2020

Voss, Kim, and Irene Bloemraad. 2011. *Rallying for immigrant rights: The fight for inclusion in 21st century America*. Berkeley: University of California Press.

5

Winooski

Up to this point in this book, I have moved from the international to the national to the local scales in my examination of refugee resettlement. In this section, I will also move between scales as I look in greater depth at different kinds and sizes of smaller cities. In this chapter, I examine the case of Winooski, a small suburb of Burlington that like its larger neighbor has both an older and a much more recent history as an immigrant destination. What does resettlement look like in such a location?

A suburb in Vermont—a state with few cities, let alone large cities or metropolitan areas—is of course different from a suburb in California, Texas, or New York, not only in size but in form and function. The relationship between a forty-thousand-person city and a neighboring seventy-five-hundred-person town is qualitatively different from that between the core sections of a mega-city and its outlying districts. But examining such dynamics at this micro-scale can offer important insights into the lived experience of refugees in newer destinations. As we have seen in Chapter 3, a significant number of refugees have been placed in similar contexts, in the exurbs and suburbs of relatively small cities.

© The Author(s) 2020
P. S. Bose, *Refugees in New Destinations and Small Cities*,
https://doi.org/10.1007/978-981-15-6386-7_5

Within Vermont, there is a long history of autonomy at the local level. It is one of the few remaining regions in the US Northeast to engage in intensive participatory governance and budgetary decision-making through administrative mechanisms. These include the annual Town Meeting Day in which citizens discuss and debate all manner of proposals for civic improvement and expenditures put to them by mayors, city councils, municipal boards, village and town representatives, and city managers—depending on the size and structure of each locality (Bryan 2010). Such small-scale and intense participation by residents in the running of their own communities has been much-lauded (Robinson 2011; DeSantis and Hill 2004). Yet such traditions are not without their flaws.

To an outsider like myself, the familiarity and small scale of this kind of local involvement can just as easily seem insular and parochial as it might to others seem a measure of engagement. If one does not know local customs and traditions, or is not already part of social and professional networks, then how does one become acquainted with them? How does one participate if one is identified as an outsider by immigration status, skin color, accent, religious observance, gender, or other markers of difference? As a number of scholars have noted, local politics is often an arena through which xenophobia and anti-immigrant sentiment are channeled and made manifest (Longazel and Fleury-Steiner 2011; Hopkins 2010; Gilbert 2009). It is not just that one may not know how to access networks; many newcomers are often actively discouraged from joining them. This is equally true of low-income, racialized, or other marginalized populations, whose participation in city boards and local government may be openly or implicitly discouraged (Patel et al. 2016).

Decentralization can also lead to a certain kind of duplication of services that are both inefficient and at times redundant. Many Vermont towns have their own police, fire, and ambulance services rather than pool resources, for example. Attempts to organize on a more regional or at least county level often run into opposition in the name of decentralization and a fierce protection of local autonomy. While a Chittenden County Regional Planning Commission does exist, its attempts to engage in multi-town planning initiatives are often hampered by the demands of its individual constituent members—a fact that I have seen personally in my years serving on brownfields and other advisory committees of this commission. And the Burlington metropolitan area—despite having the most extensive public transportation system in Vermont—struggles with delivery because of factionalism and the competing demands of smaller rural towns and communities versus larger urban centers, both of which fall within the Green Mountain Transit (the local transit authority) service area. Again, I have seen these conflicts play out firsthand, during my time serving as a Transit Commissioner and former head of its strategy committee. Even attempts to create a shared emergency dispatch service within Chittenden County have led to controversy and opposition among some first responders and the general public in recent years (Dawson 2018).

It is thus important not to valorize uncritically a concept like 'local governance' in my examination of a smaller community, just as it is important not to uncritically accept an embrace of 'alternative transportation' in Chapter 7 on refugee mobilities or 'local food' in my examination of refugees and food practices in Chapter 8. Instead, I will explore in this chapter the parallel, sometimes symbiotic, and often fraught relationships between neighboring communities of differing sizes and contexts and what these mean for the refugees who have been placed in each. It is also important not to blur the distinctions between places and to remember instead that Winooski is its own independent town. It has its own institutions, governance, and traditions, and it is important to remember this rather than simply to subsume Winooski into the broader Burlington area and identity.

I detail the story of refugees in Winooski in four parts in this chapter. In the first, I look more closely at the concept of the suburb itself to set part of the context for Winooski. In particular, I explore the relationship between ethnicity and place and between the ethnic enclave and its newer manifestation of the so-called ethnoburb. In the second part of the chapter, I introduce Winooski itself and talk briefly about its history and development. In the third, I describe refugee resettlement in the town. I conclude with results from a Photovoice project conducted in Winooski that parallels the one completed in Burlington.

Refugees, Ethnic Enclaves, and Suburbs

Immigration, whether of people moving from former imperial peripheries to cores (e.g., South Asia or the Caribbean to the UK or North and West Africa to France) or from 'old worlds' to settler societies (e.g., Europe, Asia, and Africa to the US, Canada, and Australia), has long been centered on large metropolitan areas. This is not surprising when one looks at the bulk of immigrants in the nineteenth and twentieth centuries, when those who made such journeys settled overwhelmingly in major cities. In the nineteenth century, this was especially true of so-called gateway cities like New York, San Francisco, or Chicago—where immigrants often first arrived on US shores, some of them moving on through transportation hubs to destinations further inland.

As ports of entry and places of geographical proximity to sending countries, it is not surprising that such cities became both gateway and host to large immigrant populations. Those who did not move onto other destinations tended to cluster in distinct enclaves—often in central, core, or downtown areas of cities. Some of this was intentional; living near those from a similar background linguistically or culturally can often make adjusting to a new life smoother. It might make obtaining jobs or housing, navigating educational opportunities, or simply getting around in a new place much smoother. Of course, historically, the development of ethnic enclaves in immigrant-destination cities was not always (or even mainly) optional; the creation of so-called ghettoes in which new immigrants congregated was a result of available (usually poor quality) housing, restrictive laws and city ordinances, and mounting xenophobia and racism, especially in the late nineteenth and early twentieth centuries (Portes and Rumbaut 2014; Roediger 2005).

Specific neighborhoods in gateway cities thus became marked as immigrant or ethnic—a Chinatown, Little Italy, or Little India. Today, such spaces have been sanitized, sanctified, commodified, and incorporated into many large metropolitan cities' marketing of themselves as 'global.' Where once they were undesirable, today they are marked as exotic destinations as signaled by the presence of signs in different languages, restaurants serving ethnic cuisines, businesses offering ethnic goods, and the bodies of racialized others. The ethnic enclave runs counter to the notion of the melting pot or of immigrant assimilation, to the expectation that after a few generations a group will lose the hyphen in their identity and simply become 'American' or 'Canadian' (such fantasies of course leave out the inability of some—especially those phenotypically different or racialized as Other to ever become fully part of such identities in the way that white immigrants might be able to 'melt' into a national imaginary). But what has been called 'persistent ethnicity' is not simply an imposition from without; as Portes and Rumbaut (2014: 63–64) point out, there is also a great value for members of new communities to have such spaces:

> For members of the immigrant generation, spatial concentration has several positive consequences: preservation of a valued lifestyle, regulation of the pace of acculturation, greater control over the young, and access to community networks for both moral and economic support.

Immigrant enclaves have also themselves played an important 'gateway' function within many larger metropolitan areas, serving as home to succeeding waves of immigrant communities. East Harlem in New York City, for example, has been host to Jewish, Portuguese, Italian, Puerto Rican, Dominican, and Mexican immigrants (Bell 2013). Kensington Market in Toronto has similarly been home to Scottish, Irish, Jewish, Italian, Eastern European, Caribbean, Vietnamese, Central American, and African immigrants (Li 2015). The Pilsen neighborhood in Chicago was one of the largest settlements of Poles outside of Poland in the late nineteenth century and today has an extensive Mexican population (Pero 2011). Jackson Heights in Queens, New York, contains a diverse array of immigrant groups from Salvadoran to South Asian and many others as well (Miyares 2004). Similar histories are evident in many other cities, not only of the Global North, but in the Global South as well—Dubai, Mumbai, Lagos, Manila, Hong Kong, Sao Paulo, and Bangkok all have their own immigrant and ethnic enclaves as well.

Yet while this pattern of immigrant enclaves in large metropolitan areas has characterized the late nineteenth and much of the twentieth centuries, more recent decades have seen the rise of new trends, especially the emergence of ethnic groupings on the suburban fringes of large cities. In the Global South, this has meant the development often of gated communities and luxury residential complexes meant for local and transnational elites alike. As I point out in some of my earlier work, such patterns extend not only to megacities like the ones mentioned above but even to secondary cities like Kolkata, India (Bose 2015). More relevant to the question of refugee resettlement in the US, however, has been the emergence of what Li (2009) has described as the 'ethnoburb.'

Since the 1980s, immigrants in the US have been moving in significant numbers from traditional gateways to the South, Northeast, Northwest, and Midwest regions and to rural and small towns as well as larger secondary cities. A number of studies have pointed out that the largest immigrant group—Latinos—have settled in the suburbs rather than central parts of cities or in small towns at some distance from the metropolis (Furuseth and Smith 2008; Kasinitz et al. 2008; Zuniga and Hernandez-Leon 2005). They are not the only ones, however; a number of other immigrant populations also have made their homes in suburban settings (Singer et al. 2008; Li et al. 2016). This trend mirrors one visible in other settler societies like Canada (Mukhtar et al. 2016) and New Zealand (Johnston et al. 2008).

Does the ethnic enclave look different from the ethnoburb? In many places, the ethnoburb takes the characteristics of the ethnic enclave or neighborhood in the central city—signage, restaurants, shops, people—and grafts it onto the suburban form especially popular in North America. That is to say that the ethnoburb is not so much the suburb that historically developed in the early part of the twentieth century in gateway cities like London, New York, and Paris—a blending of city and country by providing affluent denizens the ability to live on the edge of growing metropolises and have access to more space—and more the iconic North American suburb of the post-Second World War period. This is the suburb that is associated with the American Dream—sprawling, car-centric, tied to the development of the interstate highway system, focused on the nuclear family, white picket fences, White Flight, consumer culture, and malls. The movement of immigrants into this space is fraught with tensions, as many more recent studies have shown (Tam 2019; Walker 2018; Fittante 2018; Jones-Correa 2008).

As I turn to the second of my cases of immigrant neighborhoods in Vermont—the town of Winooski—it is important to keep all of this context in mind. Winooski is its own town, distinct from but connected to its larger neighbor, Burlington. It is a bedroom community rather than suburbia in the ways that we often imagine the latter, but one that has historically been host to an immigrant population that is situated outside of the main downtown enclave described in the previous chapter on Burlington. Winooski was one of the main settlement sites for laborers coming from Ireland and Quebec in the nineteenth and twentieth centuries; today, it is home to refugees from Africa and Asia.

Winooski the City

Across a river from Burlington lies the tiny community of Winooski, population under 7500 (US Census Bureau 2020). It is a working-class town, once conceived as a bedroom community for Burlington commuters, but has a long history of settlement by French-Canadian and Irish immigrants. Where Vermont's population is 97% white, only 77% of Winooski's is—nearly 15% of the population is Asian (US Census Bureau 2020). Unlike many Vermont towns, Winooski has actually grown over the last decade—albeit by only 1%, nearly the same rate of growth as Burlington. Almost all of that growth is due to the refugee resettlement program. Along with the Old North End of Burlington, the area near Winooski's main street is one of the two most densely populated refugee enclaves in Vermont (Table 5.1).

Winooski is a much smaller city than Burlington (7500 versus 43,000 residents, while Rutland is in-between with over 15,000 residents) and is a little less white (78–85%). It is considerably poorer (over 30% of residents live in poverty compared to 24% in Burlington), though rent and housing prices are comparable with its wealthier neighbor. As with Burlington, those refugees who have become more economically established do not stay in Winooski—many move on to the neighboring towns of Essex, Essex Junction, and Colchester. But many refugees do stay in Winooski—it has a significantly higher foreign-born population than Burlington as well as a higher proportion of languages other

Table 5.1 Selected characteristics of Winooski, Vermont, and the US

Demographic measure	Winooski	Vermont	US
Per capita annual income	$26,274	$33,238	$32,621
Poverty rate (%)	31.0	11.0	11.8
Median house/condo value	$221,800	$223,700	$204,900
Median gross rent	$1117/month	$972/month	$1023/month
Foreign-born population (%)	17.9	4.6	13.5
Language other than English (%)	21.1	5.7	21.5
Unemployment rate (%)	4.1	3.1	4.8
White population (%)	78.7	94.2	76.5
Asian population (%)	14.9	2.0	5.9
Hispanic population (%)	2.5	2.0	18.3
Black population (%)	3.0	1.4	13.4

Source US Census Bureau (2020)

than English spoken at home. A number of Winooski residents work in schools and colleges within the metropolitan area; 14% are in the professional, scientific, and technical services sector while another 10% are in educational services (US Census Bureau 2020). Retail workers comprise a further 14% of Winooski's workforce while manufacturing in this former industrial city is the occupation of just 11% of its current population. Hospitality and construction make up 8% each while healthcare and social services account for 7% of local workers. Much of this work is concentrated in two places in Winooski—for hospitality, retail and food services workers along the Main Street corridor and for those in manufacturing in one industrial park located just off it (Image 5.1).

Winooski, named by the Abenaki as the 'land of the wild onion' or the 'onion river,' was inhabited by indigenous communities for over a thousand years before European contact. Its colonial history, like that of Burlington and Rutland, is grounded in its life as an industrial city. It is located by a river whose steep waterfalls powered the expansion of woolen mills and textiles industries, which attracted many immigrant laborers. The mills were the backbone of the local economy; in the late nineteenth and early twentieth centuries, more than half of local residents were employed by them, with many others directly reliant on the textile industries (Feeney 2002). During two world wars and high demand for textiles, the city boomed; but in peacetime and especially

Image 5.1 Winooski Main Street corridor

after Second World War, the mills and the city that was dependent upon them fell on hard times. As one long-time resident and former city employee recounted:

> This was a vibrant city during the war [WWII] because of the mills and Fort Ethan Allen. Then the base closed and the mills started closing in the mid-50s and all of a sudden all of the businesses – all the bars and restaurants on Main Street – they all started shutting down too. It wasn't just something that affected Winooski, it was bad for Burlington too.

For the next few decades, Winooski stagnated. Housing prices fell, local industries were few and far between, and the small town struggled with its place in a changing Vermont. Not many of the back-to-the-landers who came to Vermont in the 1960s and 1970s settled in Winooski, but some of the radical ideas they brought to the state took hold in the small town. In 1979, for example, Winooski became somewhat infamous when its mayor and community development office floated the idea of building a one-square-mile dome to cover the entire city as a way of saving on heating costs and conserving energy and the city applied for federal funds to explore the feasibility of the project (*New York Times* 1979; Lange 2017). This vision never came to fruition (creating such a dystopia seems impractical at best) but illustrates the quirkiness that characterizes Winooski for many locals as another city employee told me:

> I know, everyone still talks about the dome. And it makes us seem like something out of the *Simpsons*. But if you think about it, trying to keep the town affordable makes sense, even if covering us all up in a plastic bubble or a giant snow globe doesn't.

Winooski did not go through the same cycle of revitalization that Burlington did during the 1980s—much of the 1980–2000 period was characterized by investment in historic preservation rather than new construction (Lindholm and Cengeri 2014)—but by the early 2000s the city began to slowly follow its larger and wealthier neighbor through a similar set of transformations. Many of the old mill and other industrial sites were remade into new housing and office space, especially for star-tups connected to IT and services. A large traffic circle was installed in the middle of downtown main street and a string of popular restaurants and bars now surround it. New condominiums, a community college, and heritage buildings hosting entrepreneurs and maker spaces give this part of the small city an air of gentrification and revitalization.

Yet move a few blocks off of the main street and the challenges of Winooski persist. Nearly a third of residents fall below the poverty line and a large proportion of students in the local school are considered low income, qualifying for free or subsidized lunches. There are no grocery stores in Winooski, only a Costco and a Shaw's located across the highway in the neighboring town of Colchester, both of them diffi-cult to reach without a car. While the Main Street Revitalization Project in Winooski has focused on (re)building sidewalks and foot traffic in the downtown corridor (City of Winooski 2020) and further up Main Street a number of smaller grocery stores dot either side of the road, there are currently no sidewalks leading to the larger supermarkets, making them inaccessible for residents without a personal vehicle. Many refugees living in Winooski are particularly vulnerable to this lack of mobility, which I explore further in Chapter 7. I turn in the next section of this chapter to the placement of refugees within the town.

Refugees in Winooski

While urban development, tech startups, and a bustling culinary scene are all heralded as signs of a revitalized Winooski, the most significant change to the city in the past two decades has been the addition of a large immigrant and refugee population. As the town's history shows, this is not the first time, as the markers of earlier generations of Irish and French-Canadian immigrants can still be seen in local churches, tombstones in cemeteries, and family names of local businesses and streets can all attest to the refugee presence. In the school district, nearly twenty different languages and fifty different national origins are found within the student body (Winooski School District 2020). This is not surprising given that nearly 20% of the town's population is foreign-born, far in excess of any other town in the entire state. And this group is overwhelmingly composed of refugees resettled over the past twenty years (Table 5.2).

We can see here that the vast majority of refugees in Winooski arrived from Bhutan (mostly between 2008 and 2016). The two large earlier waves of refugees (from Vietnam and Bosnia, respectively) saw some settlement in Winooski, but accurate numbers are not available from USCRI-VT (which does not track movement beyond the first year); anecdotally, several staff members did mention placing arrivals from both groups initially in the town, but not in as large numbers as with more recent groups. While Bhutanese and Burmese refugees parallel the

Table 5.2 Refugee resettlement in Winooski 2002–2020

Country of origin	Numbers settled
Bhutan	465
Burma	40
Croatia	4
Dem. Republic of Congo	20
India	1
Iraq	60
Nepal	1
Somalia	4
Total	**595**

Source WRAPS (2020)

numbers placed in Burlington, the main outlier are Iraqi refugees who have been resettled in Winooski in far greater numbers (in two waves, in the 1990s following the first Gulf War and again after 2005 and the invasion of Iraq) than in Burlington (Image 5.2).

Much smaller than its larger neighbor, defining distinct neighborhoods is not as easy in Winooski as it is in Burlington. It is just over a square mile in total area, bordered to the north by the town of Colchester and to the south by Burlington's Old North End; indeed, one might argue that the refugee neighborhood stretches across this entire section of the metropolitan region and the two cities. Yet the physical barrier between the Old North End and Winooski is significant; the Winooski River that divides them lies at the bottom of steep hills between both neighborhoods and makes travel between them more complicated than simply walking across a few streets. Winooski is the most densely populated town in Vermont, albeit the smallest of its incorporated cities. Most

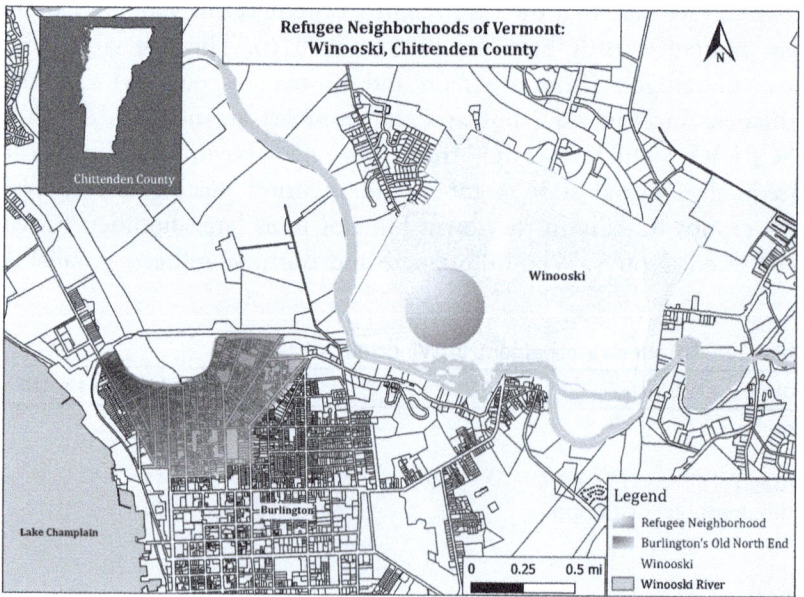

Image 5.2 Winooski refugee neighborhood (*Source* All basemap data comes from the Vermont Center for Geographic Information. Authorship: Refugee Resettlement in Small Cities, Lucas Grigri, March 24, 2020)

of its housing lies on either side of Main Street (also Vermont Route 2), beginning from a bridge connected to Burlington on the south to just before the Interstate Highway 89 in Colchester.

What has made Winooski an attractive destination for refugees? As with Burlington's Old North End, it has a long history of immigrant settlement; it was its own ethnic enclave, not an 'ethnoburb' as such, but an ethnic enclave outside of the core of the metropolitan area. Again, similar to Burlington, that history was long past; decades passed between the French-Canadian and Irish histories of Winooski and the arrival of newcomers from Africa and Asia in the 2000s. A member of the city's community and economic development office commented on the continuities and distinctions between these two moments:

> I think the history of Winooski is both a blessing and a curse. It's been a city of immigrants since it began, a lot of heritage with French and Irish immigration when the Mills opened. It's really interesting being involved with the Senior Center where there are folks who primarily speak French still. There's a refugee high school student who was on a city commission a few years ago who used to say nothing is different, the only difference is skin color.

Another city employee suggested that despite the differences between older and newer residents, Winooski's history meant at least some level of understanding of what it meant to arrive in a newer home:

> I think that it's a much more visible difference for folks arriving but I don't think it mirrors very much the challenges that French migrants saw, Irish immigrants, Bosnian immigrants. I do think that on some level there is a bit of cultural understanding of what that experience can be like that's been passed on through some of the families of longer-term Winooski residents.

The idea that Winooksi's experience with past waves of immigrants (much like Burlington's Old North End) made it hospitable to newer arrivals seems to be a common narrative, at least among the city officials I interviewed. However, the availability of (somewhat) more affordable housing seems to have been a much more immediate consideration. Another city official stated:

> I think we by virtue of our affordability and proximity to Burlington tend to be one of the two spots that people land in. I think VRRP makes a point of looking at us because we are next door and we have such a high proportion of rental stock. We are 70% rental and our Code Enforcement Department has made a lot of effort to make sure that rental stock is kept at a quality level. I think this is why we are so popular with refugees.

What the official is referring to here is the fact that USCRI-VT (at the time called the Vermont Refugee Resettlement Program or VRRP) has its head offices in neighboring Colchester and has long worked with a number of landlords in Winooski (as it has in Burlington's Old North End) to place new arrivals. The USCRI-VT offices are themselves not that accessible—there is one bus that serves it and without a car these offices are certainly not walkable. However, a number of other refugee community offices are also present in Winooski, including those of the Somali Bantu Association of Vermont, the Vermont Bhutanese Association, and the Islamic Society of Vermont. A mosque was in nearby Colchester but recently moved to larger premises in South Burlington. Many of these community offices are supported with space and financial resources by the city of Winooski.

What advantage do city officials see in supporting specific ethnic communities and refugees at large? When I put this question to them, many echoed the sentiments of municipal authorities in other small cities across America I described in Chapter 4. The theme of diversity was front and center, as this city official said:

> I think we've really managed to double down and show that we value the diversity refugees bring and view it as very much as a strategic advantage for us.

Another stated:

> I think as a smaller city in trying to kind of establish ourselves it is unique and kind of allows us to carve out our little niche here in Chittenden

County. I think that that's actually been something we viewed as really valuable and so both for reasons of wanting to do the right thing and also because it's really helpful for our community we've really wanted to do resettlement well and I think of across the board in our city structures tried really hard to incorporate more cultural competency more awareness of the various needs of folks that we see, you know the wide variety of folks we see in our services.

And while unfamiliarity with serving newcomers—or at least a significant lag in the time spent doing so—might pose a challenge for a small city, it is the very size of a place like Winooski that some of the municipal authorities see as a strength. Here again, a staff member in the community economic and development office speaks:

I think our small size is really powerful and helpful. It is a community where you know the city manager, the school superintendent, the police chief, they are all going to pick up the phone when you call and so I do think that that's really helpful. I think it's really cut down on the bureaucratic layers that sometimes muddle things when you're trying to deliver services.

Said a member of the mayor's staff:

I think in terms of a small city sort of scale issue that you know there's more contact. You have to ask yourself, do newcomers reach out to you, do they actually come and participate, do they come to school meetings, or after school programs or the parks and I think the answer is mostly yes, because we're so small, because they get to know us.

Such sentiments were not uncommon, and not only among city officials. The achievement of members of the Bhutanese community—success in schools and starting new businesses—became emblematic of this particular population's success. A number of Bhutanese refugees began to purchase homes a scant five years after the first members of the community first arrived in Vermont. Some of these were in Burlington's New North End and a few others in South Burlington and Essex, yet a handful were in Winooski, where a number of refugees stayed on past their initial placement and not only bought homes but became landlords in their own right, often to other newer refugee arrivals (Picard 2013).

The successes of Winooski's resettlement program were publicized beyond the little town itself. During the controversial attempts to expand the resettlement program to Rutland (detailed in Chapter 6), such stories became especially prevalent, as advocates for resettlement argued that Rutland could use Winooski as a model for economic development and focused on the ways that new arrivals could help a community grow (Keck 2016). Others talked about the successes of refugee integration in Winooski and tried to dispel common misconceptions regarding refugees, culture clashes, and the potential for rising crime rates (Dritschilo 2016).

As with Burlington, it is clear in Winooski that the impact upon the landscape of the town made by refugee arrivals is significant. And in this town as well, I set about documenting the evidence of newcomers in the neighborhood and found much to record. Through interviews with residents (refugee and non-refugee alike) and other key informants, as well as through a careful, street-by-street documentation of spaces within the Winooski—especially along the Main Street corridor—I catalogued what uses and functions I saw in each (Image 5.3).

I categorize these spaces in terms of those functions into eight broad groupings: community centers, food and drink, grocery markets, other businesses, public resources, public spaces, and religious institutions. Community centers could take many forms—an official space with a dedicated purpose, like a regular senior center or a more ad hoc youth program meeting area. Food and drink included restaurants, food trucks, and fast food outlets. Grocery markets—and increasingly ethnic grocery markets carrying goods popular particularly with Bhutanese—were especially visible along the Main Street corridor in Winooski. Other businesses were varied—a phone store, thrift stores, and clothing shops. Public resources mainly meant small offices maintained by local service providers that worked with refugee (and other) clients in the areas of mental health, or food pantries or tax services among others. Public spaces were mainly neighborhood parks and green areas. Religious institutions in Winooski were primarily formal churches and informal temples.

Visualizing Winooski - Area of Focus

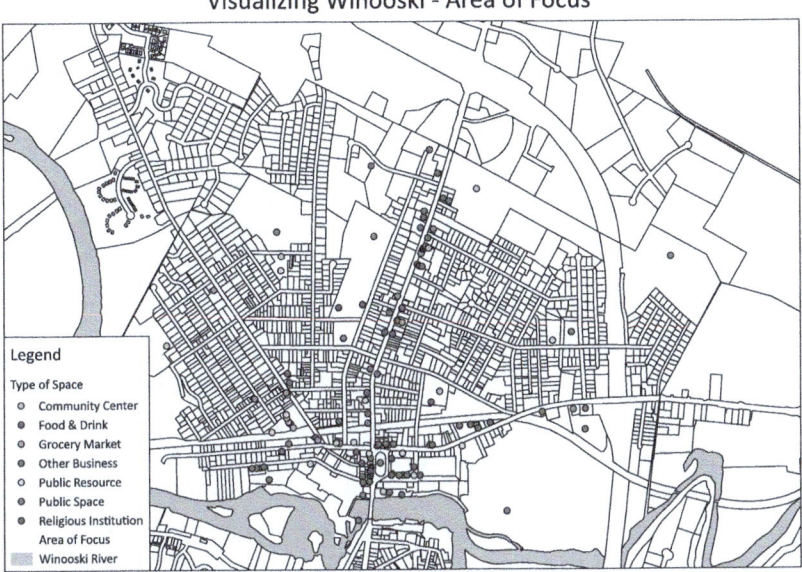

Legend

Type of Space
- ○ Community Center
- ● Food & Drink
- ◐ Grocery Market
- ● Other Business
- ○ Public Resource
- ◐ Public Space
- ● Religious Institution
- Area of Focus
- Winooski River

Image 5.3 Visualizing Winooski's refugee neighborhoods (*Source* Vermont Center for Geographic Information [VCGI]. Authorship: Lucas Grigri, Tilden Remerieltch, & Emma Talt, Refugees in Vermont Project, NSF Award#1359895, April 26, 2016)

Just as I found the Old North End Community Center to be a central hub for refugee support activities and connections in the Burlington neighborhood, so too in Winooski I found that a community center was an integral part of the community of newcomers. There were in fact several main areas where refugee activity seemed to be centered: Culinary jobs and housekeeping jobs were mostly to be found near the traffic circle (the new restaurants and the renovated condominiums and office spaces), a second set of hospitality services at hotels near the highway toward the northern boundaries of the town, a set of manufacturing jobs in the business park also to the northwest part of town, and both social services and housing clustered near the O'Brien Community Center, to the southwest of town (Image 5.4).

Image 5.4   O'Brien Community Center

Again, much like the O.N.E. Community Center in Burlington, the value of the O'Brien Community Center has much to do with accessibility. AALV for some time maintained an office in this building and still has some presence (though USCRI-VT does not). But it contains health services, a greenhouse for farmers, a gym, a library, and several other city services. There is a bus stop, a market, a park, and a community garden nearby. Many houses of refugees are in the immediate vicinity, as are the offices of the main ethnic community associations. Inter-faith, inter-ethnic, and intra-community events are common at the O'Brien Community Center. Legal clinics, tax advice, immigration assistance, citizenship classes, literacy and English classes, parenting courses and support, traditional arts, and community justice initiatives can all be found there. Little surprise then that it is a hub for the local refugee population. While such centralized services and hubs are common in many other countries with a less fragmented refugee and immigrant integration structure or even in larger metropolitan cities, in smaller cities like Winooski they are less common.

To this point, I have been examining resettlement in this refugee neighborhood through the lens of key informants and outsiders like myself. But what do refugees think of their neighborhood? I turn in this last part of the chapter to their perspectives to examine these more fully.

Photovoice: Refugee Images of Winooski

As with Burlington, I again used the technique known as Photovoice to analyze refugee perceptions of the neighborhood in which they live. I recruited twenty refugee individuals settled in Winooski within the previous five years and asked them to take photos of and discuss their views about their neighborhood. The purpose of incorporating refugee voices into planning processes was a little different in Winooski from that in Burlington; in the latter, it had been driven by the need of neighborhood planning assemblies and city councilors who had noted the lack of refugee participation as a problem. In Winooski, it had been the mayor's office and the community and economic development office that had flagged this as a concern. As in Burlington, I hoped that conducting a Photovoice project in Winooski might add another source of information to bring diverse voices into the planning processes of a city undergoing an already extensive process of transformation.

My instructions to participants were the same as I had given to the cohort in Burlington: walk around the neighborhood and take pictures. The prompts to guide their activities were also the same:

a. Take 3 pictures of things you want to see changed in your neighborhood
b. Take 3 pictures of things you want to see stay the same in your neighborhood
c. Take 3 pictures of things that represent US/Vermont to you in your neighborhood
d. Take 3 pictures of things that represent home/community to you in your neighborhood.

Participants then sent these pictures to me along with explanations of why they had chosen each image (interpreters were provided where necessary). A follow-up session was held consisting of each neighborhood group collectively meeting to discuss a selection of photos that I had curated. I focused on images and places that were common across multiple participants as well as those that revealed contested or multifaceted uses of particular spaces.

Table 5.3 Photovoice themes—Winooski

Category	Theme #1	Theme #2	Theme #3
Things to change	Bus/transportation	Housing quality	Graffiti
Things to stay	Community center	Ethnic stores	Restaurants
US/Vermont	City Hall	Flag	Own home
Home/Community	Community center	Own home	School

The results of the project in Winooski were as fascinating as that I discovered in its neighboring city. The following were some of the most common responses grouped by theme (Table 5.3).

In both cities, one of the most valued places is the community center—the O'Brien Community Center in Winooski and the O.N.E. Community Center in Burlington's Old North End. And again, the flag and one's own home appear as somewhat literal responses to the respective prompt in each category. One of the most interesting differences in responses between the two groups had to do with things they wanted to see changed. In Winooski, the lack of adequate public transportation was a recurring theme, as visualized thus (Image 5.5).

One participant said:

> I don't understand why the bus comes into Winooski from Burlington, goes all around the town and then back to Burlington. When our kids go to school they have to go all the way to Burlington before they can get to school, just because we live on the wrong side of the bus route. Why can't the bus be better?

Another added:

> There is one bus stop here. Only one that is close. And it doesn't go to the work or to the school. That has to change.

Yet another remarked:

> The bus is horrible. It is good when it comes. It just doesn't come enough.

Image 5.5 Participant photo of empty bus stop

Such responses are not surprising given how underserved Winooski is in terms of the bus service compared to Burlington. I will revisit this question more fully in Chapter 7.

While a number of Burlington participants had pointed to potholes and infrastructure more broadly, Winooski participants focused more specifically on housing. This was somewhat surprising given that the state of housing in disrepair in the Old North End and Winooski is not markedly different. But the area of the Burlington neighborhood is somewhat more spread out than that of Winooski. The photos from our participants in Winooski tended to focus primarily on houses, as well as on graffiti (in this case mirroring another issue raised by the Burlington cohort) (Image 5.6).

Said the participant who took the above photo:

This is a house that a refugee family has to live in. I know this family. When winter came the windows had holes in them. They had to wear all their clothes in the house. And the landlord would do nothing. This is not right.

Image 5.6   Participant photo of a house in disrepair

Another pointed out a difficulty for refugees as renters:

> It is difficult to fix your house because you don't own it. What if you don't stay there the next year? Still, it is difficult to live here when nothing gets fixed. That is one thing I would like to see made better.

One thing that Winooski participants agreed represented the US and Vermont to them is the Town Hall—in such a small community, it is much more central than perhaps the one in Burlington, where City Hall is located downtown and in the midst of the main pedestrian thoroughfare and shopping district. In Winooski, it is much more integrated into the small town and is frequented more often by refugees in need of different services as it is a short walk from their homes (Image 5.7).

As with Burlington, ethnic stores and restaurants were points of pride for many participants (Images 5.8 and 5.9).

Image 5.7 Winooski City Hall

Image 5.8 Ethnic restaurants Winooski

Image 5.9 Ethnic grocery stores Winooski

One participant said:

I love being able to get food from my community, just as I walk by. There are more and more of these restaurants now.

Another added:

When we first came here there was nothing like this. Not even the Vietnamese restaurants – maybe one. Now there are so many and they serve the best food.

On ethnic groceries, another participant added a similar note:

It was so difficult when we first came, there were only the gas stations and the grocery stores you could not get to without a car. Now there are our own stores!

When we look at a small town like Winooski in the context of refugee resettlement, a complex story emerges. There are many parts of many histories here—ethnic enclave, bedroom community, mill town, post-industrial decline, ethnoburb, and urban revitalization. Refugees have played a significant part in the latest phase of its story, one that has engendered both hope and fear as we will see as we turn from a narrative of refugee resettlement as success in these last two chapters to a case of aborted resettlement in the next.

References

Bell, Christopher. 2013. *East Harlem remembered: Oral histories of community and diversity*. London: McFarland and Company.
Bose, Pablo S. 2015. *Urban development in India: Global Indians in the remaking of Kolkata*. London and New York: Routledge.
Bryan, Frank. 2010. *Real democracy: The New England town meeting and how it works*. Chicago: University of Chicago Press.

City of Winooski. (2020). Main Street Revitalization Project. Available from https://www.winooskivt.gov/Faq.aspx?QID=62.

Dawson, Corey. 2018. Town Meeting Day: Consolidated dispatch service in Chittenden County on the ballot. *Vermont Digger.* March 4. Available from https://vtdigger.org/2018/03/04/town-meeting-day-consolidated-dispatch-service-chittenden-county-speed-emergency-response-times-officials-say/.

DeSantis, Victor, and David Hill. 2004. Citizen participation in local politics: Evidence from New England town meetings. *State and Local Government Review* 36 (3): 166–173.

Dritschilo, Gordon. 2016. Winooski describes positive refugee experience. *Barre-Montpelier Times-Argus.* July 1. Available from https://www.timesargus.com/article/rh/20160701/news01/160709954/0/sports/.

Feeney, Vincent. 2002. *The great falls on Onion River: A history of Winooski, Vermont.* Winooski: Winooski Historical Society.

Fittante, Daniel. 2018. The Armenians of Glendale: An ethnoburb in Los Angeles's San Fernando Valley. *City & Community* 17 (4): 1231–1247.

Furuseth, Owen, and Heather Smith. 2008. From Winn-Dixie to tiendas: The remaking of the New South. In *Latinos in the New South: Transformations of place,* ed. Heather Smith and Owen Furuseth, 1–18. Aldershot: Ashgate.

Gilbert, Liette. 2009. Immigration as local politics: re-bordering immigration and multiculturalism through deterrence and incapacitation. *International Journal of Urban and Regional Research* 33 (1): 26–42.

Hopkins, Daniel. 2010. Politicized places: Explaining where and when immigrants provoke local opposition. *American Political Science Review* 104 (1): 40–60.

Johnston, Ron, Michael Poulsen, and James Forrest. 2008. Asians, Pacific Islanders, and ethnoburbs in Auckland. *New Zealand. Geographical Review* 98 (2): 214–241.

Jones-Correa., M. 2008. Race to the top? The politics of immigrant education in suburbia. In *New faces in new places: The changing geography of American immigration,* ed. Douglas Massey, 308–340. New York: Russell Sage.

Kasinitz, Philip, John Mollenkopf, Mary Waters, and Jennifer Holdaway. 2008. *Inheriting the city: The children of immigrants come of age.* New York: Russell Sage.

Keck, Nina. 2016. In Winooski, many see refugee resettlement as economic advantage. *Vermont Public Radio.* June 13. Available from https://www.vpr.org/post/winooski-many-see-refugee-resettlement-economic-advantage#stream/0.

Lange, Bernie. 2017. The Winooski Dome: How you (almost) paid for it. Available from https://www.mychamplainvalley.com/news/the-winooski-dome-how-you-almost-paid-for-it/. Accessed February 8, 2020.

Li, Wei. 2009. *Ethnoburb: The new ethnic community in urban America*. Honolulu: University of Hawaii Press.

Li, Na. 2015. *Kensington market: Collective memory, public history, and Toronto's urban landscape*. Toronto: University of Toronto Press.

Li, Wei, Emily Skop, and Wan Yu. 2016. Enclaves, ethnoburbs, and new patterns of settlement among Asian immigrants. In *Contemporary Asian America: A multidisciplinary reader*, 3rd ed, ed. Min Zhou and Anthony Ocampo, 222–236. New York: New York University Press.

Lindholm, Jane, and Ric Cengeri. 2014. Winooski: Where it's been and where it's headed. *Vermont Public Radio*. December 9. Available from https://www.vpr.org/post/winooski-where-its-been-and-where-its-headed#stream/0.

Longazel, Jamie, and Benjamin Fleury-Steiner. 2011. Exploiting borders: The political economy of local backlash against undocumented immigrants. *Chicana/o-Latina/o Legal Review* 30 (1): 43–64.

Miyares, Ines. 2004. From exclusionary covenant to ethnic hyperdiversity in Jackson Heights. *Queens. Geographical Review* 94 (4): 462–483.

Mukhtar, Maria, Jennifer Dean, Kathi Wilson, Effat Ghassemi, and Dana Wilson. 2016. "But many of these problems are about funds…": The challenges immigrant settlement agencies (ISAs) encounter in a suburban setting in Ontario, Canada. *Journal of International Migration and Integration* 17 (2): 389–408.

New York Times. 1979. Dome may shelter a whole town. *New York Times*. November 18. Available from https://www.nytimes.com/1979/11/18/arc hives/dome-may-shelter-a-whole-town.html.

Patel, Sejal, Richard Sliuzas, and Yola Georgiadou. 2016. Participatory local governance in Asian cities: invited, closed or claimed spaces for urban poor? *Environment and Urbanization Asia* 7 (1): 1–21.

Pero, Peter. 2011. *Chicago's Pilsen neighborhood*. Charleston, SC: Arcadia Press.

Picard, Ken. 2013. Vermont Bhutanese graduate from being renters to homeowners-and landlords. *Seven Days VT*. March 13. Available from https://www.sevendaysvt.com/vermont/vermont-bhutanese-graduate-from-being-renters-to-homeowners-and-landlords/Content?oid=2243077.

Portes, Alejandro, and Ruben Rumbaut. 2014. *Immigrant America: A portrait*, 4th ed. Oakland: University of California Press.

Robinson, Donald. 2011. *Town meeting: Practicing democracy in rural New England*. Boston: University of Massachusetts Press.

Roediger, David. 2005. *Working towards whiteness: How America's immigrants became white: The strange journey from Ellis Island to the suburbs*. New York: Basic Books.

Singer, Audrey, Susan Hardwick, and Caroline Brettell (eds.). 2008. *Twenty-first century gateways: Immigrant incorporation in suburban America*. New York: Russell Sage.

Tam, Christina. 2019. Beyond the immigrant enclave: Differentiating between coethnic neighborhoods for the study of health and social problems. *GeoJournal* 84 (4): 983–999.

US Census Bureau. 2020. Winooski City Quick Facts. Available from https://www.census.gov/quickfacts/winooskicityvermont. Accessed February 9, 2020.

Walker, Kyle. 2018. Immigrants in US suburbs. In *The Routledge Companion to the Suburbs*, ed. Bernadette Hanlon and Thomas Vicino, 193–207. New York: Routledge.

Winooski School District. 2020. English Language Learners. Available from https://www.wsdvt.org/english-language-learners/.

Zuniga, Victor, and Ruben Hernandez-Leon (eds.). 2005. *New destinations: Mexican immigration in the United States*. New York: Russell Sage.

6

Rutland

If the last two chapters focused on examples of relatively successful resettlement experiences, this chapter examines a case of failure—the planned placement of Syrian refugees in the southern Vermont town of Rutland. Instead of an anticipated 200–250 Syrians to be resettled there over 2016–2017, a grand total of 17 individuals in three families were ultimately accepted. And while those three families have thrived, a succession of travel bans and cuts to the USRAP have meant that none others have followed. It is for these reasons that this chapter looks so different from the two that precede it. The resettlement in Rutland is recent—only four years since it began—and only a fraction of the expected refugees has been ultimately placed there. Thus, there are no maps to show the extent of changes to the local environment and no photos of significant places in this chapter. Instead, I focus here on the story of how Rutland was selected as a resettlement site, why and how the process failed, and what this tells us about refugee resettlement in contemporary America and especially in smaller cities and towns.

I begin by looking at the logic of placing refugees into cities in decline, especially in so-called rustbelt areas of the US. This helps to contextualize why Rutland wanted (and was approved for) refugees in the first place.

© The Author(s) 2020
P. S. Bose, *Refugees in New Destinations and Small Cities*,
https://doi.org/10.1007/978-981-15-6386-7_6

In the second section, I introduce Rutland itself and give an overview of its context and demographics. In the third part of the chapter, I explore the process through which the town was determined to be an appropriate site for resettlement. In the final section of the chapter, I look at the controversies that arose—both locally and nationally—and led ultimately to the closure of the program in Rutland. I thus situate the case within the broader conversation about refugees in non-traditional locations as well as within the anxieties that confront resettlement agencies and programs at the current moment. As in the rest of this book, in this chapter I use material from a larger project that looks at refugee resettlement outside the gateway communities in the US, in particular some of the parallel processes of refugee resettlement in rustbelt and other small cities in the US.

An issue I want to return to at the outset of this chapter is that of research ethics and in particular participant confidentiality. If the challenge with a small state like Vermont is to keep the identities of informants hidden, the task becomes all the more daunting when describing an even more specific case and an even smaller context. That is the situation with Rutland—the major players are well-known locally, as are their perspectives and attitudes. My description and analysis of this case are based on a series of interviews with key informants—resettlement officials, municipal and state authorities, refugees themselves, local community members—that detail the process of selecting and trying to have the city approved as an official resettlement site. Also included is my account of respondents' thoughts on the controversies that would ultimately derail the initiative. They are presented here not as official representatives from particular organizations or to voice official positions but rather to help provide insight into these complex dynamics.

Interviewee responses were coded and categorized as I analyzed this data in order to look for common themes regarding the goals of resettlement, the challenges that arose, and the potential ways forward. I have highlighted some of those themes and insights in this chapter. The specific quotes used in this chapter are meant to be illustrative of the dynamics at the heart of my story about refugees in Vermont—the tensions between embracing newcomers on the one hand and rising anxieties and xenophobia regarding them on the other. The voices of key informants feature perhaps more prominently in this chapter than in other parts of this book. And yet the highly charged nature of the controversy and the relatively small number of actors means that I have had to obscure the identities of speakers as much as possible—not to change their words or their meanings, but to be judicious in terms of what I have revealed and whose particular views are featured. This has meant not only masking identities but also leaving some particularly illuminating quotes on the cutting room floor, as they would have fairly easily identified the speakers. Such decisions also lie behind my identification of other speakers in places not as small as Rutland through broad labels; I identify state refugee coordinators, health coordinators, mayors, city officials, resettlement agency staff, or federal government workers only by a broad job title and a vague geographic region—West, Southeast, and Northwest, for example.

Refugees and Rustbelt Cities

The idea of how to reinvigorate a city in decline is of course not unique to Rutland, to Vermont, or indeed to the US. Many smaller towns, cities, and rural areas are facing the struggles that confront Rutland, with businesses losing customers, city services underfunded, schools seeing a precipitous drop in enrollments, and facing closures themselves. In a number of cases in often very different contexts such decline has been staved off or indeed reversed by the arrival of immigrants, especially labor migrants (Fonseca 2008; Nelson et al. 2015; Associated Press 2016; Pottie-Sherman 2018; Kordel and Weidinger 2019). Increasingly, politicians and civic leaders have turned to the idea that resettling refugees may be one strategy to turn around their cities. Even in places like Lewiston, Maine, where an influx of Somali refugees was famously opposed by the then-mayor in 2002, nearly two decades later the story is one of success, of a reinvigorated downtown and business district, strengthened schools and local agriculture, among other accomplishments (Ellison 2009). This is not to suggest that tensions do not linger (Galofaro 2017), but in Lewiston as in many other smaller cities across the US, newcomers have changed the face of their new homes for the better (Misra 2019).

As I went across the US as part of my larger study of refugee resettlement, I perceived a sense of faith in the benefits of welcoming refugees
expressed by many speakers. For some the value of refugee newcomers
lay in the diversity they might bring to newer immigrant destinations:

> Well, I think the impact in the smaller communities is that it also
> increases the community's idea of what's beyond themselves.

- State Refugee Coordinator, West

> You know, for the community that's welcoming them, I think just the
> whole diversity that they bring to that situation. In addition to that,
> there's also that sense of just that newness they bring, because your
> community are either going to have a sense of wanting to help the
> refugees, or not. And certainly, for the ones that want to help, there's
> also that sense of contributing to that community as a result of helping
> out that population.

- State Refugee Health Coordinator, Midwest

> We have other immigrants as well, but we are not a gateway city, we
> don't have—we're not a destination for many immigrants. We have some
> enterprises that do attract foreign workers but it's small numbers. We
> have a history of immigration, but it's small numbers. I think the refugee
> program, the refugee resettlement, the fact that we are resettling refugees
> adds significant cultural diversity and a more global view of the world.
> And it helps to revitalize the neighborhoods that they go into.

- State Refugee Coordinator, Midwest

Such statements reflect a number of realities in many of the smaller cities
and towns outside of larger metropolitan areas in the US. As in the case
of Rutland, in such cities the population is relatively homogenous and
there has been little history of welcoming non-white immigrant groups.
Refugees are thus an important way of changing the demographics of
these cities. And like Rutland, many such cities—in the rustbelt but
beyond it as well—are struggling with aging populations, youth out-
migration, the loss of local jobs and workers (and the foundations of a

local tax base connected to them), and more broadly a shifting set of relationships to the global economy. Unlike larger metropolitan areas with longer histories of immigration that might additionally be more demographically diverse, many smaller communities may seem less attached to the outside world; in the US as in much of the rest of the world, this can feel like the separation of two solitudes, whether of a rural-urban or a political divide. For such reasons it is thus not surprising that a significant number of interviewees described the addition of refugees as a way of allowing smaller communities to widen their sense of self. This could take multiple forms—exposure to new languages, foods, religions, and traditions for the majority population, the ability of children to encounter more difference in schools and within youth activities, and the possibility of connecting the experience of those living in smaller cities to the wider world.

Others across the country spoke of a more direct motivation for resettling refugees—the opportunity to use the arrival of newcomers to revitalize the cities and neighborhoods they settle into. The sentiments expressed in the previous quotes and the general sentiments of those I spoke to in many parts of the US are widespread—that refugees are potential drivers of urban renewal. There are many ways that this potential may be realized: Refugees may start new businesses or provide more and newer consumers for existing ones. Refugees may be a stable source of rental income for landlords in many smaller cities and may even become homeowners in their own right. A number of respondents in my travels spoke of both individual success stories and the improvement of entire neighborhoods as a result of refugees moving in by purchasing homes and beautifying lawns and gardens and investing in renovations.

> Yeah, I mean, as I said, I think our recent refugees have actually brought better statistics to the high schools, graduation, college enrollment, college attendance, grade advancement… lots of small businesses, lots of participation in the workforce… we've had a lot of home purchases by the Bhutanese populations, I mean, well over a hundred, I mean, it's in the hundreds. And they fix up these homes, they really fix up the whole

streets and the whole neighborhoods. I think it's good for the state culturally. I mean, people wouldn't say this but, not being from X, I think it's
one of the ways that X is able to kind of join the global community.

- City Manager, Northeast

We have quite a few ethnic restaurants, we have other stores, grocery
stores, and we have some other businesses that … cater primarily to
their ethnic community but in other situations they can cater to a more
mainstream population. So, we have that business situation. We have a
lot of home ownership among refugees. We have increased the tax base,
economically. I'm thinking, speaking specifically in economics here. The
contributions that refugees make to the growth, to the economic vitality
of the community is very measurable. It's a big part of how we make the
neighborhood that they were placed in which was kind of falling apart,
come back to life. We really expand our thinking as a community a great
deal by having refugees present. The arts are more vital, cultural events
are occurring weekly, international types of things that are happening in
many cases because we have a diverse refugee population.

- State Refugee Coordinator, Northwest

Both of these speakers describe resettlement in terms of vitality. Yet
others used even more explicit warnings, not simply suggesting that
smaller and rustbelt cities should welcome refugees, but rather that such
places would not even *survive* without refugees. The discourse is at times
desperate and reflects another set of anxieties regarding demographic
change—that the populations of certain cities and towns are aging or
disappearing and thus unable to sustain economic and social vitality.
Refugees here represent a lifeline to continued viability:

Well this is really interesting right now with a lot of smaller cities dwin-
dling in size as their own children move to the big city, or industry that
has kept a smaller community alive for decades decides to close and move.
So sometimes refugees actually keep communities alive, or keep businesses
alive. So that is definitely one impact, supporting smaller communities,
and reinvigorating local business. Refugees then would tend to open a
little restaurant or community store that caters to their needs. So, you
start to see business development in smaller communities.

• Resettlement Official, Federal Agency

When we first moved here, the only places who would rent to us were in the neighborhoods no one wanted to live in. They were falling apart – not full of crime but they were not good. We have made them better. Now everyone wants us in their neighborhoods and to rent their houses and even the city has a program to help our families buy houses because they know we will make the city better.

• Ethnic Community Based Organization (Refugee) official, Southeast

I don't care where we get people from. I'll take 'em from Syria, from California, from Africa, from Spain, from Mexico, from New York City, I don't care. We're losing people, all the young people and the families, they're all moving out and I'm afraid in a few more years there'll be more empty houses and boarded up businesses if we can't get these refugees to come. I'll take anyone, anyone who'll make my city look lived in again.

• City Mayor, Northeast

Sentiments like this were common among many respondents, that without refugee arrivals, the future looks bleak for small cities in the US, especially those outside the orbit of larger metropolitan areas. How does Rutland fit into such perspectives, contexts, and scenarios? In what ways do such views resonate and how did they manifest during the towns own abortive attempt at refugee resettlement? And how were not only these positive views of refugee resettlement reflected in this small Vermont town, but also a backlash against newcomers that was also evident in other such places across the US?

Rutland the City

Burlington occupies at least some space in the US imaginary, thanks in no small part to Bernie Sanders' presidential campaigns, to its draw as an outdoor leisure destination and to nationally known brands such as Ben and Jerry's ice cream. And Winooski as part of the greater Burlington metropolitan area falls to some extent within that broader ambit, even if it is itself perhaps less visible to the broader public and has its own quirks and particularities that set it apart from its larger neighbor. Rutland, on the other hand, is little known outside of Vermont. And what is known about it in Vermont is rarely positive. Rutland has a bad reputation for many in the state. Residents call may themselves 'Rutlanders' with some pride. But others will use the name 'RutVegas' ironically and to denigrate a blue-collar town with a reputation for high rates of crime, drug use, addiction, and poverty—even if the actual statistics do not always bear out the perception that Rutland has any of these things in greater numbers than its neighbors (Barcellos 2019) (Image 6.1).

Image 6.1   Rutland

Located in the south-central part of Vermont, it is the state's third largest city with a population of 16,495 (US Census Bureau 2020). Its history is primarily as an industrial town focused on marble quarries with work drawing in mainly European immigrants in the late nineteenth and early twentieth centuries. As with many similar industrial towns all across the country, it has undergone considerable decline in recent decades, with its waning fortunes tied to shifts in both the local and global economies. Particular concerns facing the town reflect a kernel of truth in some of the stereotypes and caricatures it seeks to resist. These include an aging population, out-migration of youth, and a significant opioid addiction crisis (Levitz and Calvert 2016). Like many other formerly prosperous industrial towns, Rutland seems to be perpetually re-inventing itself, as local newspaper stories are often filled with tales of new businesses setting up shop, art galleries and green energy projects abounding, young people returning to the city, and a downtown undergoing an urban revival (Flagg 2012; Costello and Jaye 2016; Amore 2018).

And yet Rutland struggles to shrug off the label of decline, not only in perception but in terms of socioeconomic reality. The population of Vermont, as previously noted, has long been decreasing—but drill down deeper into such statistics at the town level and it becomes clear that what population growth there is remains concentrated in the metropolitan area surrounding Burlington. Of the 252 cities, towns, and villages in Vermont, only a third saw any kind of population growth between 2010 and 2020, most of it negligible and, only eleven towns had growth rates approaching or exceeding the national average (Wertlieb 2020). Of those eleven towns, all but two are located in Chittenden County, mostly within the Greater Burlington area or within fifty miles of the state's main city.

At the other end of the spectrum is Rutland. Much of the population loss in Vermont has been in rural towns and villages but Rutland stands out as an urban area that has seen similar kinds of decline. It is the city in Vermont that has lost the most people in recent years, nearly 4.5% of its population in the last decade alone (Petenko 2019). The demographics of the town compared with Vermont as a whole and with the rest of the nation are as follows (Table 6.1).

Table 6.1 Selected characteristics of Rutland, Vermont, and the US

Demographic measure	Rutland	Vermont	US
Per capita annual income	$28,962	$33,238	$32,621
Poverty rate (%)	14.1	11.0	11.8
Median house/condo value	$152,800	$223,700	$204,900
Median gross rent	$776/month	$972/month	$1023/month
Foreign-born population (%)	2.9	4.6	13.5
Language other than English (%)	5.0	5.7	21.5
Unemployment rate (%)	3.0	3.1	4.8
White population (%)	96.2	94.2	76.5
Asian population (%)	1.7	2.0	5.9
Hispanic population (%)	1.4	2.0	18.3
Black population (%)	1.4	1.4	13.4

Source US Census Bureau (2020)

Overall then, Rutland is generally poorer, whiter and somewhat less expensive than either the rest of the state or the country as a whole. Where nearly 15–20% of Burlington and Winooski are non-white, those numbers slip considerably in Rutland to less than 5% of the city. Manufacturing remains the dominant industry in town employing just under a quarter of residents, with retail, construction, hospitality and food services, and educational services all employing significant numbers (US Census Bureau 2017). The demographic challenge posed by an aging population coupled with youth out-migration has also meant a decline in the local tax base and an inability to make investments in retaining skilled workers.

Refugees in Rutland

For all of these reasons, the idea of refugees in Rutland First began to take hold by 2015. The city had never before hosted refugees. But it soon emerged as a candidate for the process of expanding resettlement sites across the US described in Chapter 2. But why this town? In the previous chapter, I showed that general public opinion in Vermont has been strongly in favor of the refugee resettlement program. A common sentiment expressed in each of the five years when I asked where refugees should be placed was that this should happen evenly across the state. Such preferences aligned with two other views. The first was that perhaps the Burlington metropolitan area was over-stretched in terms of its own capacities. As a staff member of the resettlement agency stated:

> We had explored the possibilities of placing refugees in other towns, mostly because Burlington officials had complained for some time that they were bearing the full brunt of integrating newcomers and if this was meant to be a state program then more communities in the state should be sharing the responsibilities.

On the other hand, other cities and towns across the state had begun to ask why they had not been chosen as resettlement sites. If refugees had had such a significant impact in other locations—as was so often reported in local media—why could they too not benefit? There were good reasons to be wary, however. There had been an earlier attempt—in the late 1990s when a small group of Eastern European refugees had been settled in Barre, a small central Vermont town of less than 10,000 people close to the state capitol of Montpelier. This experiment was seen as something of a failure since a majority of those resettled moved to Chittenden County within a few years as they continued to feel somewhat uncomfortably visible within the local community. From the perspective of some local leaders, they felt as though they had not been sufficiently prepared to receive an influx of newcomers. One said:

> Thinking back on it, I wish we had spent more time letting the local service providers know a bit more about who was coming and what to expect. We had a problem with some clinics and other providers not wanting to take refugee clients and we had to spend a lot of time explaining their backgrounds and that they could not simply refuse to serve them because of the language difficulties or other differences. That didn't help the refugees feel very welcome.

But in the following years, resettlement in the Burlington area had been widely hailed as a success. Those who arrived stayed for the most part. Employment was high for newcomers and many of their children excelled in sports and academics in local schools. Refugees opened new restaurants, ethnic markets, and grocery stores. Some were even able to buy homes in a relatively short period. There were negative stories and outcomes as well, as the previous chapters on Burlington and Winooski and those in the next section on embodied experiences explore more fully. But overall the story was an appealing one.

Little surprise then that other towns in Vermont were interested in benefiting as well. By 2011 a number of towns had approached the resettlement agency to explore the possibility of expanding the number of sites. At least one received serious consideration in 2013—including scoping studies funded by the federal government—but in the end while this town had sufficient employment and affordable housing to support resettlement, it did not have enough support within the local school system to sustain a resettled population. As another resettlement agency staffer said to me:

> Yeah, we considered XXX town. People kept telling us 'well there's all these jobs out there, there's 80 refugees everyday going out to XXX, why don't you see if we can put people out there?' So, we got a grant to do a scoping study and we did a scoping study and it basically said housing is cheaper, jobs are here, but we have no services. So, we didn't put people out there. Which is kind of what you want us to do, right? Can you put people out there? No. Okay. Move on.

This example of careful consideration and review very much debunks the notion that resettlement has been foisted upon local communities by the federal government and its proxies with no regard for the capacity or consequences. But of course, such dynamics are not known by many who are not intimately involved with them—as we will see with the misinformation and misconceptions about the Rutland case.

By 2015, the idea of new resettlement communities in the US had arisen once more, not only in Vermont but across the country, and especially in light of the dramatic increase in forced migration from Syria and North Africa and the seeming capacity of the US to accept more refugees. As a result, at least seven Vermont towns once again approached USCRI-VT to inquire about their suitability as resettlement sites. Out of such initial and preliminary conversations, Rutland emerged as a prospective candidate to host refugees. The interest from Rutland came initially and primarily from its mayor. One of his advisors describes it thus:

> He really became convinced looking specifically at data of refugees and migration patterns that core towns in rural areas, like Brattleboro in Windham County, Rutland in Rutland county, Middlebury in Addison County, that demographically across the country that these were areas that were in decline. Pretty easy to see, there's rural to urban migration, automation is going to affect the economy, you gotta do something and this was his plan.

Another member of the mayor's staff echoed the mayor's focus on this aspect of decline:

> It's not that hard to see and he would say that demographics are destiny. If your share of young people is constantly declining, you're going to have huge issues. He would talk about Winooski—he wouldn't talk about this on the campaign trail because no one in Rutland wants to think anything nice about Winooski—but cerebrally thinking about this, about how much better Winooski is doing now than 30-40 years ago, it was pretty easy for him to draw the line. He really thought this is the single most impactful thing we can do for Rutland: people, just people. Don't care who they are. And he really would say this on the campaign trail, too: 'If you can get me 100 families from Nebraska, I'd pay for them to come. I don't care who they are, it's just population, more dollars spent.' So that was his economic mayoral imperative. That was one side. The other side was 'my family is Greek immigrants to Rutland, Rutland is a city of immigrants, we have an obligation to hold a door open, I'm a Christian, the Bible says refugees.'

This last sense of a moral obligation to accept refugees was an important motivating factor not only for the mayor but others in the community as well, especially. Whether stirred by the images of civilians fleeing violence in Syria or outrage at travel bans and immigration restrictions, many residents of Rutland felt a sense of duty to help potential newcomers. For the mayor, his own experience as a military veteran intensified his commitment. As another of his staff said:

> I don't know if I have ever had a more emotional conversation in politics than the day that Trump signed the executive order [the travel ban], he and I probably talked on the phone for an hour and at one point he just screamed as loud as I ever think I have ever heard anyone scream into the phone "I can't believe I shot people for this shit" and then kept bringing up the picture of the kid dead on the beach in Syria. Emotionally for him, he really struggled with the Trump transition and that aspect I think made him dig his heels into how he was right to do it in the first place.

Certainly, neither the mayor nor the resettlement agency was unaware of the controversies into which they would be stepping, as the summer of 2015 and sympathy for refugees quickly turned into a backlash by the fall and the terrorist attacks in Paris in November 2015. Additionally, proponents of Rutland as a resettlement town did not want to repeat the mistakes that happened with Barre. Accordingly, the approach taken was meant to be much more deliberative and consultative. Local leaders—primarily the mayor and his staff as well as state and USCRI-VT officials—set out to hold multiple meetings with various stakeholders. These included local school officials, employers, landlords, social service providers, and healthcare agencies. Their idea was to properly assess whether the town had the capacity to accept newcomers, especially those fleeing the various traumas of war. Like Lewiston and many other small cities across the country, there continued to be hope that Rutland's decline might be reversed through the arrival of refugees (Henderson 2016).

Backlash

However, the plans to take a deliberative approach to any proposed resettlement quickly became derailed through a combination of both local and national politics. As the city announced that it would be seeking to resettle 100 Syrian refugees beginning in the fall of 2016, a backlash grew (Keck 2016a). At the local level critics—especially those on city council—complained that plans had been hatched in secret, that the general public had not been consulted, and that as a result trust had been broken between the city and its citizens (Davis 2016). A group called Rutland First began to organize against the proposed resettlement, bringing in prominent anti-refugee activists like Ann Corcoran (founder of Resettlement Watch) to speak against the plans and challenging the mayor and resettlement officials on their actions, asking that a public vote be held on the proposed resettlement. Many of the concerns noted by the group echoed the same themes of the national debate on refugees, with security, issues with vetting, the possibility of economic fraud, the possibilities of migrants bringing infectious diseases into the community, and the unraveling of the existing social fabric heading the list of anxieties (Keck 2016b). Against such fears and concerns, the mayor and director of USCRI-VT both strongly defended the decision on placing refugees in Rutland, arguing that the community had plenty of resources to help support resettlement (MacQuarrie 2016). In the words of a staff member with the resettlement agency:

I am not going to put anyone into that community unless I can be sure they have enough opportunity, support and a clear pathway to success. For all the criticism we have received from some, in my view it really is a small minority of people who are being vocal. There are a lot more who have been just as active if not more in reaching out to help us.

And indeed, at the same time that Rutland First became active so too did another grassroots organization called Rutland Welcomes, one focused on building support and services at the neighborhood level, with over twenty separate groups spread across the city and hundreds of volunteers ready to assist newcomers integrate. A Facebook group counted 2400 local members for Rutland Welcomes, while a warehouse downtown was filled with goods and supplies to help the newcomers (Keck 2019a). At the same time, Rutland First members had their own social media groups and went door to door soliciting support to oppose resettlement, with fears of Sharia law and Islamic customs at the top of their concerns.

The decisions regarding Syrians in Rutland was for the most part taken out of locals' hands by travel bans and the cuts to the USRAP—both in refugees admitted and programs to support them—over the next three years. But the local effects were also significant. First and foremost, his staunch support for resettlement cost the mayor his job. After winning his first five elections for mayor handily, in 2017 the mayor lost the Rutland municipal election. As his election staff recount:

So, he went from winning every election by 30 to losing by over 20. I talked with him and I looked at the numbers and I don't know what explanation you can possibly arrive at, other than refugees. I have to go back and look at the turnout number but we were doing a fair bit of organizing with the Rutland Welcomes group to make sure everyone gets out and votes for us. That was our base and it just did not matter.

When I asked how important the refugee question was in the local campaign, the mayor's political advisors said it was central, but not the only one. The mayor's disputes with the firefighters' union regarding a new contract played at least some role in his downfall, as did an ongoing feud with the Board of Aldermen (city councilors) who complained that his lack of consultation and inclusion on planning for refugee resettlement reflected a broader trend of sidelining them on important matters. One of those aldermen ended up opposing and eventually defeating him in the mayoral election in 2017, running a campaign that opposed both the mayor personally and the refugee resettlement program more generally on process issues. The two became enmeshed so that, as one of his staff put it:

It was all that anyone could talk about – why he was doing it if it was making people so upset. What did it say about him as a person, not just as mayor? So, if it was enough for people in the New York Times and NPR to be paying attention to it, we certainly knew that he couldn't walk down the street without getting heckled about it or someone coming up and hugging him in tears about it. So, it was pretty intense.

It was of course not only the mayor's political fortunes that were affected by the resettlement controversy. The resettlement issue was as deeply divisive in Rutland as immigration more generally has become in America. Another staffer in the mayor's office related this story:

He was with an NPR reporter in a café in Rutland doing an interview and it was the day that Trump signed the executive order and he had to go tell this table of women who had been all excited about the refugee thing that they were not going to come and they all cried. And then some table of rednecks overheard and cheered and yelled at them in the café. So, it was that kind of, you know, it was very divisive, and you knew.

Postscript: Rutland Now

How are we to assess what happened in Rutland, Vermont, a new resettlement site that stalled after only a handful of planned hundreds of refugees from Syria ended up being resettled? Is this just a cautionary tale of trying to develop solidarity networks and services in an era of xenophobia? Of a town that cannot save itself with new blood even when it can little afford to reject such help? Of one that holds onto its traditions and local autonomy even as it faces decline?

The truth is that the story is much more complex than it might sometimes seem. The former mayor has been vocal in public about having no regrets about his attempts or his stance, though he does regret what might have been—many more Syrian families made safe in a new home, and Rutland made stronger by an influx of newcomers. Again, one of his political advisors on whether the former mayor had second thoughts about his actions:

> No, he has made it very clear to me and to others that he would do it all over again. He said to me 'You know, if I gave up my office to bring two families into a refugee center in god knows where in Rutland then that's a pretty good deal.' He's still convinced that this is the only way we could've reversed population loss – and if you look at what's happened he's probably not wrong.

The reality is that the victory of those who sought to stop resettlement in Rutland has done nothing to address the kinds of demographic decline outlined at the outset of this chapter. Rutland is still the city that is losing the most population in Vermont. Ironically, the same city councilors who opposed refugees have since spent nearly $150,000 on marketing campaigns to try and attract new residents to Rutland—a campaign that has yielded a total of 22 families at a far higher cost than the city would have had to spend to support refugees (Keck 2019b).

There have been other, unanticipated outcomes from the Rutland experience. For some, the gains have been immediate and personal—the alderman who most vocally opposed resettlement became mayor, while the town treasurer who was also a key figure against refugee resettlement earned a federal post in the US Department of Agriculture shortly afterward (Keays 2017). Among proponents of refugee resettlement, several prominent members won elections in their own right, to the city's board of aldermen, for example (Keays 2018). Perhaps more substantially, the divisive debate helped to politicize city residents more broadly, leading to the founding of its first NAACP chapter and the establishment of high school clubs meant to support newcomers and local college initiatives working with immigrant families (Keck 2019a).

What of the refugees themselves, those who actually did arrive in Rutland? Did they flee the controversy and end up in Burlington or in Albany, New York or another location? In fact, they did not. They laid low upon first arriving, not wanting to inflame the contentious situation any further (Sari 2017). But each of the families has thrived, learning English, acquiring stable jobs, buying cars, and in one case building a house with the help of Habitat for Humanity (Keck 2019c). Their transition and adjustment to a new life have gone well, if not always smoothly. As the former mayor says, their success is bittersweet—not for them, but for the potential that others like them might have brought to Rutland if not for the fears that enveloped their arrival for some.

The Rutland refugee resettlement failure may well be taken as an illustration of the importance of scale in determining outcomes in civic politics. Despite the passion that Rutland's former mayor brought to his advocacy and the supporting activism of the Rutland Welcomes group, the move failed primarily because xenophobia and misinformation can take hold of a small community much more extensively and quickly than larger ones. Political events on the national level, specifically the US-wide travel ban, were indeed forceful deterrents to Rutland's ambition to be a sanctuary for refugees, but again, their impact was heavier in Rutland than in larger communities. In thinking about the realities of refugee resettlement, then, scale must be recognized as a determining factor.

References

Amore, B. 2018. Did Rutland join the cutting edge? Art pioneers at 77 Gallery. *The Barre Montpelier Times Argus.* August 25. Available from https://www.timesargus.com/did-rutland-join-the-cutting-edge-art-pio neers-at-gallery/article_182c2c03-0e06-564e-bff9-40ecd0e70639.html.
Associated Press. 2016. Reborn Maine mill town offers lessons amid refugee crisis. *UK Daily Mail.* February 8. Retrieved from http://www.dailymail. co.uk/wires/ap/article-3436758/Reborn-Maine-milling-city-offers-lessons-amid-refugee-crisis.html.
Barcellos, Kate. 2019. Rutland city police report drop in city crime. *Rutland Herald.* February 28. Available from https://www.rutlandherald.com/news/local/rutland-city-police-report-drop-in-city-crime/article_c3025590-adf1-595d-bbee-f0c1a79fb50f.html.
Costello, Steve, and Terry Jaye. 2016. Reimagining Rutland. *Mountain Times.* July 21. Available from https://www.mountaintimes.info/reimagining-rut land/.
Davis, Mark. 2016. Critics of Rutland refugee plan grill alderman, resettlement officials. *Seven Days VT.* May 25. Retrieved from http://www.sevendaysvt. com/OffMessage/archives/2016/05/25/critics-of-rutland-refugee-plan-grill-aldermen-resettlement-officials.
Ellison, Jesse. 2009. Lewiston, Maine, revived by Somali immigrants. *Newsweek.* January 16. Available from https://www.newsweek.com/lewiston-maine-revived-somali-immigrants-78475.
Flagg, Kathryn. 2012. Leaving RutVegas: A blue-collar city reinvents itself. *Seven Days.* February 1. Available from https://www.sevendaysvt.com/ver mont/leaving-rutvegas/Content?oid=2183476.
Fonseca, Maria Lucinda. 2008. New waves of immigration to small towns and rural areas in Portugal. *Population, Space and Place* 14 (6): 525–535.
Galofaro, Claire. 2017. How a community changed by refugees came to embrace Trump. *AP News.* April 19. Available from https://apnews.com/

7f2b534b80674596875980b9b6e701c9/How-a-community-changed-by-refugees-came-to-embrace-Trump.

Henderson, Tim. 2016. Rutland, other shrinking small towns, see hope in refugees. *Valley News.* August 20. Retrieved from http://www.vnews.com/Shrinking-small-towns-see-hope-in-refugees-4222723.

Keays, Alan. 2017. Trump taps Rutland treasurer for federal post in Vermont. *VT Digger.* November 5. Available from https://vtdigger.org/2017/11/05/trump-taps-rutland-treasurer-federal-post-vermont/.

Keays, Alan. 2018. Democrats grab Senate seat in Rutland, win one of three spots. *VT Digger.* November 7. Available from https://vtdigger.org/2018/11/07/democrats-grab-senate-seat-rutland-county-win-one-three-spots/.

Keck, Nina. 2016a. 100 Syrian Refugees are headed to Rutland. *Vermont Public Radio.* April 26. Retrieved from http://digital.vpr.net/post/100-syr ian-refugees-are-headed-rutland.

Keck, Nina. 2016b. Vermont town debates Syrian refugee resettlement program. *Vermont Public Radio.* July 1. Retrieved from http://www.npr.org/2016/07/01/484381701/vermont-town-debates-syrian-refugee-resettlem ent-program.

Keck, Nina. 2019a. Three years after the Rutland refugee debate, the city still needs people. *Vermont Public Radio.* September 24. Available from https://www.vpr.org/post/three-years-after-rutland-refugee-debate-city-still-needs-people#stream/0.

Keck, Nina. 2019b. 'Magical place for us': Syrian family finds new home in Rutland. *Vermont Public Radio.* September 23. Available from https://www.vpr.org/post/magical-place-us-syrian-family-finds-new-home-rutland#stream/0.

Keck, Nina. 2019c. He was the mayor who brought refugees to Rutland. His regret? Not bringing more. *Vermont Public Radio.* September 22. Available from https://www.vpr.org/post/he-was-mayor-who-brought-refugees-rutland-his-regret-not-bringing-more.

Kordel, Stefan, and Stefan Weidinger (eds.). 2019. *Processes of immigration in rural Europe: The status quo, implications and development strategies.* Cambridge: Cambridge Scholars Publishing.

Levitz, Jennifer, and Scott Calvert. 2016. Vermont's radical experiment to break the addiction cycle. *Wall Street Journal.* December 23. Available from https://www.wsj.com/articles/vermonts-radical-experiment-to-break-the-addiction-cycle-1482510297.

MacQuarrie, Brian. 2016. Vermont city prepares Syrian refugees with welcome, wariness. *Boston Globe.* May 13. Retrieved from https://www.

bostonglobe.com/metro/2016/05/12/vermont-city-prepares-for-syrian-ref
    ugees-with-welcome-wariness/nfs6Z8QbcQZQzMmlqZm26I/story.html.
Misra, Tanvi. 2019. The cities refugees saved. *CityLab*. January 31. Available
    from https://www.citylab.com/equity/2019/01/refugee-admissions-resettlem
    ent-trump-immigration/580318/.
Nelson, Lise, Laurie Trautman, and Peter B. Nelson. 2015. Latino immigrants
    and rural gentrification: Race, "illegality", and precarious labor regimes in
    the United States. *Annals of the Association of American Geographers* 105 (4):
    841–858.
Petenko, Erin. 2019. As Vermonters leave small towns, Burlington region
    grows. *VT Digger*. October 3. Available from https://vtdigger.org/2019/10/
    03/as-vermonters-leave-small-towns-they-flock-to-burlington-region/.
Pottie-Sherman, Yolande. 2018. Austerity urbanism and the promise of
    immigrant-and refugee-centered urban revitalization in the US Rust Belt.
    Urban Geography 39 (3): 438–457.
Sari, Kymelya. 2017. Family of Syrian refugees arrive in Rutland as reset-
    tlement begins. *Seven Days Vermont*. January 19. Retrieved from http://
    www.sevendaysvt.com/OffMessage/archives/2017/01/19/family-of-syrian-
    refugees-arrive-in-rutland-as-resettlement-begins.
US Census Bureau. 2017. Rutland City Vermont. American Factfinder.
    Retrieved from https://factfinder.census.gov/faces/nav/jsf/pages/commun
    ity_facts.xhtml?src=bkmk#.
US Census Bureau. 2020. Vermont QuickFacts. March 4. Retrieved from
    https://www.census.gov/quickfacts/map/IPE120213/50/accessible.
Wertlieb, Mitch. 2020. Census report numbers highlight Vermont's population
    decline. Vermont Public Radio. January 9. Available from https://www.vpr.
    org/post/census-report-numbers-highlight-vermonts-population-decline#str
    eam/0.

7

Mobility

The last three chapters offer insights into what refugee resettlement looks like in terms of place in Vermont: What has happened to some of the towns that newcomers have gone to or were supposed to go to? In this final section of the book, I turn to the scale of individual bodies, experiences, hopes, and outcomes. I have always been fascinated by the ways in which cultures and individuals and landscapes within which they are situated transform and affect one another. Such relationships help us to understand both people and place much better. In the three foregoing chapters, I still draw upon some of the opinions and perspectives of key informants in refugee resettlement in Vermont and elsewhere, but in the present chapter more than in the rest of the book, my attention is focused more on the experiences of the refugees themselves than on the those of officials, authorities, and leaders of organizations. What have been the experiences of refugees—individuals and communities—upon arriving in Vermont?

There are many categories of experience that I could focus on—I could use the themes of gender, race, class, sexual orientation, or political ideologies, for example, to distinguish between and highlight common

© The Author(s) 2020
P. S. Bose, *Refugees in New Destinations and Small Cities*,
https://doi.org/10.1007/978-981-15-6386-7_7

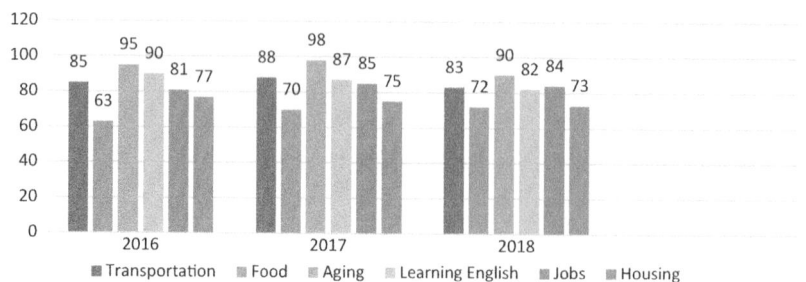

Fig. 7.1 What is the most important part of success after arrival?

contexts. I could look at employment, health, education, housing, transportation, civic integration, or other important elements of the resettlement process. Indeed, in my research projects, which have evaluated the effectiveness of resettlement in Vermont, these are key categories that I have examined through surveys, interviews, and focus groups. But I have chosen in these three final chapters to explore themes in which all of these issues, identities, and perspectives are present and significant. The ways through which we understand experiences in each chapter underscore the importance of the gendered, classed, and racialized nature of resettlement, for example, as well as the ways in which work, housing, civic life, and opportunities structure the refugee's relationship to new homes and communities in Vermont. In this final section of the book, I look at mobility, food, and aging as representative of the refugee experience at the level of the individual and their ethnic group or community. In a survey I conducted in 2016–2018 with one hundred refugees who had been resettled in Vermont during that period, when asked what they considered to be the most significant factor in a successful integration outcome, the top answers were as follows (Fig. 7.1).

Learning English was the leading answer across all three years, but it is also a necessity articulated by the USRAP and immigration narratives more generally. It is also an experience that is as influenced by how refugees actually access their language classes—walking, driving, or taking the bus to them—as by their use of new skills (to gain citizenship or to gain knowledge in particular industries, for example). The need to gain employment for working-age refugees is also an immediate priority reinforced by resettlement agents and the USRAP structure, as is housing.

The other three sets of answers represent a more comprehensive and nuanced set of categories that I see as more broadly representative of embodied experiences of resettlement. I have included, for example, a number of responses that focused on various elements of the resettlement process including education (including K-12, post-secondary, literacy, and adult education), childcare and eldercare, youth and mental health services, and recognition of prior skills under the category of aging. Similarly, the category of food includes access to familiar cuisines and ingredients, working or shopping in ethnic grocery stores, markets and restaurants, and farming. Finally, I broadened the category of transportation to look at mobility more generally, as the utility of travel as a foundation for broader success was a recurring theme with many respondents. The three thematic categories I have chosen to focus on are thus more complex than housing, employment, and English language learning alone.

In this first chapter of this section, I focus on the first of these themes, the idea of mobility. What does mobility mean for those who have been resettled in Vermont? By mobility I mean much more than just an analysis of daily movements or the availability of transportation alone, but rather, I ask what the ability to access different places, processes, people, and opportunities has meant for refugees in Vermont. The 'mobilities turn' in social sciences has significantly challenged our understandings of a wide range of flows—of capital, labor, commodities, people, and ideas—and suggested more complex ways of understanding these relationships (Cresswell 2012; Urry 2016; Sheller and Urry 2016). In the same vein I am interested in how refugees in Vermont experience their new surroundings and their ability to move into and through them.

In particular, I focus on refugees' ability to access a range of opportunities and needs that either enable or limit their participation and integration into new societies. I argue that the mobility of refugees in Vermont is about much more than convenience and utility—being able to travel to jobs, health care, and educational resources leads to a better quality of life outcomes, a sense of independence and agency, and a more established presence within their new communities. Conversely, limitations on movement and mobility may have profound effects on refugees' notions of community, integration, and perhaps even citizenship itself—effects that may also be felt in the broader population but given the more tenuous place of refugees in their new homes may be more pressing.

The chapter is divided into four parts. In the first I detail some of the literature on migration and mobility to explore some of the findings in other contexts. In the second I look more closely at some of the impacts of constrained mobilities upon the daily lives of refugees in Vermont. In the third I look specifically at the gendered dimensions of refugee mobilities in Vermont. And in the final part of this chapter, I examine the relationship between refugee mobilities and both alternative transportation and car culture in their new homes. The analysis in this chapter (especially for the last three sections) is based on a series of surveys, interviews, and focus groups I have organized with various refugee communities between 2006 and 2020.

Migrants and Mobility

The study of mobility in a multiplicity of forms has been an important theoretical exploratory tool in a range of disciplines in recent years. Cresswell (2010) suggests that a mobilities framework is an interdisciplinary one that draws on much more than positivist and technocratic traditions concerned with the utilitarian function of transport. Mobilities research utilizes traditions ranging from geography, urban studies, sociology, and the humanities to situate itself. Cresswell describes mobility as a 'geographical fact that lies at the centre of constellations of power, the creation of identities and the microgeographies of everyday life' (Cresswell 2010: 551). Jensen (2011) similarly argues that mobilities research is important not for its descriptive capabilities but for the potential of such work to make critical interventions in the contemporary crises of modernity by engaging directly with the question of power. A flat notion of mobility—where all subjects have undifferentiated access and power—is at odds with the realities of the world in which we live. Indeed, Urry suggests that what he calls 'network capital'—the ability to unfold one's life through highly interconnected, networked societies—'points to the real and potential social relations that mobilities afford' (2012: 27). Conversely, the lack of such capital can lead to disparate experiences of mobility and profound consequences—as seen, he suggests, in a case such as Hurricane Katrina in terms of who could and who could not escape the effects of the storm.

One of the key contributions of mobilities research is then a focus on the construction of meaning rather than a mapping of movement— Cresswell (2010) urges, for example, that in building a bridge between mobilities research and transport geography, the focus should be not only on travel times alone but what those travel times signify. When we think about refugees and mobility, therefore, the complexities of what the latter word means for refugees should not be lost. These are, after all, individuals and groups for whom movement itself has complicated and often troubling valences. Refugees have been violently uprooted from homes, livelihoods, families, and traditions; their migrations are forced ones. Yet the refugee can also experience a great deal of stillness—for example, those marooned in refugee camps in Nepal, Kenya, and Lebanon for months, years, and generations by protracted conflicts with no end in sight (Loescher and Milner 2005). Often, they are physically restricted to the camp space, barred from working or going to school outside of its boundaries, and barred from integrating into their host country's society in multiple other ways. If and when they are resettled, unlike other immigrants, refugees have little say on where they might go—it is not chain migration, family reunification, or economic opportunities that drives the flow, but rather the directives of the state and its agents that determine where one will be placed (Haines 2010; Bloemraad 2006). Once in their resettlement site, refugees may choose to relocate to another place (as other immigrants) but in the US at least to do so would mean relinquishing significant initial financial assistance (Pipher 2002). For such reasons, the vast majority of refugees in Vermont have remained in their original settlement site (the same is not necessarily true across the US where secondary migration continues to be significant, at least after the first year).

The aspect of refugee mobility with which I am primarily interested in this chapter, however, is that experienced by refugees once they have arrived in their new homes in Vermont. Mobilities research has much to offer such an inquiry, extending the extant literature that is for the most part centered on the study of transportation services and access for immigrants as a broad category and to a limited extent on the experiences of refugees as well. Several important analyses of immigrant travel behavior have begun to highlight more systematically the crucial role that mobility plays in the acculturation process (Tal and Handy 2010). For example, Blumenberg and Smart (2010) and Lovejoy and Handy (2011) demonstrate the utility of carpooling by immigrants in California as a way of strengthening social networks and overcoming shared obstacles. Chatman and Klein (2009) illustrate the reliance of foreign-born populations on bicycling, public transit, walking, and shared private transportation as a way of adjusting to the demands of a new environment. Similar studies in Canada indicate a high use of transit among immigrants (Heiz and Schellenberg 2004), and indeed Lo, Shalaby, and Alshalalfah argue explicitly that access to 'transit needs to be recognized as a key ingredient for the success of the immigrant settlement process' (2011: 470).

Additionally, multiple studies have shown the adverse effects of constrained mobility on the lives of immigrants. For example, transportation barriers appear as among the most significant challenges to accessing both employment and health care for Burmese Karen refugees in Texas (Mitschke et al. 2011). In Neidell and Waldfogel's (2009) research on immigrant children in Head Start programs across the US, parental access to transportation—rather, the lack of it—emerged as an important factor for low rates of participation. Outside of the North American context, Abdelkerim and Grace (2012) highlight in their study of refugees and immigrants from Africa in Australia the deleterious impact that a lack of personal mobility has had on self-sufficiency and political agency. Similarly, Uteng suggests that 'constrained mobility [is] a constitutive factor of social exclusion' (2009: 1057) in the case of non-Western immigrant women in Norway. Issues of safety (especially for women and particularly at night) in accessing destinations and the costs associated with reaching destinations have been emphasized across all of these studies. Such themes are repeated in the narratives repeated by refugees in this chapter—ad hoc strategies to overcome obstacles through cooperation, for example, and a sense of isolation and dependency when these barriers cannot be removed. Accessibility, then, is the second important conceptual framework in which this chapter and my arguments regarding refugee mobility are based.

While mobility as a concept has been focused on the notion of flows broadly understood, accessibility is generally understood as referring 'to the ability to reach desired goods, services, activities and destinations' (Litman 2011: 5), usually in a timely fashion. It is not movement per se that is the goal, but rather the ability to reach specific destinations. The effect of not being able to reach destinations therefore has been at the root of much of the work in transportation and accessibility. For many European researchers, this dynamic has been framed around questions of integration and exclusion—in which members of a given society are excluded from full and vigorous participation because of their lack of access to services such as public transit (Clifton and Lucas 2004; Lucas 2006; Lyons 2004). In the US context, the idea of accessibility is often grounded in the concepts of environmental justice, civil rights, and anti-racism (Deka 2004; Hanson and Guiliano 2004; Bullard et al. 2004). The focus here has been on the displacements caused by transportation planning and projects (Freilla 2004; Forkenbrock and Schweitzer 1999), on the lack of investment in infrastructure serving working class and racialized neighborhoods versus affluent, white suburbs (Ramsey 2000; Nogrady and King 2004), and on the disconnect between certain populations and the destinations they seek to reach.

This last, the so-called spatial mismatch hypothesis proposed by Kain (1968) and others has been especially influential and argues that jobs have followed middle-class white populations to the suburbs while minorities such as African-American populations remain trapped in hyper-urbanized concentrations in inner-cities. Similar studies have suggested that such trends have continued over subsequent decades and that in order to reach their jobs (primarily in the service sector), marginalized groups have been forced to undertake so-called reverse commutes from central cities to the suburbs (Kennedy 2004). Indeed, this phenomenon has been so widely recognized as to have federal programs dedicated to addressing the gap, such as the Job Access and Reverse Commute Program (JARC) (Cervero 2004). Some scholars have suggested that the spatial mismatch hypothesis needs to be reformulated to look more specifically at mode choice rather than geographic distance alone (Grengs 2010; Blumenberg and Manville 2004; Kawabata and Shen 2007). From this perspective, access to certain forms of transportation—especially the personal automobile—is of more significance than the distance between home and work (Blumenberg 2008; Horner and Mefford 2007). Others argue that traditional notions of spatial mismatch do not correlate with new immigrant settlement patterns. Liu and Painter's (2012) study of job decentralization and employment opportunities in sixty of the largest metropolitan areas in the US shows that immigrants are more spatially mismatched than the White population, though less so than African-Americans. This mismatch is increasingly being offset, they argue, by the movement of certain immigrant groups to suburban areas or what Li (2011) refers to as 'ethnoburbs.'

Yet even if the idea of spatial mismatch needs to be updated to take new demographic and economic realities into proper context, the issue of accessibility to jobs and other opportunities for various populations remains a crucial one. For example, in their study of transit equity in Toronto between 1996 and 2006, Foth et al. (2013) suggest that while contrary to popular perception, the socially disadvantaged groups in their research did not have lower levels of transit access than many others in the region in terms of travel time, distance, and employment destinations, this does not take into account quality or reliability of transport—when the latter are factored in, these marginalized populations may be seen to be continuing to have diminished economic opportunities compared to the broader public. Similarly, Paez et al. (2012) distinguish in their review of a range of measures of accessibility between what they call positive and normative definitions—how far is it reasonable to travel versus how far one ought to travel. Indeed, Morency et al. (2011) suggest that when a wider number of factors than space-time are taken into account, there are significant differences between the accessibility afforded low-income, elderly and single-parent households than the general population in three Canadian cities. The impact of a lack of accessibility has significant implications on economic self-sufficiency (Rogalsky 2010; Garasky et al. 2006; Jacobsen 2005) and socialization (Miller and Rasco 2004; Shen Ryan 1992)—especially important considerations for refugees under the USRAP, where self-sufficiency is a paramount concept. Scholars who have followed in this line of analysis and critique have urged, therefore, that those who advocate 'smart growth' and less-automobile-centric modes of regional development must avoid planning that reinforces transportation racism and entrenches existing inequities (Haynes et al. 2005; Schweitzer and Valenzuela 2004). In light of such scholarship, what are we to make of the experiences of refugees with mobility in Vermont?

Vermont and Refugee Mobility

When I first arrived in Vermont, mobility seemed like an obvious question to ask about, not only because so much of the research on immigrants had focused on this issue, but because my own experience in other cities and in Burlington as well made it clear that this was a central concern. I was also personally quite aware of the challenges— moving from large cities where public transit was an integral part of the landscape, I found it quite difficult in my first years to navigate the small city and the surrounding rural areas without a car and quickly abandoned my plans to live without one as I had in my previous years in Toronto. As I began to build relationships with local refugee communities and service providers, I heard time and again that transportation was a major issue—a fact that has not changed in the decade and a half since.

The first two studies that I therefore conducted in Vermont—both funded by the US Department of Transportation—were on refugee mobilities (Bose 2013, 2014). The first was based on two surveys conducted with 300 recently arrived refugees (10% of those who had arrived in the past decade) and 30 service providers who worked with them to ask about their experiences of and perspectives on travel in their daily lives. The second used focus groups and interviews with both women and elderly refugees to gauge what their more specific experiences might be. As I have said in previous chapters, the vast majority of refugees and all of those I worked with in these two studies had been settled in the Burlington metropolitan area. I also wanted to know whether refugee experiences in Vermont are distinct from those of the broader public. I thus also compared my survey responses from refugees to the travel behavior of the general population by using the 2012 Transportation Survey conducted at the county level with 519 residents (Resource Systems Group 2012). While the questions asked in these studies are not identical, there is enough overlap between the inquiries to yield some interesting comparisons. I found, for example, that the refugee population had lower levels of satisfaction in the local public transportation system than the general population did and a greater desire for car ownership than other residents—an observation I will return to in the last section of this chapter.

Comparing refugee and general population responses helped to establish a baseline that allowed me to see whether refugee travel behavior mimics that of the broader population or whether it has unique characteristics. There were many similarities in responses. Vermont has a cold climate, a relatively rural natural landscape, few urban spaces, not much industry, is mainly agricultural, and has little in the way of a developed public transportation infrastructure—realities that remain valid regardless of whether one has long roots or is a newcomer to the state. But what became quickly clear through my research was that refugees were experiencing even greater levels of inaccessibility and inconvenience than the general population and that the effects of this lack of mobility were intensifying already existing challenges to their adjustment process.

Many of my interviewees—much like the general population—listed the climate of Vermont and in particular the challenges of snow and ice to be of significant concern. Such weather conditions—and navigating them by various modes of transport—are unfamiliar to many of the refugees. One suggested:

> Due to the snow in Vermont, it is very important to have a car here. Without a car it's very hard to commute long distances and cannot get on time to places.

Said another:

> I think you should own a car especially during the weekends and in the winter

Yet others recounted how much the weather conditions can prove an especially hazardous obstacle:

> I fell last winter. I live alone. There was no transportation and with limited English I couldn't ask for help. Snow and ice make travel very hard

The lack of sidewalks, especially in Winooski, was a common theme for respondents:

> No sidewalks in many places, hard to walk in snow and ice

Such conditions lead many to look to car ownership to address the problem:

> Yes we do own a car right now. And I think it important because to get to places we really require one especially to get to work and also sometime to do the laundry and grocery before the car it was terrible because carrying everything on the back or strolling you know the 15 minute walk during the winter was terrible, it was absolutely cold and the hands were freezing so it was difficult at that time and it was a short lift at that time now we do own a car

Of course, weather alone is not the only issue for newcomers. The ability to simply reach other places—learning how to do so—seems at times insurmountable. As one refugee told me:

> The most important challenge the newcomers are facing is riding the bus to get to far away appointments

At the core of this criticism seems to be the distance to destinations and the inability to use transit to bridge this gap (also due to language barriers). As another refugee put it:

> The most challenge is the transportation. We live very far away, it is hard to go for shopping

Yet another stated:

> Learning bus schedule is difficult because of language, cannot get to places because of language and travel

Even if the bus schedule was comprehensible, the four major clusters of refugee neighborhoods—three in Burlington and one in Winooski—are served by only two buses on limited routes. The sheer distance between three of the locations—in the New North End, Winooski, and Riverside—means that walking to many destinations is not an option (Image 7.1).

Travel times to important destinations came up repeatedly as a serious issue. This was especially true when it came to jobs—the cornerstone of the USRAP's approach to resettlement—as this individual stated:

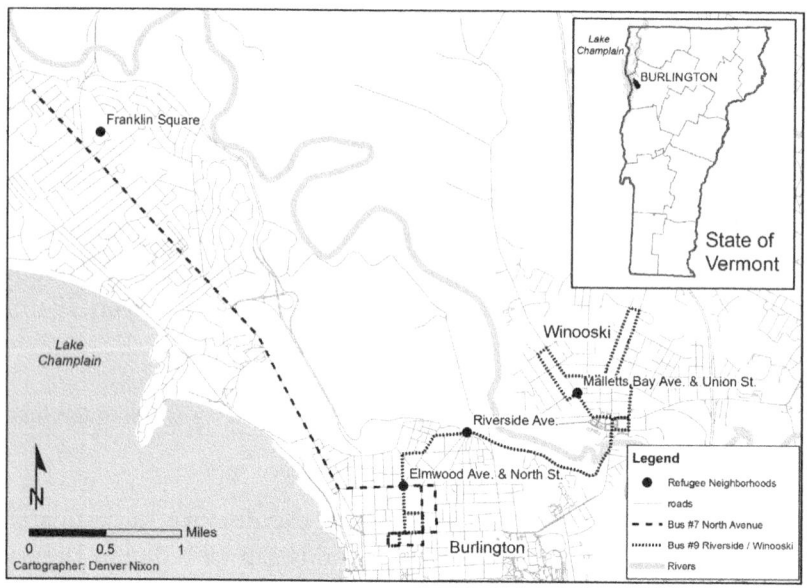

Image 7.1   Refugee neighborhoods and transit access

My friends and I, we use carpooling when we go to work every day at 10:45 pm because there is no public transportation running at this time. Sometimes we get to work late, which may result in a job loss. I feel that transportation is the most important issue for most people, especially for many refugees who cannot easily afford it

Many refugees in Vermont faced with such circumstances rely on similar ad hoc solutions comparable to those used by immigrants in other contexts, as identified by Blumenberg and Smart (2010)—carpooling with coworkers, relying on the generosity of friends, neighbors and often service providers, and on the willingness of employers to arrange transportation or overlook late arrivals to work. Refugees also revealed other coping mechanisms for offsetting their lack of adequate transportation to work.

For example, several of the former refugees who work at my university and at the university hospital—two of the major employers of refugees—mentioned a 'delicate dance' involving carpooling and the handing over of prime parking locations to coworkers coming for the next shift. Others mentioned an 'early morning stroll' of workers one can see coming and going from Winooski along one of the major streets during the early hours of the morning. Among the service providers, it became clear through surveys and interviews that many organizations provide support well beyond their mandate, with scarce resources dedicated to providing rides for clients to and from appointments, work, and shopping, helping refugees to learn bus schedules and the public transit system, assisting with obtaining taxi vouchers for medical appointments and even teaching clients how to drive. For service providers, transportation emerges as a key challenge to a successful resettlement experience in terms of employment. One stated:

Transportation is a serious barrier to refugees looking for work. The bus schedule usually does not accommodate second shift and third shift workers. Even first shift workers cannot get to their destination via bus on Sundays

Another echoed these sentiments:

> Some are able to pass the driver's license test and get a car in order to
> work late shifts and carpool. Most clients, however, spend hours per day
> commuting on one or more bus, walking or riding a bicycle (or a combi-
> nation). If the bus routes reached further, operated more frequently and
> on the weekends, newly arrived refugees would have a greater likelihood
> of becoming economically self-sufficient

Geographic distance/spatial mismatch was a consistent theme in both
surveys and interviews—many businesses are seasonal and ill served by
transit, as with a local inn and farm estate:

> Bus doesn't go to Shelburne Farms where I work. Takes me 70 min. I
> take the bus to the museum and then walk or bike or hitchhike.

Another, employed at the same business, said:

> There is no bus at late evening and nighttime. More newcomers (refugees)
> who work at nighttime (second and third shifts) have to pay for taxi or
> co-workers for their transportation.

One of the major new employment sites—an industrial park with
multiple businesses in the town of St. Albans—is located 30 miles
away, a significant challenge for survey respondents with full- and part-
time jobs there (nearly one-third of our respondents). Other jobs most
immediately available to refugees are with large institutional employers—
hospitals, hotels, a few manufacturing plants, schools, universities, retail,
and food services—but many of these are part-time, shift-based, and
often late-night positions. It is little wonder then that despite all the
other challenges refugees face—enormous hurdles in learning a new
language, having their existing skills and training recognized, and understanding a foreign workplace culture—the most significant barrier to
employment reported by respondents (85.3% of them) is transportation.
And despite creative solutions to overcome barriers to travel, a significant
number of respondents (75.3% of them) reported either turning down
work or being unable to apply for a particular job because of lack of
transportation.

My research shows that another accessibility issue identified by refugees was the relocation of various medical services—including orthopedic, pain management, physical therapy, cardiac rehabilitation, and gynecological—from several different locations in Burlington to a hub in the town of South Burlington. While the centralization of these various offices along Tilley Drive is potentially more convenient for some users, such benefits are undercut for those without access to a car by the fact that the nearest bus stop is half a mile away from the various clinics and offices—a relatively major undertaking for those with a range of medical needs and conditions. As one service provider notes:

> There are increasing numbers of health-related appointments for resettled refugees at orthopedics, cardiologists, Maitri and other health care providers on Tilley Drive in South Burlington. Of utmost concern is lack of a bus to Maitri, the often-preferred pre-natal care clinic for Africans, who already have high-risk of dropping out of care in VT.

This situation is of considerable concern for a large number of stakeholder groups—including low-income, elderly, and physically challenged individuals—but has an especial impact on newly arrived refugees. A full third of our respondents in the refugee survey listed this as their top priority with regard to transportation challenges during their resettlement experience. In particular, the relocation of the offices of Maitri Health Care for Women—a group of female healthcare providers offering alternative and holistic approaches especially popular among many refugee women—was seen as one of the most problematic. Getting to and from medical appointments in general was listed as an important priority for many respondents within the refugee community. One reported showing up to an appointment by bus and finding—in the midst of a snowstorm—no sidewalk leading from the bus stop to the medical facility and promptly got back on the bus. In his words:

> I was told how important it was to make all of my medical appointments. So, I went. But I couldn't even see the road. I got back on the bus. I came to fix my back, not get hit by a car

Weather, jobs, and health care were all significant concerns for refugees I spoke with. So too was the ability to access English language training. Language acquisition is often seen as crucial for a successful adjustment to a new home. We see such a belief expressed by the general public (as evident in the Vermonter Poll discussed in Chapter 3), by service providers, and by refugees themselves. The need is certainly clear—nearly half of the respondents in the refugee survey listed their English skills as basic. Accessing English Language Learning (ELL) programs is therefore a necessity rather than a luxury—yet for many refugees simply getting to the classes is a challenge. While every refugee resettled in Vermont is entitled to participate in a wide variety of ELL opportunities, some 24% of survey respondents reported being unable to attend a class due to transportation issues. While some classes are held in community centers in both refugee neighborhoods, many others are offered in the evening and in locations at some distance away. Even the Vermont Refugee Resettlement Program offices in Colchester—where many classes are held—are miles away from refugee neighborhoods in Winooski and Burlington with a unreliable bus service connecting them.

Mobility is also a concern for education beyond language acquisition. Service providers noted the lost opportunities for children, for example:

A lot of my Head Start children ride the SSTA van to school. The hours aren't great. Many children get to school at 10:30 and get picked up at 2 pm. They are missing out on opportunities at school for education and social interactions with other children. By the time they arrive at school, open playtime is over and children are going outside. Then the children have lunch, rest time and many children leave in the middle of rest time

Another stated:

I feel that there is a large need for transportation of young children to their childcare settings for refugee populations who do not own a car or may only own one car. It is very challenging for parents to take a bus to drop their child off at preschool and then wait to take another bus to work or school. Many children are being denied access to an early education because of transportation challenges. More SSTA services would be very helpful to this population and would also increase later school success for refugee children.

Similar to the service providers, refugees themselves were concerned about the negative impacts that diminished transportation options would have on their children's education and welfare. 75% of respondents expressed concerns that their children were missing out on educational opportunities because of the lack of transportation. One said

> It is so difficult to get our children to school for the start of school. We get them there for the school bell but they cannot go for the preschool or afterschool. The older boy brings his sister and brother home so they cannot do the other activities.

Being unable to travel to and from school in a timely fashion means particular impacts on young children attempting to acclimate to new educational systems, language, and social networks.

The findings from my studies suggest that for refugee families and individuals for whom transportation is less of a challenge—because they live closer to their travel destinations or to transit options, or due to their access to a car—their acclimation to a new environment is potentially much smoother. Indeed, those for whom transportation is less of an obstacle have considerable advantages over those who do not live either in close proximity to the work, stores, services, and schools that they need to reach, or lack access to modes of transport that render such distances manageable. Access to viable transportation options—both public and private—is clearly lacking for refugees in Vermont and this gap acts as a significant barrier for the adaptation of refugees to their new homes. Furthermore, limited transportation options can in substantial ways restrict the autonomy and independence of refugees, leaving them dependent on the services and schedules of others, which in turn can adversely affect their ability to seek and secure gainful employment, receive necessary medical care, and access other goods and services vital to both basic survival and social advancement. Such limitations are even more apparent when we look at the ways that race, class, and gender intersect to affect newly arrived refugees.

Gendered Dimensions of Mobility

In the follow-up study to my initial survey of refugee mobilities, my team and I focused on the specific experiences of women—first by re-analyzing the original data in terms of gendered responses to see if there were any differences between men and women, and second by conducting in-depth interviews with 30 of the approximately 150 women we had surveyed.

That travel behavior is diverse according to a range of variables is not a new insight. Such distinctions are not merely apparent and notable; they have clearly observable and often negative impacts upon socioeconomic outcomes including health, employment opportunities, self-sufficiency, and education (Hanson 2010). In the context of rural transportation in the so-called developing world, for example, Fernando and Porter suggest that 'women often carry a heavier burden in terms of time and effort spent on transport, and that, with less access and control over resources, they have fewer opportunities than men to use transport technologies that could alleviate their burden' (2002: 2). Similarly, Kwan's research (1999) on access to urban opportunities (in terms of job access) indicates specific gendered distinctions based on space-time constraints and locational proximity. Hanson (2010) argues that in fact mobility and gender are inextricably intertwined and initiatives meant to imagine and support new modes of sustainable transportation must take such relationships into account. Other research has highlighted the dual impacts of both aging and gender on the ability to lead an active life among senior populations within urban settings; in Dupuis, Weiss and Wolfson's study (2007) found that three times as many female respondents as men reported limitations to their lifestyles as a result of barriers to their mobility.

My research with female refugees settled in Vermont echoed such findings. Even before I had started my first survey, both service providers and refugee participants voiced the concern that a broadly based study aimed at all refugees might not get at the differential impacts of transportation barriers felt by women. Many participants suggested that more research was needed to understand whether women used particular modes of transportation more or less than men, and whether they felt their resettlement experience has been affected by transportation in different ways compared to the experienced of male members of their communities. Given the traditionally less prominent social positions occupied by women in certain of the refugee communities, it is important to question whether these patterns were being reproduced in their new homes and perhaps even intensified due to transportation limitations or if conversely, new forms of mobility are creating new forms of social interaction and relationships.

What I discovered were significant gender-based differences for refugees in Vermont in terms of travel patterns, choices, and options. While many similar experiences are reported regardless of gender—living relatively far (at least 30 minute) from most destinations or the need to make round-trip journeys at least once a day, for example—there were notable distinctions between male and female responses. While both men and women needed to make daily journeys, men reported making multiple trips each day at a rate three times as high as women. In the larger survey, a majority of men listed commuting to work and school as their primary reason for traveling while among women medical appointments and shopping for groceries and household goods were the top reasons.

Women also showed greater levels of willingness to embrace alternative modes of travel, especially walking and using transit than the general male refugee population. However, most female respondents articulated a sense within the refugee community as a whole that private vehicle ownership was an important component of a successful acculturation experience. They explained this was because of the greater levels of independence, flexibility, and self-sufficiency that cars provided in their lives, as I will relate in greater detail in the final section of this chapter. Most female respondents also did tend to use the bus on a more regular basis than men; they also suggested to more recent arrivals that they rely on transit to get around (Fig. 7.2).

But the theme that emerged most clearly from my interviews with women in the Vermont refugee communities was that barriers to mobility had a significant and negative impact on their independence. Many interviewees reported having to rely on others—whether friends,

What are some of the things you recommend for newcomers to the
community in terms of travel?

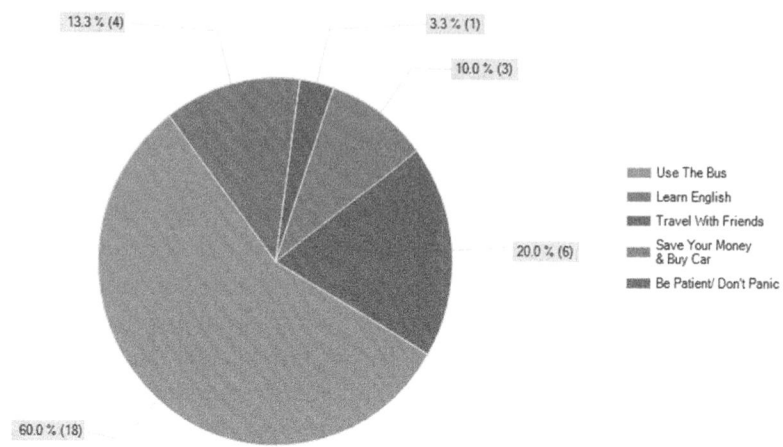

Fig. 7.2 Female interviewees' recommendations

family, other members of their communities, service providers, caseworkers, or volunteers through the resettlement agencies—to assist them.
As one told me:

> Transportation is the biggest challenge. We also do not have a car and
> always have to ask people to assist us

Another said:

> If I had a car then I would be self-dependent, I wouldn't have to rely on
> other people to help me move from to one place to another. It would be
> very easy and could go anywhere in a convenient way. I would feel that I
> am very independent

The sense of discomfort in always asking for a ride is also evident in this
quote:

> You need a car it is very necessary to have one because some grocery store is very far. It is very hard to ask friend all the time because they go to work. If they are on their way to grocery it is easy to go with them, but it is hard to ask if they aren't going. It is very necessary to have a car

And again:

> It would be nice to have a car. We have to always ask for help. It is hard to get many things from the market. My husband also goes to work with someone who has a car.

For many of the respondents, the dependency was quite often within the family, where those who did have greater levels of mobility tended to be male members—usually husbands and sons (Image 7.2). This is a pattern that emerged repeatedly, as the following female refugees told me:

> My husband owns a car
>> We have a car my husband drives it
>> We own car, my husband only drives
>> My husband drives me
>> My son drive me to garden
>> Yeah we have a car now. My husband drives to work and sometime to go to shopping we take a car, he will drive me
>> My husband recently just bought a car, I do not know how to drive a car yet. He takes a car to work and for shopping car is very convenient and also to commute for my husband's job
>> We have one car. I do not drive but my husband and son drive it. If we have our own car then it is very easy, if we have to go to Costco we do not have to ask other people we can easily go during the holiday. Even to go to work is very accessible and can come sooner to home after work. If we have a car then it is very convenient.
>> One of my sons has a car, but he has to take it to work and the other is very ill so he cannot drive a car. I cannot travel without help

I present all of these quotes to emphasize the significance of the dependency part of this dynamic—even when a personal car can help to overcome the family's reliance on others and outsiders, it is often unable to perform the same function for women within the family. Part of

Image 7.2   AALV Van

this had to do with a lack of familiarity or experience with driving in their countries of origin, part of it included cultural barriers regarding women driving within some of the communities, but the single largest reason was an inability for women in particular to get driver's licenses. This last has been a sore spot in Vermont for years, with some in the refugee communities accusing the local department of motor vehicles of racism in their treatment of those seeking to both learn how to drive and become licensed. This issue has been significant enough to have been taken up by the Vermont State Legislature to try and overcome such barriers.

The issue of cars of course brings us to the last section of this chapter—the question of refugees, modes of travel, and car culture itself.

Newcomers and Cultures of Travel

Burlington, as Chapter 4 notes, prides itself on certain aesthetic, cultural, and political commitments that on the one hand render it unique within Vermont and on the other hand aligns it with a set of parallel places across the US—Boulder, Colorado or Austin, Texas, or Portland, Oregon, for example. These are all places that are liberal or progressive in their politics, somewhat small-scale in their physical footprint, and wide in their embrace of alternative practices in environmental, health, and food cultures, as I note at greater length in the next chapter. Such patterns are so commonly known that they have become stereotypes, parodied in popular media such as the sketch-comedy show *Portlandia.*

One way in which Burlington fits into such a milieu is through its adoption of alternative modes of transportation. These include a city-wide plan for bicycling and pedestrian corridors, the purchase of electric buses for its transit authority and subsidies for carshare programs and personal electric bicycles (City of Burlington 2020). There are also a number of local bicycle advocacy organizations and bicycle shops that work closely with refugees, providing secondhand bicycles and trainings for those who wish to repair their own. Such services are important but a question that many such alternative transportation organizations and advocates have asked me is why there is not greater adoption of these other modes by newly arrived refugees.

An obvious answer would be utility—cars offer convenience and ability to access destinations that are otherwise difficult to reach because of distance or time. It is clear from the quotes in the previous sections that *not* being able to get to places has a compounded effect upon refugee families and individuals. Other refugees echoed these sentiments:

> We do not have a car. It will be very convenient. We could go anywhere we wish to. It will be easy to go anywhere. I think it is very important part of the resettlement process

Yet another said:

> Yeah I think that every family need to have a car to make their life very easier because VT we have lots of cold days raining, winter. Taking a bus is convenient but you can save a lot of money taking a bus but if you have job, children then it is good to have a car because it will make your life easier

One interviewee noted her preference for transit yet said that despite this she recognized the significance of having a car:

> In reality I do not feel like it is important, but especially here feels like you need to have a car in order to get a job

Like this woman, a majority of the refugees I interviewed or surveyed reported that they used the bus and were on the whole pleased with their experience. And more than male respondents, they were more interested in walking or taking the bus than driving, not least because of the difficulties in obtaining a license. But refugees across multiple communities and genders spoke about what having a car enabled, not only in utilitarian terms but in aspirational ones, as voiced by this refugee:

> I can't afford to buy a house right now. But I can buy a car. It will be my first step to being an American.

Another refugee echoed this sentiment:

> I want to be like other Americans. I want to drive a car, I want to own, maybe more than one cars. Young people here know that to be a grownup you need to have a car.

When I return to my original survey on refugee mobility, I see that while some 85% of respondents use the bus, 90% aspire to eventually have a car—even while being generally satisfied with the transit experience (at a far higher rate, it should be noted, than the general population). The responses above suggest three distinct themes: first that owning a car oneself—as opposed to relying on someone else's vehicle—greatly enhances mobility; second, ownership signifies independence, and third, it means achieving social and cultural legitimacy. A preference for cars is about more than mode choice or the convenience of being able to access destinations for many of my respondents.

Several refugees spoke of future plans to purchase cars and tied these explicitly to their integration:

> We work and save money and buy the used car then later update some better car. We hope to get new car same time as citizenship, as citizenship present.

Another respondent told us that getting a car was her advice for newer arrivals:

> I will tell people to work hard save up money and buy a car. So most of the refugees use bus, very rare not to. I think we work so hard so we need car to go to places much faster, be like other people here. You want to succeed in America, you get a car.

Some respondents expressed their appreciation in providential terms:

> I am very happy to have a car. I have never imagined that someday we will have a car and will drive someday. I am very happy that god helped us get a car and helped us own one.
>
> Yeah thank lord, we are very lucky because everyone has a car and makes life very easier

In sum, my research into refugee mobilities in Vermont suggests that the lack of access to desired and required destinations may lead to negative outcomes—fewer job opportunities, poorer health, and missed chances to improve skills and education. Refugees are told upon arrival that they must become economically self-sufficient in order to integrate into American society, that they must maintain good health to be functioning members of their new communities, and that they must learn English and better their educations to improve their social standing. Yet missing out on jobs because they cannot reach them (or reach them on time), missing medical appointments due to a lack of transportation, and having skills stagnate and lessons go unlearned because they cannot get to school put these key elements of the refugee's successful transition to new homes in jeopardy.

But as I have argued in this chapter, the issue is much more than practicality. Instead, my studies have suggested that existing transportation hierarchies that place the car at the top of the pyramid are reinforced through the refugee resettlement (and more broadly immigrant acculturation) process. It is not merely that cars provide greater levels of mobility and improve outcomes—it is that owning and operating one's own car is a seemingly logical and obvious outcome of bettering one's adjustment to a new society, one that in the context of the general publics of the US, Vermont, and the Burlington metropolitan area is firmly articulated as a car culture. For refugees arriving in Vermont, therefore, it is not surprising that they would reflect such beliefs and practices. Or as one of my respondents put it:

> Without transportation there is no possibility in this state. Car is very important.

References

Abdelkerim, A., and Marty Grace. 2012. Challenges to employment in newly emerging African communities in Australia: A review of the literature. *Australian Social Work* 65 (1): 104–119.

Bloemraad, Irene. 2006. *Becoming a citizen: Incorporating immigrants and refugees in the United States and Canada*. Berkeley: University of California Press.

Blumenberg, Evelyn. 2008. Immigrants and transport barriers to employment: The case of Southeast Asian welfare recipients in California. *Transport Policy* 15: 33–42.

Blumenberg, Evelyn, and Michael Manville. 2004. Beyond the spatial mismatch: Welfare recipients and transportation policy. *Journal of Planning Literature* 19 (2): 182–205.

Blumenberg, Evelyn, and Michael Smart. 2010. Getting by with a little help from my friends…and family: Immigrants and carpooling. *Transportation* 37: 429–446.

Bose, Pablo S. 2013. Building sustainable communities: Immigrants, acculturation and mobility in Vermont. *Research in Transportation Business and Management* 17: 81–90.

Bose, Pablo S. 2014. Refugees in Vermont: Mobility and acculturation in a new immigrant destination. *Journal of Transport Geography* 36 (2014): 151–159.

Bullard, Robert, Glenn Johnson, and Angel Torres (eds.). 2004. *Highway robbery: Transportation racism & new routes to equity*. Cambridge, MA: South End Press.

Cervero, Robert. 2004. Job isolation in the US: Narrowing the gap through job access and reverse-commute programs. In *Running on empty: Transport, social exclusion and environmental justice*, ed. K. Lucas, 181–196. Bristol: Policy.

Chatman, Daniel G., and Nicholas Klein. 2009. Immigrants and travel demand in the United States: Implications for transportation policy and future research. *Public Works Manage Policy* 13 (4): 312–327.

City of Burlington. 2020. PlanBTV Walk Bike. Available from https://www.burlingtonvt.gov/planbtvwalkbike.

Clifton, Kelly, and Karen Lucas. 2004. Examining the empirical evidence of transport inequality. In *Running on empty: Transport, social exclusion and environmental justice*, ed. Karen Lucas. Bristol: Policy.

Cresswell, Tim. 2010. Mobilities I: Catching up. *Progress in Human Geography* 35 (4): 550–558.

Cresswell, Tim. 2012. Mobilities II: Still. *Progress in Human Geography* 36 (5): 645–653.

Deka, Devajyoti. 2004. Social and environmental justice issues in urban transportation. In *The geography of urban transportation*, 3rd ed, ed. Susan Hanson and Genevieve Guiliano, 332–355. New York: Guilford Press.

Dupuis, Josette, Deborah R. Weiss, and Christina Wolfson. 2007. Gender and transportation access among community-dwelling seniors. *Canadian Journal on Aging* 26 (2): 149–158.

Fernando, Priyanthi, and Gina Porter. 2002. Introduction: Bridging the gap between gender and transportation. In *Balancing the load: Women, gender and transport*, ed. P. Fernando and G. Porter, 1–14. London: Zed Books.

Forkenbrock, David J., and Lisa Schweitzer. 1999. Environmental justice in transportation planning. *Journal of the American Planning Association* 65 (1): 96–112.

Foth, Nicole, Kevin Manaugh, and Ahmed El-Geneidy. 2013. Towards equi-table transit: Examining transit accessibility and social need in Toronto, Canada, 1996–2006. *Journal of Transport Geography* 29: 1–10.

Freilla, Omar. 2004. Burying Robert Moses's legacy in New York City. In *Highway Robbery: Transportation racism and new routes to equity*, ed. Robert D. Bullard, Glenn S. Johnson, and Angel O. Torres, 75–99. Cambridge, MA: South End Press.

Garasky, Steven, Cynthia Needles Fletcher, and Helen H. Jensen. 2006. Transiting to work: The role of private transportation for low-income households. *Journal of Consumer Affairs* 40 (1): 64–89.

Grengs, Joe. 2010. Job accessibility and the modal mismatch in Detroit. *Journal of Transport Geography* 18 (2010): 42–54.

Haines, David. 2010. *Safe Haven? a history of refugees in America*. Sterling, VA: Kumarian Press.

Hanson, Susan. 2010. Gender and mobility: New approaches for informing sustainability. *Gender, Place and Culture* 17 (1): 5–23.

Hanson, Susan, and Genevieve Guiliano. 2004. *The geography of urban trans-portation*. New York: Guilford Press.

Haynes, Kingsley E., Jonathan L. Gifford, and Danilo Pelletiere. 2005. Sustain-able transportation institutions and regional evolution: Global and local perspectives. *Journal of Transport Geography* 13 (3): 207–221.

Heiz, Andrew, and Grant Schellenberg. 2004. Public transit among immi-grants. *Canadian Journal of Urban Research* 13 (1): 170–191.

Horner, Mark W., and Jessica N. Mefford. 2007. Investigating urban spatial mismatch using job housing indicators to model home-work separation. *Environment and Planning A* 39 (6): 1420–1440.

Jacobsen, Karen. 2005. *The economic life of refugees*. Bloomfield, CT: Kumarian Press.

Jensen, Anne. 2011. Mobility, space and power: On the multiplicities of seeing mobility. *Mobilities* 6 (2): 255–271.

Kain, John F. 1968. Housing segregation, Negro employment, and metropolitan decentralization. *Quarterly Journal of Economics* 82: 175–197.

Kawabata, Mizuki, and Qing Shen. 2007. Commuting inequality between cars and public transit: The case of the San Francisco Bay Area, 1990–2000. *Urban Studies* 44 (9): 1759–1780.

Kennedy, Lori. 2004. Transportation and environmental justice. In *Running on empty: Transport, social exclusion and environmental justice*, ed. K. Lucas, 155–180. Bristol: Policy.

Kwan, Mei-Po. 1999. Gender and individual access to urban opportunities: A study using space-time measures. *The Professional Geographer* 51 (2): 211–227.

Li, Wei. 2011. *Ethnoburb: The new ethnic community in urban America*. Honolulu: University of Hawaii Press.

Litman, Todd. 2011. *Measuring transportation: Traffic mobility and accessibility*. Victoria: Victoria Transport Policy Institute.

Liu, Cathy Yang, and Gary Painter. 2012. Immigrant settlement and employment suburbanization: Is there a spatial mismatch? *Urban Studies* 49 (5): 979–1002.

Lo, L., A. Shalaby, and B. Alshalalfah. 2011. Relationship between immigrant settlement patterns and transit use in the Greater Toronto Area. *Journal of Urban Planning and Development* 137 (4): 470–476.

Loescher, Gil, and James Milner. 2005. *Protracted refugee situations: Domestic and international security implications*. New York: Routledge.

Lovejoy, Kristen, and Susan Handy. 2011. Social networks as a source of private-vehicle transportation: The practice of getting rides and borrowing vehicles among Mexican immigrants in California. *Transportation Research a* 45: 248–257.

Lucas, Karen. 2006. Providing transport for social inclusion within a framework for environmental justice in the UK. *Transportation Research Part a: Policy & Practice* 40 (10): 801–809.

Lyons, Glenn. 2004. Transport and society. *Transport Reviews* 24 (4): 485–509.

Miller, Kenneth, and Lisa Rasco. 2004. *The mental health of refugees: Ecological approaches to healing and adaptation*. Mahwah, NJ: Lawrence Erlbaum Publishers Inc.

Mitschke, Diane, Aaron Mitschke, Holli M. Slater, and Consoler Teboh. 2011. Uncovering health and wellness needs of recently resettled Karen refugees from Burma. *Journal of Human Behavior in the Social Environment* 21 (5): 490–501.

Morency, Catherine, Antonio Paez, Matthew Roorda, Ruben Mercado, and Steven Farber. 2011. Distance traveled in three Canadian cities: Spatial analysis from the perspective of vulnerable population segments. *Journal of Transport Geography* 19: 39–50.

Neidell, Matthew, and Jane Waldfogel. 2009. Program participation of immigrant children: Evidence from the local availability of Head Start. *Economics of Education Review* 28 (6): 704–715.

Nogrady, Brian, and Anna King. 2004. Transit activism in Steel Town, USA. In *Highway robbery: Transportation racism and new routes to equity*, ed. R.

Bullard, G. Johnson, and A. Torres, 121–144. Cambridge, MA: South End Press.

Paez, Antonio, Darren Scott, and Catherine Morency. 2012. Measuring accessibility: Positive and normative implementations of various accessibility indicators. *Journal of Transport Geography* 25: 141–153.

Pipher, Mary. 2002. *The middle of everywhere: Helping refugees enter the American community*. New York: Harcourt Books.

Ramsey, K. 2000. Riding the freedom bus in LA. *Forum for Applied Research & Public Policy* 15 (3): 77–80.

Resource Systems Group. 2012. *Chittenden county regional planning commission transportation survey*. Burlington: CCRPC.

Rogalsky, Jennifer. 2010. The working poor and what GIS reveals about the possibilities of public transit. *Journal of Transport Geography* 18 (2010): 226–237.

Schweitzer, Lisa, and Abel Valenzuela. 2004. Environmental injustice and transportation: The claims and the evidence. *Journal of Planning Literature* 18: 383–398.

Sheller, Mimi, and John Urry. 2016. Mobilizing the new mobilities paradigm. *Applied Mobilities* 1 (1): 10–25.

Shen Ryan, A. (ed.). 1992. *Social work with immigrants and refugees*. New York and London: Haworth Press.

Tal, Gil, and Susan Handy. 2010. Travel behavior of immigrants: An analysis of the 2001 National Household Transportation Survey. *Transport Policy* 17: 85–93.

Urry, John. 2012. Social networks, mobile lives and social inequalities. *Journal of Transport Geography* 21: 24–30.

Urry, John. 2016. *Mobilities: New perspectives on transport and society*. New York: Routledge.

Uteng, Tanu Priya. 2009. Gender, ethnicity and constrained mobility: Insights into the resultant social exclusion. *Environment and Planning A* 41 (5): 1055–1071.

8

Food

The previous chapter explored refugee lives in terms of mobilities—how does the ability—or the lack of it—to access particular locations affect resettlement outcomes? In this chapter, I also examine access issues but in this case the access being sought is to the familiarity of tastes, of cuisines, of ingredients, of smells, of crops, and of cultures. I focus thus in this chapter on the relationships between food and migrant identities and explore some of the ways in which refugees attempt to forge connections between old and new homes through their consumption practices as they engage in gardening and farming, open restaurants and search for familiar and preferred ingredients.

It is clear from my research that food practices and options for newcomers in a changing Vermont are significant components of refugee identities, ways of forging and maintaining linkages to things left behind—or alternatively of challenging and transforming them. Food in this sense can be a symbol or a carrier of tradition and nostalgia, and it can also be a tool to help one adjust to a new set of realities. Knowing how significant food practices have been for immigrants in other contexts, the second set of research projects I undertook after arriving in Vermont—following closely on the heels of my initial studies

© The Author(s) 2020
P. S. Bose, *Refugees in New Destinations and Small Cities,*
https://doi.org/10.1007/978-981-15-6386-7_8

of refugee mobilities—focused on food. This became central to my broader project as well to map, understand, and evaluate the refugee experience as it relates to resettlement.

I began to investigate what food meant to newcomers by conducting a series of ethnographic, semi-structured interviews with a range of respondents. This included speaking with shopkeepers, restaurant owners, food suppliers, and farmers and gardeners. I have also been able to conduct participant observation of a number of food-related events and practices, including community celebrations held by various refugee groups, community gardening and farming workshops, farmers' markets and community-supported agriculture programs, and toured the pantries and kitchens of refugee households themselves. What I discovered in these various spaces confirms the arguments put forth by much of the existing literature on food, migration, and culture—that there are strong, deep, and lasting ties between people, place, and identity that are expressed on the plate and in the palate. At the same time, my studies shed light on some of the unique contexts for newcomers in Vermont with regard to their culinary habits and desires.

I explore these relationships in this chapter in four parts. In the first I discuss some of the scholarship on the importance of food in creating a complex sense of 'home' for immigrants in their new homes. Next, I introduce the contemporary food culture of Vermont and how newcomers (refugees and migrant farmworkers in particular) might fit within it. In the third part of the chapter, I examine in greater detail the (re)emergence of ethnic grocery stores and restaurants in refugee neighborhoods in Vermont. Such prominence has already been noted by participants in the Photovoice project results presented in Chapter 4 on Burlington and Chapter 5 on Winooski, highlighting such places as significant ones in refugee lives. In the final part of this chapter, I look at an innovative refugee agriculture program in Vermont meant to provide access to land and the ability to grow culturally significant crops for newcomers.

Migrants and Food

The connections between people and place are forged, maintained, and contested through multiple cultural forms, including many food-related practices (Counihan and Van Esterik 2012). This is particularly true when we think about migration within and across borders, and between and beyond continents in an age of globalization. Whether arriving in a traditional immigrant gateway, being a newcomer in an unfamiliar region, or dreaming of a distant or ancestral homeland from an overseas community, food and drink have often played a major role in maintaining social, cultural, and kinship ties to other places (Fernández-Armesto 2002; Matt 2007; Etzold 2016; Sarkar 2019). This complex, multifaceted relationship between food and migration has become a topic of increasing interest to scholars intrigued by the role that food has played within the acculturation process—highlighting, for example, tensions and struggles within communities and individuals as they negotiate hybrid identities (Ray 2004). Others have pointed to tensions—many of them fruitful—in the food and migration dynamic, including a clash between syncretism and parochialism in the encounter between various migrant groups, available foodstuff, and competing traditions (Kershen 2017; Diner 2009; Gabaccia 2000; Alibhai-Brown 2009; Moffat et al. 2017). These processes are an important part of identity construction for communities both old and new and perform a crucial function in narrating stories about difference and familiarity to migrants and established populations alike.

Migrant communities are not, of course, a new phenomenon, as earlier chapters have pointed out. They have existed for centuries and in many ways complicate modern notions of geographic and political boundaries. They are often multifaceted social organizations, interwoven in the contemporary context with legacies of colonialism and emerging trends toward cultural, economic, political, and social globalization. Generations of migrants have flourished away from their 'homelands,' often establishing distinct cultural identities and differences as expressed through art, music, language, religion, and food practices. Indeed, the hallmark of so-called ethnic enclaves—whether in downtown neighborhoods or the newer ethnoburb (Li 2009) discussed at the outset of Chapter 5—is a preponderance of ethnic cuisines, food carts, corner stores, supermarkets, street festivals, and restaurants (King 2004). Through the creation of such spaces and culinary preferences, different émigré groups have forcefully asserted their sense of self and difference. At the same time, food has helped many migrants to forge and maintain a significant sense of attachment to particular places—whether old or new, currently lived in or recalled through nostalgia. As Ray argues,

> Food is particularly potent as a place-making practice because it links the land to the hearth and the hearth to the heart through the mediation of produce. As Alice Watters, noted chef and culinarian, says: "If you see the same ingredients every place you go, you lose a sense of time and place. Then nothing is special." That is exactly why immigrants crave some of the distinctive products of their homeland, notwithstanding time or place. (Ray 2004)

It is important to make the proviso, however, that not all immigrants and migrants relate to land and food in the same ways. Migration itself takes many forms; as the chapters in the first section of this book note, there are multiple factors that both push people out of old homes and pull them toward new ones. The differences between undocumented farmworkers and legally resettled refugees, for example, lead to very different experiences of precarity and different kinds of access and relation to food. The refugee neighborhoods that are the focus of this book and explored in the previous section offer an opportunity for visibility and legitimacy on the landscape that Latinx farmworkers in rural Vermont rarely have. And while refugees might open restaurants or shop at ethnic grocery stores, the fears of detection and deportation force migrant farmworkers to lead lives often at the margins of Vermont society, seeking anonymity or relying on others to provide them with food that advertises their identity (Mares et al. 2020).

Regardless of their origins or their current status, these two particular groups of newcomers to Vermont tend to stand out from longtime residents in their new homes as well as other in-migrant groups. Race and ethnicity have much to do with this; Latinx farmworkers and refugees are phenotypically, linguistically, and culturally distinct from most other

Vermonters. Processes of racialization subject both sets of communities apart from those around them; they also render refugees and migrants as substantially different from those of other immigrant groups, such as the transnational elites that have so often been the focus of the study of migrant cultural practices in general and foodways in particular.

Mannur (2005: 90), for example, has suggested that the eating habits and indeed the very lives of specific migrants—especially so-called model minorities—have been valorized through global media in its preoccupation with fusion cuisines and elaborate cooking shows featuring glamorous hosts such as Padma Lakshmi and Ming Tsai:

Certain types of fusion are considered "cuisine" while others are dismissed as mere forays into poor eclectic food. Increasingly, fusion cuisine as offered by chefs such as Ming Tsai is part of the upscale culinary market, commanding higher prices than "merely" ethnic restaurants.

Mannur argues that these distinctions between what becomes valued as 'cuisine' and what remains simply sustenance for the working classes demands our attention to what she terms 'culinary fictions' in the production of migrant identities (Mannur 2010). It is important, therefore, as I embark on this particular examination of food, migration, culture, and identity in contemporary Vermont, not to reify or exoticize the eating habits, preferences, or options of the refugees. As Ray (2004) notes in his study of food in the context of another transnational migrant population:

For the middle-class Bengali migrant, all the trouble with food has to do with two things: home and heritage. Both are about defining one's self in terms of a place and a past, and that makes the middle-class Bengali migrant a quintessentially modern subject. In the process of showing that, I take nostalgia seriously and critique the assumption that migrants are somehow more traditional than other.

It is crucial not to take for granted that 'ethnic cuisines' (and dominant representations of them) are the ultimate or 'authentic' expressions of identity. To take seriously this caveat is often challenging because frequently when one sets out to look for the impact of refugees on a particular landscape, restaurants, and grocery stores are an obvious and visible marker of difference—indeed what one might expect to find in an ethnic neighborhood. And certainly, a preponderance of these was noted both by my cataloguing of refugee neighborhoods and by participants in the Photovoice project. An association between ethnic enclaves and modern (especially global) cities is often 'proven' by the presence of eating establishments that cater to 'other' tastes. These might be expressed through street festivals and cultural celebrations, markets, and grocery stores filled with culturally specific goods, or restaurants and food stalls catering to specific populations and cuisines. We also see the assertion of particular identities through language and the naming of certain forms of cuisine, through street signs, menus, and the adoption of particular brands and types of food in grocery stores.

But the presence of 'ethnic' food in neighborhoods and cities is not merely about describing difference or a way for cities to market themselves to tourists and global (or local) audiences seeking the exotic and unexpected. As Koc and Welsh (2001) suggest in their examination of Toronto (a city with a significant immigrant population) differences in cuisine are not simply about catering to elite curiosities or increasing civic boosterism. They show us instead the ways that Toronto—as seen in its culinary landscape—has been shaped and reshaped by waves of different diasporas over time, transforming neighborhoods through the arrival and integration of new people, ingredients, markets, and restaurants. Restaurant spaces in particular are seen by the authors as points of community building within the diaspora groups and as a point of contact and exchange between multiple cultures. Scanlon's (2010) study of Mexican restaurants, restaurateurs, and customers in Atlanta and Houston similarly focuses on the naming, decoration, and placing of restaurants within each metropolitan area as a negotiation between owners and patrons over the role of these spaces within their cities. Trying to balance between the needs and desires of different customers—community insiders seeking familiar food and outsiders seeking an 'authentic' experience—has led to mixed and sometimes unexpected acculturation outcomes for these neighborhoods as a whole. This is a familiar dynamic evident in many other cities and ethnic neighborhoods (Szanto 2015; Blake 2018; Khojasteh and Raja 2017; Han 2018).

It is clear from such work that a critical focus on food practices in the urban landscape can tell us much about the ways in which the city itself is made and remade through a set of diverse processes related to food production, consumption, distribution, idealization, and imagination. Many of these processes are overlapping while others are dissonant with one another. The emergence of specialized cuisines in restaurants and food stands can equally tell multiple stories—about the changing demographics of a city, about an Orientalizing obsession with exotic tastes, or about gentrification in particular neighborhoods. Similarly, the changing location and character of food venues can illuminate the new ways in which we can think about the city and its denizens—where food deserts emerge and are reified, how restaurant districts come to be produced and reproduced, where conflicts over the meaning of community play out in the siting of gardens and food carts alike.

In the context of the urban, food has long played an important role in the spatial ordering of cities. From the granaries, cisterns, and market squares around which ancient citadels were built to the dizzying array of restaurants, edible gardens, concession stands, and supermarkets that characterize many contemporary cities, food, and foodways have helped to shape and define the structures in which diverse communities live. In the changing landscapes of twenty-first-century cities, food retains its role as a unifier, a liminal boundary between cultures, and often a site of struggles over social justice and the right to the space itself. In this sense, food can act as much more than a marker of place or culture—in important ways the specific practices we see in particular places can help us to understand cities and communities themselves.

I have so far mainly discussed ethnic enclaves and neighborhoods and the roles that markets, grocery stores, and restaurants might play in their development. Yet it is not only in the realm of the downtown core, the refugee neighborhood or the 'ethnoburb' that we see the connections between food, culture, and identity. The focus of this book is on the cities (of varying size) of Vermont; yet the boundaries between these and their semi-rural and rural peripheries are constantly blurred in terms of where refugees live, work, and recreate. Of particular note for refugees in Vermont is another foodscape of especial importance, one that has increasing resonance in scholarship and practice of migrant transna-tionalism today—urban agriculture, both farming and gardening. This example, as we will see presently in greater detail, tells us about a number of overlapping narratives—about self-sufficiency and food security, about the growing of familiar foods, and about new uses for underutilized lands and brownfield sites.

The possibilities for urban agriculture—as distinct from large-scale commercial agriculture or subsistence farming in rural areas—are complex, especially when located within peri-urban areas, which, as we will see, is where the refugee agriculture programs in Vermont have been placed. But urban gardening and farming programs have become increasingly popular in multiple contexts and cases despite the often-marginal land and complicated politics involved (Horst et al. 2017; Clendenning et al. 2016). Scholars have looked at the role that urban agriculture can play in combating gentrification and reversing the decline of metropolitan cities (Walker 2016; Jung and Newman 2014), as crit-ical social justice education (Reynolds 2017) and improving governance, democracy, and participation (Camps-Calvet et al. 2016).

Urban agriculture is no panacea or silver bullet, however. Kato et al. (2018), for example, look at the challenges for an urban farming organi-zation with on-site CSA markets and community- and entrepreneurial-gardens located in a working-class, predominantly black neighborhood in New Orleans as it works to rebuild not just neighborhoods but entire wards and arguably a city itself recovering from political, social, economic, and ecological disaster that has extended far beyond (and long before) one hurricane. Not only is there a competition for available land with speculators and developers, the participation of minority and racial-ized communities is often far from assured. Conway (2016) suggests similar barriers when looking at home-based or backyard gardening as well. This is not an uncommon phenomenon when one looks at so-called alternative food movements as I discuss in greater depth in the next section.

Vermont and Food Cultures

Both Burlington and Vermont have gained an increasing prominence in recent decades for their presence within certain kinds of food scenes. Part of Burlington's identity as of a kind with the Austin-Boulder-Portland-Asheville-nexus of alternative college towns in the US is its alternative foodie culture (Thompson 2016). It is not the presence of fusion restaurants or fancy cafes that mark its distinction but rather the number of farm-to-table eateries, micro-breweries, and rustic bakeries that establish the city's membership in the alternative food fraternity. This is true of the state more generally; over the past few decades, Vermont has developed a reputation as a hub for alternative food practices. It has a long history as a rural, agricultural state, but today Vermont leads the US in the number of farmers' markets and CSAs programs per capita, has a significant percentage of certified organic farmland, and boasts innovative programs such as the Farm to School and Vermont Gleaning Collective Initiatives (Rosenfeld 2010; Conner et al. 2019). Maple sugar production has long been tied to Vermont's own cultural identity, as have artisan cheesemaking and small-scale dairy production.

For newcomers to the state, however, Vermont's food systems networks, traditions, and opportunities are less apparent and less accessible. Latinx farmworkers are crucial to the survival of the aforementioned dairy farms. For those that are family-run in particular, their inability to attract skilled labor from within the state has led to increasing consolidation and in the case of many family-run farms, increasing farm closures. And yet the Latinx farmworkers who sustain many operations find themselves often isolated and vulnerable, trying to remain out of sight of border patrols and ICE officers and thus remaining highly dependent upon farm managers and owners to provide them with food (Mares 2019; Radel et al. 2010). Most farmworkers work in a northern county that is close to the Canadian border, and not surprisingly, their own precarity and sense of insecurity is thereby heightened. The jurisdiction of immigration authorities in the US always extended one hundred miles south of the border but in the present anti-immigrant era of the Trump administration, such enforcement has been made more visible and has intensified.

What migrant farmworkers do have access to is often fast food or unhealthy options bought in bulk from big box stores. An innovative program developed by colleagues at my university has for over a decade aided Latinx farmworkers to grow small gardens and harvest fresh vegetables for them to supplant these meager and limited options. But as one of the founders of this program Teresa Mares (2019: 116) states in her study of this population:

> Our project team is also aware that no matter how many gardens we plant or how successful they may be, they are just one small part of addressing basic needs year-round. It is imperative to underscore that with Vermont's short growing season these gardens are only productive for a few months out of the year. While most of the gardeners make an effort to freeze, dry, and otherwise preserve foods for the winter months, all remain dependent on others to do the majority of their shopping for them—often the manager or owner of the farm who rarely speaks Spanish. In this way, their ability to choose and have regular access to food in these northern borderlands—particularly fresh foods with cultural significance—remains compromised, and their practices of food sovereignty remain constrained.

Refugees, as I have pointed out earlier, do not suffer from the same kinds of fears of detention and deportation as Latinx farmworkers. Yet refugees too find themselves navigating an unfamiliar foodscape upon arrival. In Chittenden County, where many thousands of resettled refugees have arrived over the past 40 years, food security and food sovereignty remain elusive to many new arrivals—a fact noted in studies of hunger within the county (Stokes 2017; Conway 2018). Vermont's growing season is short, weather patterns are confusing and food preservation methods are unfamiliar to newcomers. Crops that refugees may know how to grow may not do as well in this new soil, while new pests, agricultural practices, and harvesting techniques present additional challenges. Added to the many other obstacles facing refugees—transportation, employment, housing, and education—food security is a central barrier to effective integration.

One might expect that an appetite to overcome such obstacles might be high given the strong levels of support for refugees indicated in the Vermonter Polls discussed in Chapter 3, the progressive sensibilities of Burlington and Winooski, and the presence of so many alternative food initiatives in the area. And as we will see presently, there have been attempts to marry Vermont's agricultural identity and farming knowledge to the needs, preferences, and knowledge systems of some newcomers. But as many scholars have noted, food sovereignty movements and social justice are not always well-aligned. Slocum (2007: 526), for example, argues that processes of racialization are deeply embedded within such spaces:

> Whiteness emerges spatially in efforts to increase access to healthy foods, support farmers and provide organic food to consumers…The connections among property, privilege and paler skin are evident in alternative food practice. There is a physical clustering of white bodies in the often-expensive spaces of community food—conferences, farm tourism, community supported agriculture and alternative food stores.

Other scholars have similarly critiqued alternative food spaces and programs for the ways in which they cater to or at least align with middle-class white values and experiences and can marginalize others based on class, race, gender, sexuality, ability, or other differences (Parker et al. 2019; Guthman 2008; Alkon and McCullen 2011; Smith 2019).

Vermont, as I discussed in Chapter 3, has a long and at times sorry record of linking a rural and bucolic countryside with specific racialized identities, as seen particularly through its eugenics history. Beyond this extreme, from the late nineteenth century onwards, the state has invested explicitly in a white agrarian identity in its self-promotion. As Vanderbeck (2006: 247) suggests

> Images of the true Anglo-Saxon, Protestant Yankee Vermonter were employed to lure potential tourists and second-home buyers who were seeking not only attractive scenery but the kinds of "authentic" rural social relations that were disappearing from the rapidly industrializing landscapes of much of the rest of America. Put another way, a particular Vermont whiteness became a marketing tool.

How do those who do not fit neatly or clearly into such visions of a Vermont landscape negotiate their place in it? How do they manage their relationships with a dominant Vermont food culture that may be as much about show as it is about production or consumption? In the final two sections of this chapter, I return to the question of migration, food, and culture to examine the ways in which tastes distinct to newcomer cultures appear in refugee neighborhoods and an urban agriculture program to explore these complex dynamics at greater length.

Home Pantries, Grocery Stores, and Restaurants

In an era of globalization, where we often expect our grocery stores and restaurants to carry ingredients and dishes from across the world, fulfilling the food desires of new migrants might seem straightforward. After all, we can find tomatoes from Mexico, bananas from Ecuador, saffron from Spain, or rice from India in our supermarket shelves. And yet for many of the refugees I interviewed, their adjustment to life in Vermont has meant adopting new cuisines and new ingredients into their diet. A complaint that we heard on a regular basis is that familiar foodstuffs are not available. Several Bhutanese refugees voiced these sentiments:

> I am used to eating spicy foods, with different spices. The only things you can find here are some Indian foods which are similar but not the same. And you cannot find proper sweets at all.
> We don't eat food from Vermont. Nothing more than cheese and maple syrup.
> We eat American food. There's none of our food here. We don't have a choice.

Such sentiments were echoed by a number of the African refugees I interviewed:

> Where can we get African food here? Even if there is African food it is not Somali food. I would have to go to Montreal or Boston to get real African food.

If we don't cook it, there is none of our food. And it is difficult to find the right spices.

It's alright, we can still cook our food at home. But at school, the children must eat American.

Such complaints are not uncommon, of course, to anyone moving into a new area where there are few others from the same background. And like other immigrants and newcomers, the refugees I spoke with mentioned several different coping mechanisms. One was simply to start trying new foods, as some told us:

We buy milk. We drink milk in Nepal but less milk, more quantity and varieties here.

Bread, fruits very little in Nepal, but here there's a lot of many many fruits. In Nepal too expensive, here can afford.

Our eating has not changed but we try some US Food: sandwiches, pizza, cookies, roast chicken.

As I explored the pantries of refugee households, I saw evidence of these new products—row upon row of sugary breakfast cereal in one home for example. When I asked why the family had so many, the mother replied:

We don't actually like these cereals because you have to eat them with cold milk. Back home we don't drink cold milk, only hot. Our volunteer gives us these cereal boxes. We don't eat them but we make sure every morning that our daughter does with cold milk so that she can learn to eat American.

That particular turn of phrase—'eating American'—was one that was repeated by multiple respondents. For some that meant learning new customs and rituals:

I like the American food when you celebrate Christmas. I love this food and Thanksgiving—it's a bit different, different soups and breads. I don't know how to prepare it but I like it. Thanksgiving, I like it because we all live together and we all get to eat together.

On the other hand, that unfamiliarity could also be a problem. Several refugees told us that their volunteers had provided them with turkey, stuffing, and other common Thanksgiving ingredients so that they might feel part of this quintessentially American holiday. But as one said

> We didn't eat the Thanksgiving food because we didn't know how to cook the food in a box or in a can, no directions no cook. Nothing like that in our culture.

Another family told us that they simply put everything into a pot and cooked it altogether. Not surprisingly, this did not make for a delicious Thanksgiving meal. But it was not only the type of food being consumed that made it a central part of the acculturation process—*how* one ate could be an equally important component of 'becoming American':

> When I began to work at my factory job I used to eat in the lunchroom with my hands. My coworkers eat with utensils so I started to do that because I didn't want to stand out. Now I am eating at home with utensils as well, even though the rest of my family does not. Also, my hands are sore from the work and utensils are easier to eat with.

But what about those who want to retain their connection to culture and homeland through food? What if any options might they have? I discovered during my interviews that certain specialized fruits and vegetables and especially spices are much sought-after by home cooks in refugee communities. Where might these be procured if not available in local supermarkets? Some have increasingly become available through ethnic grocery stores but others are brought by family members—including later refugee arrivals and friends—upon resettlement. Extended networks of particular refugee communities also mean that some are brought by friends and relatives visiting from larger metropolitan areas.

Smaller ethnic grocery stores have begun to play a larger role in the provision of these 'tastes of home'—during the period of our study of these neighborhoods a number of newer ones opened (while a few closed as well; sustaining a small business is difficult at the best of times). The food available in many of these small grocery markets have what I would describe a 'pan-refugee' rather than a pan-Asian or pan-African character; that is, many of the foodstuffs stocked in these stores cater to multiple communities but are tailored to the particular populations nearby. One might find Asian spices, African eggplant, imported frozen goat meat from Australia, and Vietnamese hard candies all within the same store, for example.

As we can see in Chapters 4 and 5 on refugee neighborhoods in Burlington and Winooski, respectively, these grocery stores play an important role beyond providing difficult to find ingredients. Many of them also include some prepared foods familiar to particular communities—samosas, fried rice, specialty drinks, dumplings, and sandwiches, for example. Others provide comfort and familiarity simply in having products with different language, signage, or meaning. Several interviewees told us that they stopped in these stores even when they were not about to purchase anything; the grocery had become a part of making the neighborhood home (Image 8.1).

Image 8.1 Ethnic grocery store in Burlington

For many of the refugees, I spoke with this meant stops in multiple shops, supplementing an occasional trip to a larger supermarket for some staples and more regular trips to an ethnic grocery:

> We make our own roti but we buy our bread and rice from Price Chopper. We go to Central Market for all our spices.
> We buy spices from Himalayan Market because it is walking distance. We go to Costco when someone can help and drive. We buy Nepali vegetables and dal from Indian market.

But where do the ethnic markets get their own supplies? Almost all of the grocery store owners I spoke with (15 in total) described weekly trips to New York City or Boston to stock up on spices and other goods from ethnic enclaves in those larger metropolitan centers. While Montreal is much closer (a two-hour drive rather than a four-to-six hour drive to the other cities), the challenges of crossing the border—especially with commercial goods and foodstuff—make a return trip northward a non-starter. Such linkages bring into question the notion of what constitutes 'local' food—'localvore' food initiatives are also all the rage in the alternative food scene in Vermont as much as farm-to-table restaurants and CSAs. But what if the preferred food is not actually local? What if the shop is local and a key part of the neighborhood, but the goods it stocks are dependent on long journeys to make it to the shelf? Other store owners described being caught in a similar quandary. The owner of an African market said:

> If I could bring Boston and New York City closer, it would be cool. I know everyone talks about wanting to buy local but I can't get a lot of these products from Vermont.

Another African market owner emphasized the importance of her grocery for the local community regardless of where the goods originated:

> I have a little bit of everything to be like a corner store. Pasta, tomato sauce, umbrellas, fresh vegetables. It's a little neighborhood. It's not just an African store. Anyone in the neighborhood could stop and I do money grams. Money transfers. We have people from all areas. They all come

into send money. It's a little neighborhood store. I try to get a little bit of everyone's foods. They are far away from home. There's a need for ethnic foods.

The final manifestation of food on the refugee neighborhood is the ethnic restaurant. In Burlington and Winooski, there are two types of refugee-background restaurants that are most common: Vietnamese and Bhutanese-Nepali. Vietnamese restaurants have been the most successful with seven in Burlington, three in Winooski, and two more in the nearby towns of Williston and Essex Junction. Restaurants serving Bhutanese, Nepali, and Tibetan foods are fewer—one in Winooski and two in Burlington—but this type of food is available also in prepared form in a number of neighborhood grocery stores. While some refugee communities settled in Vermont have not made much of a mark—there are no Iraqi or Burmese restaurants, for example, and a Bosnian deli was short-lived—there have been attempts made to create food trucks and home catering businesses by a number of Somali and Congolese cooks, with varying degrees of success.

Travel around the refugee neighborhoods of the Old North End in Burlington and just off downtown Winooski, and you will see a number of restaurants offering pho, spring rolls, curries, hotpots, momos, dumplings, noodles, fresh salads, and other specialties. Often family-run businesses and housed in buildings that have been converted from other purposes, such as like a bus station, a laundromat, and a hardware store in three instances, they have in many cases proven to be wildly successful.

A good example is Pho Hong, started by a refugee family originally from Vietnam who settled in Burlington in the 1980s. The mother worked as a housekeeper and a janitor at the university before eventually working in a local Thai restaurant. When a space became available, the family cobbled together the money to lease a space and open their own restaurant with the mother as the head chef and designer of the menus (Gange 2019). It has proved to be a highly popular venture, one that many family members work at and that has seen lines out the door since it opened in 2012 (Image 8.2).

Image 8.2   Vietnamese restaurant in Burlington

It is, however, not clear that restaurants such as these are meant to fulfill the desire for familiar flavors for refugees themselves. They are more likely to satisfy the culinary tastes of the general public. But if ethnic grocery stores help to fill in some of the gaps for refugees in terms of familiar products, perhaps restaurants perform that other important role that scholars have noted regarding food spaces and immigrant neighborhoods—acting as a mediator and a bridge between multiple cultures and populations occupying overlapping territories. And it should also be noted here that while an ethnic restaurant may not necessarily feed a refugee community directly, food-related businesses are among the most commonly undertaken by new immigrants (Ray 2004); in this sense, they can help to sustain new arrivals in Vermont in other important ways. In the last section of this chapter, I turn to one other such example of direct and concrete sustenance: refugee agriculture.

Setting New Roots

One of the areas in which there seems a natural connection between Vermont's existing rural traditions and the experiences of refugees is farming. This is not about large-scale agribusiness—the vast fields of soy and corn or the massive hog and dairy farms found in the Midwest or fruit orchards and vegetable farms in other farming states. Vermont may be rural, but its terrain does not lend itself to large-scale production; instead, smaller family farms are more common. Such a context would seem to present a real opportunity for the many refugees who come from agrarian backgrounds in their countries of origin and have experience with subsistence farming.

In 2007, therefore, AALV (the main organization serving refugees after their first year in Vermont) launched a new program meant to capitalize on this potential and develop a relationship between refugee farmers and their new host communities. It originated as a workforce development program, training mainly female farmers from African countries to grow crops for sale in local farmer's markets, CSAs, and farm stands. The program—entitled New Farms for New Americans (NFNA)—quickly grew with the aid of substantial funding from the federal government and private donors. It is part of a set of programs funding refugee agriculture programs across the US called the Refugee Agricultural Partnership Project (ORR 2020). While most of the partner programs consist of urban and backyard gardening projects within large metropolitan cities, NFNA's locations are primarily on the outskirts of Burlington and Winooski, in an agricultural tract known as the Intervale.

The program has been widely hailed as a success both locally and nationally and has grown from an initial fifteen farmers in 2007 to over two hundred in 2020. Just over half of the participants are Bhutanese while the rest comprise Somali, Burundi, and Burmese farmers (NFNA 2020). They farm on plots that range from 1/32nd of an acre to 1/8th of an acre at a cost of between $25 and $100 per season to lease the land. For this relatively small investment, the returns are significant; NFNA estimates that the smallest ($25) plots saved those who farmed them nearly $800 per year in vegetable purchases and fed an average of between seven and nine people. Those working the largest ($100) plots saved an average of $3000 per year and fed an average of fifteen people. In 2015 alone, farmers and gardeners produced an estimated 14,000 lb of fresh, healthy, and organic food (NFNA 2015).

In the past NFNA has also participated in a range of food-related activities, including running a Community-Supported Agriculture(CSA) program featuring baskets of produce and prepared foods sold to a diverse clientele (2008–2012), a farm stand in Burlington's South End neighborhood (2011–2016), and selling produce in farmers' markets in Burlington's Old North End, New North End and Winooski (2010–2016). From its outset, NFNA has also offered a range of classes focused on farm management, budgeting, food safety, English language classes, familiarity with local crops and growing conditions, and especially cold-weather agriculture, season extension-techniques, pest-management, invasive species, and gleaning practices (Image 8.3).

The program, as mentioned, began as a workforce development initiative, meant to train newcomers to become commercial farmers. And

Image 8.3 New Farms for New Americans farm stand

some have gone on to pursue such possibilities—a handful (fifteen) have ventured trying their hand at operating their own farming operation. But it is challenging enough to maintain an economically viable farm if one has access to land, capital, and connections—how much more difficult might it be for newly arrived refugees with few of any of these assets to begin a new farming business?

In its first iteration (2007–2012), the program focused mainly on training commercial farmers and growing crops to sell to the general population, but it soon became apparent that the majority of participants were more interested in growing food they could not otherwise procure for themselves. The original structure of NFNA was to provide three tiers of participants, beginning with community gardeners (focused on individual production), who would graduate to become market gardeners (improving their gardening and marketing skills), and ultimately become independent farmers (meant to be self-sustaining and to participate fully in local agricultural markets and their own businesses). Yet in multiple surveys that I conducted with them from 2012 to 2019, participants showed scant interest in reaching that final tier. They were mainly interested in growing food for themselves and their communities, growing culturally significant crops, and having access to the outdoors.

Accordingly, in 2015 NFNA began to shift its model toward this preference by refugee participants to focus more on community gardening and less on commercial agriculture. The CSA and selling at farm stands and farmers' markets were eschewed in favor of a more robust community gardening model; some 95% of current participants grow food for their own consumption or to share with friends and family rather than for sale. One has only to visit either of the two main sites of NFNA— five acres at the Ethan Allen Homestead in Burlington's New North End and a further three across the river at the Intervale—to see the wealth of culturally distinct produce being grown in greenhouses and garden plots all around. Bhutanese farmers have favored bitter melon, mustard greens, snake gourd, water spinach, daikon radish, stinging nettle, and lamb's quarters, while also growing roselle and African eggplant. Both of the latter are also commonly to be found in African farmers' plots, along with amaranth greens and African varieties of corn. One of the Burundian farmers has been so successful with her eggplant harvests that she is one of the few participants to have pursued a commercial career; her African eggplants have been shipped as far away as Texas and Georgia in recent years. Some other farmers have been able to sell their produce to local restaurants, markets, and cafes, though again the bulk has been destined for home use and personal consumption.

There have been other attempts to build on the successes of NFNA locally. Between 2013 and 2015, for example, the program experimented with growing rice, as the director of the program describes here:

> The elders in the Bhutanese community came and asked whether they could grow rice in Vermont. We honestly didn't know. So, I looked into it and thought we'd give it a try. They did most of the work – they flooded the fields to make rice paddies and carefully harvested that first third of an acre and replanted it to be a full acre and then the next season three acres. Then we held a big ceremony and harvested the rice as the whole community, inviting others from the other refugee communities and general public to join us.

Unfortunately, while the harvest was a success, the rice was not—it was not to the taste of those who had cultivated it. It turns out that one can grow rice in Vermont—just not the kind that the refugee families from Bhutan actually wanted to eat (Image 8.4).

This was not the only initiative put into motion by NFNA. In 2013 a spin-off venture was launched in nearby Colchester under the auspices of NFNA. Called Pine Island Community Farm, it was meant to address the lack of locally available goat meat—a staple of both Bhutanese and many African households. This new initiative, with investment from the Vermont Land Trust and other partners, soon became its own entity

Image 8.4   Rice harvest for NFNA

apart from NFNA, with one Bhutanese family focused on raising goats and soon joined by an African family raising chickens and other farmers growing vegetable crops (on a smaller scale than at the other farms). The Pine Island Community Farm has had its own successes, much like NFNA (VLT 2020).

Both programs also face similar challenges. Many of the participants speak little to no English and thus the program staff are forced to act as liaisons between farmers and garden supply stores, seed distributors, and other local suppliers. The changeover in refugee populations over time means that newer food tastes and desires become apparent at a faster pace than an agricultural program can sometimes adjust to. Transportation to and from the farms is a constant challenge, none lying anywhere near local bus routes. Despite such challenges, NFNA is an innovative and evolving program that adjusts its goals and activities based on some of the perennial variables that can dictate what is and is not possible. There is a clear direction of shifting the program to be more community garden centered, with its fundamental goal being that of providing land and food access to people who may otherwise never get the chance to attempt farming in their new home (Image 8.5).

While the success of NFNA deserves celebrating in itself, it is also an indicator of the place that food holds in understanding essential conditions of resettlement and framing strategies for it. Perhaps the most thought-provoking of these conditions is that resettlement is as much an emotional issue rooted in the fundamentals of identity retention within the necessities of cultural adaptation. Recognizing food as an indispensable vector of the journey of refugees in a literal as well as metaphoric sense can only enrich thinking about the modes of resettlement and lead to measures that are at once pragmatic and principled. This has been one of the most valuable perceptions to come out of my research on food and the Vermont experience with refugees.

Image 8.5 NFNA farm

References

Alibhai-Brown, Yasmin. 2009. *The settler's cookbook: A memoir of love, migration and food*. London: Granta UK.

Alkon, Alison, and Christie McCullen. 2011. Whiteness and farmers markets: Performances, perpetuations… contestations? *Antipode* 43 (4): 937–959.

Blake, Megan. 2018. Building an unjust foodscape: Shifting governance regimes, urban place making and the making of Chinese food as ordinary in Hong Kong. *Local Environment* 23 (11): 1047–1062.

Camps-Calvet, Marta, Johannes Langemeyer, Laura Calvet-Mir, and Erik Gómez-Baggethun. 2016. Ecosystem services provided by urban gardens in Barcelona, Spain: Insights for policy and planning. *Environmental Science & Policy* 62: 14–23.

Clendenning, Jessica, Wolfram Dressler, and Carol Richards. 2016. Food justice or food sovereignty? Understanding the rise of urban food movements in the USA. *Agriculture and Human Values* 33 (1): 165–177.

Conner, David, Hannah Harrington, Sarah Heiss, and Linda Berlin. 2019. How can food hubs best serve their buyers? Perspectives from Vermont. *Journal of Hunger & Environmental Nutrition* 1: 1–15.

Conway, Tenley. 2016. Home-based edible gardening: Urban residents' motivations and barriers. *Cities and the Environment (CATE)* 9 (1): 3–21.

Conway, Meghan. 2018. *Success of food assistance programs: Metrics to evaluate provision of healthy food products across Burlington, Vermont.* BA Honors Thesis. Environmental Studies, University of Vermont.

Counihan, Carole, and Penny Van Esterik. 2012. *Food and culture: A reader*, 3rd ed. New York: Routledge.

Diner, Hasia. 2009. *Hungering for America: Italian, Irish, and Jewish foodways in the age of migration*, 3rd ed. Cambridge MA: Harvard University Press.

Etzold, Benjamin. 2016. Migration, informal labour and (trans) local productions of urban space–the case of Dhaka's street food vendors. *Population, Space and Place* 22 (2): 170–184.

Fernández-Armesto, Felipe. 2002. *Near a thousand tables: A history of food*. New York: Simon & Schuster.

Gabaccia, Donna. 2000. *We are what we eat: Ethnic food and the making of Americans*. Cambridge MA: Harvard University Press.

Gange, Jared. 2019. *Suddenly you are nobody: Vermont refugees tell their stories.* Huntington, Vermont: Burlington Graphics.

Guthman, Julie. 2008. If they only knew: Color blindness and universalism in California alternative food institutions. *The Professional Geographer* 60 (3): 387–397.

Han, Guang. 2018. From farm to Canal Street, Chinatown's alternative food network in the global marketplace. *Agriculture and Human Values* 35 (4): 905–906.

Horst, Megan, Nathan McClintock, and Lesli Hoey. 2017. The intersection of planning, urban agriculture, and food justice: A review of the literature. *Journal of the American Planning Association* 83 (3): 277–295.

Jung, Yuson, and Andrew Newman. 2014. An edible moral economy in the motor city: Food politics and urban governance in Detroit. *Gastronomica: the Journal of Critical Food Studies* 14 (1): 23–32.

Kato, Yuki, Scarlett Andrews, and Cate Irvin. 2018. Availability and accessibility of vacant lots for urban cultivation in post-Katrina New Orleans. *Urban Affairs Review* 54 (2): 322–362.

Kershen, Anne (ed.). 2017. *Food in the migrant experience*. New York: Routledge.

Khojasteh, Maryam, and Samina Raja. 2017. Agents of change: How immigrant-run ethnic food retailers improve food environments. *Journal of Hunger & Environmental Nutrition.* 12 (3): 299–327.

King, Anthony. 2004. *Spaces of global culture: Architecture, urbanism, modernity.* London: Routledge.

Koc, Mustafa, and Jennifer Welsh. 2001. *Food, foodways and immigrant experience.* Toronto: Centre for Studies in Food Security.

Li, Wei. 2009. *Ethnoburb: The new ethnic community in urban America.* Honolulu: University of Hawaii Press.

Mannur, Anita. 2005. Model minorities can cook: Fusion cuisine in Asian America. In *East Main Street: Asian American popular culture,* ed. Shilpa Davé, Leilani Nishime, and Tash Oren. New York: NYU Press.

Mannur, Anita. 2010. *Culinary fictions: Food in South Asian diasporic culture.* Philadelphia: Temple University Press.

Mares, Teresa. 2019. *Life on the other border: Farmworkers and food justice in Vermont.* Berkeley: University of California Press.

Mares, Teresa, Naomi Wolcott-MacCausland, Julia Doucet, Andy Kolovos, and Marek Bennett. 2020. Using chiles and comics to address the physical and emotional wellbeing of farmworkers in Vermont's borderlands. *Agriculture and Human Values* 37 (1): 197–208.

Matt, Susan. 2007. A hunger for home: Homesickness and food in a global consumer society. *Journal of American Culture* 30 (1): 6–17.

Moffat, Tina, Charlene Mohammed, and Bruce Newbold. 2017. Cultural dimensions of food insecurity among immigrants and refugees. *Human Organization* 76 (1): 15–27.

NFNA. 2015. *New Farms for New Americans annual report.* Burlington: Association of Africans Living in Vermont.

NFNA. 2020. *New Farms for New Americans annual report.* Burlington: Association of Africans Living in Vermont.

ORR. 2020. Refugee Agricultural Partnership Project. Office of Refugee Resettlement, Agency of Health and Human Services, Government of the United States. Available from https://www.acf.hhs.gov/orr/programs/rapp.

Parker, Barbara, Jennifer Brady, Elaine Power, and Susan Belyea (eds.). 2019. *Feminist food studies: Intersectional perspectives.* Toronto: Canadian Scholars Press.

Radel, Claudia, Birgit Schmook, and Susannah McCandless. 2010. Environment, transnational labor migration, and gender: Case studies from southern Yucatan, Mexico and Vermont, USA. *Population and Environment* 32 (2–3): 177–197.

Ray, Krishnendu. 2004. *The migrant's table: Meals and memories in Bengali-American households*. Philadelphia: Temple University Press.

Reynolds, Kristin. 2017. Designing urban agriculture education for social justice: Radical innovation through Farm School NYC. *International Journal of Food Design* 2 (1): 45–63.

Rosenfeld, Stuart. 2010. Sustainable food systems cluster, Vermont style. *European Planning Studies* 18 (11): 1897–1908.

Sarkar, Sucharita. 2019. Food, memory and everyday transnationalism in Chitrita Banerji's culinary memoirs. *Post Scriptum: an Interdisciplinary Journal of Literary Studies* 4 (2): 232–247.

Scanlon, Paul. 2010. Cuisine as an agent of acculturation: Mexican-American cultural and culinary incorporation and acceptance. PhD Dissertation. Anthropology, University of Georgia.

Slocum, Rachel. 2007. Whiteness, space and alternative food practice. *Geoforum* 38 (3): 520–533.

Smith, Bobby. 2019. Food justice, intersectional agriculture, and the triple food movement. *Agriculture and Human Values* 36 (4): 825–835.

Stokes, Hannah. 2017. *Conceptualizing and measuring food security among resettled refugees living in the United States*. MS Thesis. Food Systems, University of Vermont.

Szanto, David. 2015. *Performing gastronomy: An ecosophic engagement with the liveliness of food*. PhD Dissertation. Fine Arts, Concordia University.

Thompson, Julie. 2016. 9 ways Vermont's food scene is impossible to beat. *Huffington Post*. August 3. Available from https://www.huffpost.com/entry/vermont-food-the-best_n_57a08c6ce4b08a8e8b5f453c.

Vanderbeck, Robert M. 2006. Vemont and the imaginative geographies of American Whiteness. *Annals of the Association of American Geographers* 96 (3): 641–659.

VLT. 2020. Pine Island Community Farm. Vermont Land Trust. Available from https://www.vlt.org/pineisland.

Walker, Samuel. 2016. Urban agriculture and the sustainability fix in Vancouver and Detroit. *Urban Geography* 37 (2): 163–182.

9

Aging

In this last section of the book, I have focused on some of the main issues that participants in my various studies consider most relevant to their experiences of resettlement in Vermont. The past two chapters have focused on the broad themes of mobility and food as contributing factors of multiple conditions of refugee life—including travel, commuting transportation options, food security, farming, hunger, diverse cuisines, education, childcare, and eldercare. What does mobility mean and what kinds of opportunities can it offer? What kinds of obstacles do a lack of mobility present for improving one's life? How do food cultures structure and reformulate one's relationship to land, livelihood, and belonging? The themes of these past two chapters also incorporate many other issues and topics raised by the refugees I have worked with—housing, jobs, political representation, and the ways that gender, class, race, and sexuality have shaped the everyday lives of refugees.

In the final chapter of this section, I explore another set of embodied experience; in this case, I focus on the aging process, at two different ends of the spectrum. Along with mobility and food, the experiences of children and seniors—of education, childcare, eldercare, health, and mental well-being—were consistently mentioned by members of the refugee

© The Author(s) 2020
P. S. Bose, *Refugees in New Destinations and Small Cities*,
https://doi.org/10.1007/978-981-15-6386-7_9

communities in surveys, interviews, and focus groups as topics of significant and ongoing concern to them. Such views resonated with my own experiences—having immigrated to Canada as a child, and seeing my grandmother move from India to Canada in her late seventies only to return to India a mere six months later—has long given me a counterpoint to my later experience of immigrating to the US as a young professional.

The insights in this chapter are drawn from multiple research projects as are the others throughout this book, but several in particular are important to the discussion on aging. For my refugee mobilities study, I conducted interviews and surveys with elders (those aged sixty-five and older) within the refugee communities between 2010 and 2012 and later helped to organize focus groups and facilitate interventions designed by the state to address the needs of these populations between 2012 and 2016. Since 2014, I have also brought other concerns within my sphere of research, for example, by helping to evaluate a number of programs launched to support refugee youth navigate the educational system in Vermont and concurrently to reduce the overrepresentation of such youth in the state's criminal justice system.

In this chapter, then, I draw on findings from such projects to explore the complex understandings of what it means to come of age or to become aged as someone from a refugee background in Vermont. This focus on age and migration is an important one as is clear when one looks at the existing literature on refugees, resettlement, and integration. This is especially true given the breadth of existing studies on school-age children, youth, and young families. The research on elderly seniors is more limited but growing. In this chapter, I explore the dynamics of growing older in Vermont as a refugee in four parts. In the first I examine some of the research on aging and refugees, including some common challenges experienced across multiple communities as well as some of the innovative therapies being utilized to address them. In the second I look specifically at the experiences—and views—of refugee seniors in Vermont. In the third part of the chapter, I do the same with refugee youth. In the final part of the chapter, I describe some of the initiatives undertaken to address a number of these issues.

Age and Migration

As I have pointed out in previous chapters, the tendency to treat refugees as a monolithic and undifferentiated population is problematic in all kinds of ways. From the erasure of the particular cultural traditions and contexts of one refugee community to applying ineffective interventions based on what has worked with other populations, there are many issues that may arise from treating multiple groups and individuals as if they were the same. This is not simply about national background or ethnic origin; many Bosnian, Iraqi, and Somali refugees are Muslim, but their actual practice of Islam or cultural traditions may be quite different. Several refugees I interviewed from these communities described, for example, tensions over the programming at and direction of the Islamic Society of Vermont, though they also described commonalities that helped to forge pan-Muslim identities after arrival. Chapter 7 demonstrates the ways in which gender affects very different refugee experiences of mobility. And while the overwhelming number of refugees in Burlington and Winooski may be from a Bhutanese background, caste and class has meant differences in access to housing, employment, transportation, and social advancement.

Yet monolithic visions of refugee bodies and groupings still dominate government policy on and public perceptions of these populations. There may not be an 'ideal' age or profile of a refugee or immigrant, but an implicit (and increasingly explicit) assumption made by many nations is that working-age individuals are to be preferred. There is little room for understanding the multiplicity of identities, experiences, and backgrounds carried in the bodies of refugees and immigrants in these reductionist views. Indeed, we see the problems posed by such beliefs in the points-based immigration systems favored by countries like Canada and Australia and that the Trump administration in the US has advocated for since taking office. Such systems would shift the priorities in immigration policy away from family reunification, low-skilled labor migration, and humanitarian entries toward high-skilled and educated migrants.

I have had my own students take mock versions of these tests and they have always been taken aback by how clear it is that the state preference is so clear—for those who are between the ages of twenty-five and forty-four, for those who speak English, for those who have previous (especially advanced) education, for those who have no health issues or medical conditions; in short for those who are healthy and can become immediately productive or 'self-sufficient' in the parlance of the USRAP. Some might say that such prioritization is not unreasonable or that it is making explicit what has long been an unstated goal—yet not only do points-based immigration systems betray any adherence to international humanitarian obligations, they actively discriminate against those who do not fit into idealized conceptions of immigrant applicants. They further seem to idealize the nuclear family and penalize other forms of kinship groups, whether extended families or non-familial community groupings. If we look at the actions of the Trump administration to try and reshape immigration policy as detailed in Chapter 2, we see that many have been designed to bar those who do not already have wealth, power, and connections from coming to the US. Cutting refugee numbers and supports, limiting visa programs, and penalizing immigrants for their use (or possible use) of public services—as symbolized by the expansion of the public charge rule—are just some examples of this kind of discrimination based on identity.

Refugee elders are among the most visibly affected as a result of the fetishizing of the skilled, working-age immigrant. They are already in most cases out of the workforce; therefore, they often cannot become individually self-sufficient in the ways that the USRAP imagines. Training (or retraining) is simply not an option. Conversely, the inability to prove their exact ages in some cases, as Seibel (2016) points out, makes some refugee elders ineligible to participate in many of the supportive programs that exist for the general senior population. Feelings of isolation and disconnection are thus especially pronounced for many refugee elders, who find themselves cut off from traditional extended family networks. This is especially true for those refugee elders placed in rural areas or small cities (Winterton and Chambers 2017). As Lewis (2009) points out, this might be because they are physically separated by the resettlement process with members of the extended family located in different cities or states, or because resettlement has reshaped the family structure itself, with their children working outside of the home and grandchildren in school and other activities. Instead of occupying a position of respect and authority within their home communities, kin-groups, towns, and villages, refugee elders find themselves reduced to ancillary members of a family at best or find themselves considered a burden at worst. The shock and impact of such changes are severe, as programs specifically designed to address the mental health needs of elder refugees have pointed out (Scharrer and Coleman 2019).

Their ability to learn English is often far more limited than that of their children and younger members of their communities. The challenges of language acquisition exist not only because of advanced years, but also because in some cases refugees are illiterate in their own languages or in others the languages themselves are not written, as in the cases of the Mai-Mai and Karen. The problem of not acquiring English is especially acute for refugee elders when it comes to acquiring citizenship or driver's licenses, both of which require passing written and verbal tests (Dubus 2018). The challenges facing refugee elders is not limited to the US, of course. Common issues raised in other resettlement countries include adjusting to retirement and/or a change in life circumstance, accepting a loss of independence, finding sources of support and connection, and confronting their more imminent mortality (Türegün et al. 2018; Johnson et al. 2019). As Chenoweth and Burdick (2001: 21–22) suggest:

> These challenges are magnified for refugee elders because they are undertaken in an unfamiliar environment. The life of a resettled refugee elder can be precarious or vital depending on personal health, family support, and community resources.

For refugee youth, the issues facing them are not the same as for the elders in their communities. In part this is because there are systems—at least theoretically—in place to help them adjust to new homes. The education system in particular is supposed to help them acclimate and integrate, providing them with language and skills training for social advancement. Of course, in reality the significant differences between refugees' backgrounds, socioeconomic status and the school districts that they are placed in plays a large role in actual outcomes. As Beiser and Hou (2016) point out, the impacts of both pre-migration traumas and post-migration discrimination play a significant and often under-recognized role in the adjustment process for many children. It is not just that children may bear witness to (or are subjected to) horrific violence, deprivation, and exploitation both in the initial displacement and along the routes of forced migration and camps, it is also that the landscapes of reception upon arrival may be less than ideal and thus re-traumatize these children again.

Such challenges are not new; by the mid-1990s, scholars were noting significant achievement gaps for Southeast Asian refugee children and youth (Ranard and Pfelger 1995). In their view, the US educational system was entrenching existing inequalities and differences; those who came with higher levels of education or from more middle-class backgrounds were more able to take advantage of supports and opportunities, while accessing postsecondary education and better job opportunities. The changing demographics of refugees and the distinct needs of different groups were also difficult for school systems to adapt to quickly (Flaitz 2006). A district or individual school might work hard to reorient itself to the contexts and priorities of Bosnians but a few years later the major incoming group would be Somali or Bhutanese. New interpreters or school liaisons would be needed, materials translated into different languages, and expectations adjusted on the basis of background (Johnson et al. 2018). In the US educational system, the immediate recourse is to launch testing; as school staff in multiple locations across the US told me, they had little advance notice that a refugee child was going to arrive in their district or at their school and a part of their response to the new intake was to thus test the new student on the skills they were expected to be proficient in at that level. For the students themselves, already trying to adjust to an entirely new environment, the experience of having to endure (and adequately pass) a series of standardized tests simply adds another stressful element to the acculturation process (Juang et al. 2018). While there may be counseling and specialized courses at some school districts (Rowe et al. 2016), most do not have the resources or capacity to offer such support.

Many of my respondents suggested that the challenge for youth is not just about schools but about the lack of opportunities for younger refugees in general, especially those who do not slot into the K-12 educational system. While the latter may be flawed, it still offers structure and potential pathways for integration if not social mobility. This pattern of exclusion from higher education has been recognized in multiple resettlement countries (Schneider 2018). In Vermont, among many new refugees over the age of 18—those in the early-to-mid-20s for example—there is a feeling that their only option is to take on menial, low-wage labor, since the economic needs of their family and community are so immediate. Several individuals in this age-range that I interviewed complained that resettlement agencies pressured them to take on short-term and low-wage work instead of seeking out better longer-term opportunities. A key concern was that for even those who had prior education in their countries of origin, it was not recognized by American institutions (Kingston and Stam 2017)—a pattern of deskilling that has been widely noted for immigrants in general but is especially acute for refugees (Subedi and Rosenberg 2016).

Finally, the experience of refugee youth—at least among my respondents and more for youth than for their parents or seniors in the communities—has been shaped by American racial hierarchies and gender relations. As we will see in the third section of this chapter, children and youth in the diverse refugee communities—whether new immigrants or US-born children from refugee backgrounds—consistently speak of their experiences of racialization and gendering as they age in communities in Vermont. There are multiple layers to these processes of racialization. Children who are from African backgrounds are marked as black—seen by many (not least their parents and community elders) as disadvantageous, given the deeply embedded structural racism within US culture. It is true that for many African refugee youth, blackness also offers positive, empowering and aspirational figures and pathways for the future, but the negative aspects of racialization in the US cannot be avoided. The disciplining of youthful black bodies in Vermont mirrors that in the rest of the country, as reflected in disproportionate rates of school suspensions and encounters with the criminal justice system (State of Vermont 2018; Burlington School District 2014). As for many other refugee groups, they too find themselves racialized or othered. In some cases, the stereotypes can seem positive—some Bhutanese, Burmese, and Bosnian children are held up as exemplars of the so-called model minority (Kiang et al. 2016)—yet aggregative concepts like these are deeply reductionist and harmful to all. In the following two sections, I examine the views of refugee elders and youth in Vermont regarding their own experiences.

Vermont and Refugee Seniors

The worldwide refugee population is a generally young one; nearly seventy percent of displaced persons in the world are under the age of 18. This trend is also true in the US. In 2018, for example, out of a total of over 22,000 refugees admitted, less than 600 were over the age of 65—only 163 of them over the age of 75 (RPC 2019). Vermont has for the most part followed this pattern—with the notable exception of the Bhutanese resettlements between 2008 and 2016. In this case, a significant subset of those placed in Vermont is over the age of 65—more than 200 individuals in total. A disproportionately high number of the elderly among the Bhutanese community is not unique to Vermont; this is a trend also apparent across other parts of the US, Canada, and Australia, three of the most significant countries for Bhutanese resettlements worldwide (Di Marzo and Chapagain 2012; Reynolds and Hyndman 2015; Im and Neff 2020). The reasons for this disparity are usually attributed to the specific circumstances of the Lhotshampa expulsion from Bhutan— a wholesale displacement of an entire community during the late 1980s and early 1990s, a protracted stay in a series of refugee camps and temporary shelters in Nepal and India, and lower birth rate in those transit areas (Rizal 2004) as compared to other refugees from protracted conflicts such as the Somali Bantu in Kenya and Uganda, for example.

The unusually high numbers of elderly refugees arriving among the Bhutanese was noticed early on by resettlement agency staff in Vermont. Because previous (and other) resettled groups had far fewer elders among them, most local service providers had little experience serving the elderly refugee population and lacked information regarding their needs, resettlement experiences, and the specific challenges they might face. Over the course of my various research projects and community partnerships, I have had the opportunity to ask refugee elders directly about their experiences. Several significant and recurring themes stand out from the interviews, focus groups, and surveys I have conducted over the past decade. These were consistent across differences in age (participants ranged from 65 to 95 in age), gender, and country of origin. I highlight below three of these—the challenges of learning English, the sense of eldercare as a burden, and the desire for a communal space—as crucial factors in thinking about resettlement.

A primary concern among many refugee elders had to do with learning English and specifically about what the inability to do so might mean for citizenship and the ability to retain social services and supports. Said one Bhutanese elder:

Language is the barrier…. Other than that, everything is fine. In your sixties it's hard to learn language. After we turn sixty, we start forgetting instead of remembering.

Another, a female elder in the Bhutanese community, echoed:

I am very eager to learn English and I know the importance of English. I used to go to school with my husband but stopped going due to physical issues. I had a tutor, but they just came once. My son went to VRRP and requested another, but no one came.

As a Bhutanese elder said, lack of English made creating new connections difficult:

I have some American friends, but we don't understand each other. Sometimes we use sign language and say ok, hi or hello. I know how hard it is for my neighbor to learn my language whenever they visit us.

For many of the elders, the issues had to do with independence and the ability to contribute to the family's income. Said one Congolese elder

> The problem I have is one many of us have - they don't give us a job because they think we can't do it.

Added a Somali elder

> When I came here I was given rules for how to live here. They said that there are two things you need to do here: 1) Learn English and 2) get a job. I worked for 10 days and got injured. If people like me are old but can work then why don't we have jobs? I am still learning English but it is hard to understand me. I have been here ten years.

Another Bhutanese elder echoed the sentiment of helplessness:

> I never went to school in Bhutan or Nepal, and because of language it is hard to find a job.

For others the concern was about the citizenship test and gaining enough language proficiency to pass it. A Bhutanese elder asked me:

> I have a question about citizenship: I want to know if we can get citizenship without taking a test or interview. My biggest concern is passing test. Will I have to take the test?

Said a Congolese elder:

> I have been going to ESL classes four times a week for 7 years, but I am not making any progress. How am I going to pass the citizenship exam? How can we survive if we lose all our benefits?

Another Bhutanese elder asked for assistance:

> We request that for old people, who have a learning disability and health problems, we need assistance to pass the test.

A number of refugees suggested that they needed better access to more reliable English language tutors, complaining that some of those who had been provided by the resettlement agencies were inconsistent or ineffective. One suggestion was to find teachers from within their own communities who might be more comfortable with both language and culture and act as intermediaries of sorts.

These quotes show that many of the elderly refugees in Vermont struggle with their transition to their new home and especially their changed roles within new familial and societal formations. Their inability to learn English was symbolic to many of them of their lack of adjustment to a new environment. But it also had material consequences; the concern about not learning English and thus not acquiring citizenship was voiced repeatedly throughout my research by elders, with accompanying requests that the government change the laws or provide more accessible exemptions for them. Some refugee elders went so far as to describe their age as a 'disability.' Others took issue with the age at which one was considered an elder, arguing that this was generally much earlier than in the US. In either event, a lack of independence and purpose was expressed by many respondents, as shown in the quotes lamenting the inability to work because of poor language skills or age. The sense of eldercare as a burden was reflected by many of those who I interviewed. A Burmese elder said:

I feel very old. My children need to take care of me, so they cannot work. I wish that someone else could take care of me, or I could take care of myself.

A Bhutanese elder added

I have nothing to do all day. It is very hard to be old.

This sense of dependency was also reflected by adult refugees speaking about their experience of caring for their parents. Said one Congolese refugee:

My mother is living with me but can't prepare food for herself, so I have to prepare it for her. I work and my kids are in school, so it's hard to attend to my mother's needs.

A Bhutanese refugee added:

> My mother is 72 and doesn't speak or hear. I have to look after her, but
> I am not paid for it. I can't look for work because I have to take care
> of her. My kids are in school, but one works part-time. If she didn't we
> couldn't afford to live here.

Another Bhutanese refugee said:

> My parents are 90 years old and are home alone because my wife and I
> work and our kids are at school. They don't shop or cook at home and
> can't speak English. They have medical appointments every day, so I don't
> understand why they aren't considered disabled. I want to know how to
> get citizenship for them.

Lacking adequate capacity to support refugee elders, Vermont turned
primarily to employing a number of adult children in the various
communities (especially the Bhutanese community) to take care of
their elderly family members. But such programs are inconsistent; some
have utilized this resource while others have not. In truth many family
members are not necessarily prepared to provide the kind of care that
seniors might need.

The last significant theme that was common across all the refugee
elders I spoke with was a desire for a unique space for community gatherings, religious practice, and family reunification. Family members asked
for a community space for their elderly members, as this would reduce
their isolation and provide them with pleasurable activities, while also
making it easier for the adult children to maintain employment. There
were different ways in which the elders spoke of such a space—some
talked about a church or a choir, others a community center. For the
Bhutanese elders it took the form of a temple:

> We need social activities and places for gathering. For example, during
> ceremonies, funerals, and puja, we have to invite everyone.
> We need a temple because there is no place for us to practice our
> religion. We want to devote ourselves to practice. The older you get, the
> more you want to pray and devote yourself to God. This is the problem

all Bhutanese are facing- no temple. The language barrier is another main issue. We want to preserve our culture - we want your help to find some place.

I should note here that most of these quotes come from research conducted between 2010 and 2016; more recently a number of community spaces utilized by the refugee communities have become established, including the Old North End Community Center described in Chapter 4, several churches, and a new mosque and Islamic community center in South Burlington. The elders in the various refugee groups believe strongly that a focus on religious practice and spirituality will help to address many of the issues they see facing their communities— especially a loss of connection and contact with their pasts and their traditions. Their children and refugee youth do not evince the same belief in the power of religious centers, as I will relate momentarily.

I do not wish to conclude this section with only a negative sense of the refugee elder experience in Vermont. Along with the issues that they have raised, it was also clear that most of my respondents were deeply grateful for the opportunity to live a safe and relatively secure life. Said one Bhutanese elder (Image 9.1):

Image 9.1   Refugee elders in Vermont

I was crawling when I came to the US. Now I feel like I am in Heaven.

Another Bhutanese elder stated:

I was like a newborn when I came here. I am happy in VT because we live in peace here. I received a new life.

Yet another Bhutanese elder said:

It's peaceful and we have good security in VT. I am grateful - I have everything.

Finally, a Congolese elder stated:

I like Vermont, the farms, hospitals, schools, security. I have kids every-where in the world, Australia, Maldives, Tanzania. But I would like more, newer housing.

Vermont and Refugee Youth

As in discussing refugee elders (and other refugees in Vermont), so is it difficult to talk about refugee youth as a monolithic group. The background provided in Chapter 3 demonstrates how the range of and difference in experiences of expulsion, forced migration, stays in camps, educational opportunities, and reception upon arrival have resulted in very different outcomes and experiences. There are also differences between children who arrive as refugees and children born to refugee families in the US, not least of which are those that stem from citizen-ship itself. Since refugees are not eligible for citizenship for usually six years after arrival (they must get a green card after their first year and cannot apply for citizenship until their sixth year unless they apply via marriage), it is possible to have refugee households where the youngest children born in the US are citizens while the rest of the family are not. In this section of the chapter, however, I will look at the perspectives of older refugee youth. I have had the opportunity to interview a number of individuals from various refugee communities in Vermont and have always been struck by their ability to articulate meaningful insights from their time spent in the K-12. There are three themes in particular I will focus on in this brief review: balancing between education and family obligation, the impact of racialization on youth experiences, and the consequences of discipline within and outside schools on their lives. As with the elder communities, my information and analysis are drawn from a decade's worth of research, including facilitating discussions among educators, resettlement agency staff, parents and students, and assessing programs meant to assist refugee youth and conducting interviews and surveys with participants.

The environment of the schools themselves came up repeatedly during my research. In Chapter 7, I described the ways that lack of access to transportation presented a barrier for many refugee families, decreasing participation in pre- and afterschool activities and in recreational, athletic, and cultural occupations. Older youth talked also about their responsibilities with regard to their younger siblings. One Congolese youth said:

I don't have time to do anything else, like clubs or sports. That's because I have to get my younger sisters and brother to school on time, pick them up after and then take care of them till my parents get home. And then I'm supposed to do homework.

A Bhutanese youth stated:

I'm the oldest one. There are a lot of pressures. There are responsibilities at home. Who will take care of my parents and siblings? If I try to go to college, who will pay for the loans?

Balancing familial expectations and obligations with personal goals was a common theme. As one Somali youth put it:

We have to choose between learning English, concentrating on homework and getting a low-paying job. Usually we have to take that low-paying job and then our grades suffer.

Said a Burmese youth:

> Your success is based on luck. There is a lot of pressure for the oldest to help family- start working to help provide for family.

There have been controversies regarding the treatment of students of color in general and refugee students (especially from Africa) in particular during my time in Vermont, leading to walkouts and demonstrations staged over several years. These have been more common in Burlington and relatively rare in Winooski. In speaking with school staff as to why, the scale of the two cities was raised again. As one teacher suggested:

> We have one large integrated campus in Winooski – elementary, high school and middle school. For a lot of the refugee kids, there's an older sibling in one of the other schools or classes that they can turn to. It provides a lot of support. In Burlington you have multiple elementary and middle schools, and the big high school, none of which are close to each other.

The idea of inter-familial and inter-cultural support for refugee children was a common theme—and conversely the lack of it was a common concern—for many of my interviewees. A Somali refugee parent lamented:

> Vermont is so expensive and we are always working. Families with young kids are really suffering with a lack of parents at home, which leads to problems at school and in the community.

The pressures children and youth are under do not just have to do with balancing expectations, however. Many of my respondents talked about the significant role that race has played in their lives in Vermont. Indeed, this very point was made by one of my earliest interviewees, a Bosnian woman who arrived as a young child:

> It was really hard, those first years. Having a different last name, being Muslim, having an accent. But then the African refugees came a few years later and everything got much better, much easier.

As I have argued elsewhere (Bose 2015), refugees (and other immigrant populations) are slotted into existing (albeit evolving) American racial hierarchies. African refugees thus become black, (some) Asian refugees can become model minorities, and phenotypically at least many Bosnian or Syrian refugees might be able to whiten, as previous generations of southern and eastern European immigrants have done and immigrants from other parts of the world are unable to. For many refugee children today, race has becoming a defining experience. Said one Bhutanese youth:

> I felt so out of place. I looked different from everyone else. It was 97% white. I had to teach myself to stand up for myself. Moving from middle school where all the teachers seemed caring to high school where no-one seemed to care, it was so casual. You only hang out with others like you, which for me wasn't too many kids. I needed support and coaching and I didn't get it.

A Congolese youth similarly bemoaned a lack of support and guidance:

> My parents are very educated, so I knew I had to take it seriously. But they don't speak English so they couldn't really help. For me it was really hard, because I didn't know the English language either, or how to navigate the school system. I come from a totally different school system. Making friends was so hard - being black in a predominantly white school. Everything is questionable- no one is talking to you. Once you step out of the classroom- no friends. Different culture when it comes to friendship than what I was used to. I went from being an extrovert to an introvert. It was lonely and isolating. No support from peers, only teachers. I was so angry all the time because there were so many challenges versus the hope of moving to this country.

A Bhutanese youth stated:

> I wasn't even thinking about college at the end of senior year. The rich white kids got all of the guidance help, at least that's what I thought. I don't think the brown or black kids got as much help. But I did have one really good guidance counselor who went out of his way to help

me, pushed me, encouraged me. My parents weren't in the know, so they weren't able to help. But he helped and I got a lot of hand-holding about applications, financial aid all of it. So it worked for me but I don't know if I was just lucky.

Many of the youth I spoke with talked about the ramifications of the lack of support, especially in terms of a cascading set of effects related to suspensions and expulsions. Said one young Congolese refugee:

Teachers are so quick to see the worst in us. Not all of them but some of them. And then once you get a suspension and then maybe you get expelled and then maybe you lose your job or you get in trouble at work and then you can't keep the job. It all adds up.

A Somali youth said:

It's really hard because our parents think we're friends with the wrong people. Anytime a little thing goes wrong, everything goes wrong. Other people have a problem they get help from a guidance counselor. We do something wrong, it's the police.

This trajectory, what some scholars call 'the school to prison pipeline' (Mallett 2016), has been noted by students, parents, and community advocates alike as deeply problematic. Disciplinary problems in the schools can lead to repercussions in the criminal justice system, as the previous quotes suggest. Even for those who wish to reform, being incarcerated leaves them with few options afterward and little chance to advance, improve, or turn around their lives. Troubled youth thus have little hope of being able to reform and join/rejoin the workforce.

When I asked how supports and guidance might be improved, made more consistent and accessible more broadly to help redirect refugee youth toward more productive and fulfilling outcomes, those I spoke with identified two particular resources that they suggested held much potential. The first is the Multilingual Liaison Program, a program to provide para-educator support in the classroom and school for refugee children, which I will describe further in the final section of this chapter The second is a desire to see more involvement and participation by refugee parents in their children's education. Refugee parents have as much interest as others in their children's success, but many are hampered by work schedules, a lack of English and a lack of knowledge of the US education system to feel able or comfortable to participate. Another important initiative is thus the Parent University programs, which I will briefly describe later in this chapter.

Such programs are meant to provide a bridge between refugee youth, their families and communities on the one hand, and the new society they are joining on the other. A number of respondents saw the task of balancing as one not only between priorities and options, but between multiple cultures and identities as well, as this Bhutanese youth articulates well:

> There was a lot on my shoulders. I came to America at age 15. Ready to go straight into high school. There was a lot of pressure from home – I was the oldest one. I was used for every transaction with my parents because my English was better than theirs – store, bank, hospital etc. I had to be responsible for them. So much to juggle. Participated in English classes and the classroom. I was sent home with homework, though I didn't speak English at the time. I couldn't do it. Living in two different cultures- very challenging. Parents don't understand American culture. America doesn't understand them or me.

A Somali youth added:

> I know our parents are scared for us. But they should trust us. We will find our way. We just need some more help to get there. It is hard to be in two worlds and two cultures.

Many young refugees spoke of the importance of having their parents included in their education and their future:

> Made to feel ashamed of parents – no English, no way to interact or fit in with other parents. We need to have community gatherings with parents and teachers. Make parents feel like they are a part of the community.

Parents need to be educated about school and expectations in America. We must include parents in important discussions.

We need to have programs for parents to come and learn about the educational system. Connect parents to outside resources and you will help us. Specific things that are confusing for our parents are those that should be known by all families coming to this country.

The picture I have painted thus far of the experiences of refugee youth in Vermont seems a bleak one. Certainly, there are many challenges that children and youth have had to endure. And for young adults, those in their early twenties, the obstacles to success seem even greater, being outside of the formal education system in many cases. Yet refugee youth have also succeeded in large part in Vermont. Students from refugee backgrounds have excelled in local schools and universities, completing a range of degrees with distinction, serving as valedictorians, and earning other high honors. Others have gone onto successful careers in a range of fields, become activists and advocates for their own and broader communities. Burlington High School's top-ranked soccer team features multiple players from refugee backgrounds while a Bhutanese-born player for Winooski High School's soccer team in 2019 became the fifth Vermont athlete to score one hundred goals. My own classrooms have been filled with a number of students whose families arrived as refugees, sometimes decades ago and sometimes more recently and are passionate, engaged, and active members of our campus community. I will close this chapter, therefore, by describing some of the programs and initiatives that have helped them to achieve such success and overcome the barriers that still lie in many of their paths (Image 9.2).

Innovative Programs

As the previous section illustrated, refugee children and youth are best served by multiple forms of support both within and outside of the schools. One set of the most successful programs within Vermont schools comprise the Home-School or Multilingual Liaison programs. In the Burlington and Winooski School Districts, a number of para-educators

Image 9.2 Refugee background rap group performs at a community function

from the various refugee communities—beginning with the Vietnamese and Bosnian communities and eventually adding representatives from all of the larger refugee communities—have been added to school district staff. Some of these liaisons are based at the district headquarters while others are assigned to specific schools. Their role is to provide linguistic competency but much more: They serve as intermediaries between families and schools, negotiating, translating, and mediating between them. Their role has been described by teachers, parents, and students alike as central to success. As one teacher described the liaisons:

> They are lifesavers. I cannot tell you how many conflicts and especially suspensions and other disciplinary actions they help us avoid.

The presence of multilingual liaisons also helps to avoid the dynamic that one of the refugee youth describes in the previous section—that of children acting as translators between their teachers and their parents. Such a situation is not uncommon in immigrant contexts yet is a problematic one, not only in the inaccuracies that might arise as a result, but also because of the ways it inverts power dynamics within refugee families and can thus lead to greater strife.

While the Multilingual Liaisons are focused on building bridges beginning with youth, another program in both the Burlington and Winooski School Districts focuses on their families. Parent University is meant to provide knowledge and education to refugee families and especially parents. The US educational system can be a mystery even to the native born but it can appear especially unfamiliar and daunting to newcomers. Parent University thus introduces the structures, processes, norms, and traditions of schooling in the US to refugee parents through a series of workshops and classes spread across weeks and months (Image 9.3).

Other refugee-serving organizations also recognize the need to strengthen and support families. A number of nonprofits that serve low-income, minority, and marginalized communities, such as Spectrum

Image 9.3 Parent University Graduation 2017

Youth and Family Services, the King Street Center, and DREAM, all include large numbers of refugee children and youth in their programming. DREAM is a mentoring program that matches college students with children and youth. Its offerings include one-on-one mentoring, help with preparing college applications, summer camp, and other enrichment activities. Spectrum Youth and Family Services offer counseling services, supportive housing, mentoring programs, health services, skills development, and a multicultural youth program. The King Street Center offers summer camps as well as afterschool activities, mentoring programs, academic support, and training to enter the job market and to make healthy lifestyle choices. It also offers programs for much younger children, including preschool and early education options.

The Janet S. Munt Family Room similarly provides support for refugee families (as well as other low-income groups) including father-children groups, preschool and family programs, health and nutrition classes, and parenting classes. They have partnered with the New Americans Pediatric Clinic at the University of Vermont to offer these as well as health services at the Family Room's offices in the O.N.E. Community Center. As noted in Chapter 4, this building has emerged as a hub of activities and services for the refugee community; with the exception of DREAM and the Multilingual Liaisons, all of the other organizations discussed in this section have offices in the O.N.E. Center.

The Association of Africans Living in Vermont (AALV), which is also based in this building, offers its own suite of youth programs. In 2017 it launched a program along with a number of community partners— including Burlington's Parks and Recreation Department, the Burlington Police Department, and the Burlington School District—designed to reduce racial disparities in the criminal justice system with a focus on youth of color who are either already court-involved, those who are socially associated with those already criminally involved, or are the subjects of school-discipline, or deemed to be part of the broader population considered to be at risk of such involvement. AALV's approach has been to provide safe and productive alternatives to such activities through mentorship, community-based partnerships, mental health counseling, support for parents, and expert training for staff in aiding at-risk youth. It is a comprehensive initiative intended to reduce the disproportionate entry of youth of color into the formal justice system, expand prevention services that may help youth and families manage behaviors, family dynamics, emotional, and developmental issues that lead to justice involvement, and create strategies, interventions, systems change, and structured decision-making. AALV sought to make such interventions by providing supervised recreation opportunities, a recovery space for refugee youth, and by creating a mentoring program. It also offered a summer Youth Leadership Academy where participants were able to learn from leaders in various fields in the local community.

If it sounds as though many of the youth-centric initiatives undertaken by these various organizations are duplicative, they are. Indeed, AALV, Spectrum, and King Street saw that many of the same youth were taking part in multiple programs (and complaining that their classes and workshops were repetitive); as a result, they have been coordinating more closely so that they can expand the range of offerings and address needs more efficiently. A challenge that remains is that all of these programs, valuable as they are, remain mostly grant-funded, including the Multilingual Liaison programs. This means that there is little stability for participants or staff alike. Much work has gone into developing these capacities, yet lacking base funding they have no permanence.

This is also true for services and organizations that support seniors. There are fewer of these, though there are also fewer refugee elders than children within the community. While the needs of seniors are distinct from those of refugee youth, many supportive services for refugee elders can also be found in the O.N.E. Center. The Champlain Senior Center is located in the building and provides activities, food, and exercises for seniors. It is one of the few places in Vermont that I have seen where refugee elders and American seniors interact on a regular basis, often playing cards together or sharing a meal despite language barriers. The O.N.E. Center is also home to the Vermont Hindu Temple; while a one-room temple converted from a classroom during the renovation of an old Catholic school to a community center may not be quite what many Bhutanese elders envision when they think of a temple, it remains an important community space. The use of the community kitchen in the basement of the O.N.E. Center to serve Nepali cuisine to seniors and the use of community meeting rooms and a performance space to

Image 9.4 Bhutanese children performing traditional dance

teach music and dance to children have been mentioned by numerous refugee elders as signs that their culture and traditions remain vibrant (Image 9.4).

AALV has few programs that specifically work with refugee elders (though they are part of the organization's broader caseload) but the New Farms for New Americans (NFNA) program detailed in Chapter 8 has many elders enrolled as farmers in its programs. In my interviews with them, a good number of refugee elders reported that they have been involved in the agriculture program and really enjoy this, as it gets them outside, gives them something useful to do, and allows them to contribute to their family's food supply. Some have even earned a little income selling extra produce. NFNA has provided space for refugee elders to also garden on smaller plots of land, as a form of therapeutic practice. An earlier group of Vietnamese refugees have been using community gardening for just such a purpose for years (Image 9.5).

Finally, one of the most successful support programs for refugees in Vermont is the Connecting Cultures Program of the New England Survivors of Torture and Trauma. This is a psychology clinic based at the University of Vermont that has developed a successful practice with a range of refugee communities, primarily but not exclusively the Bhutanese. It is a trusted and well-utilized clinic that provides therapy

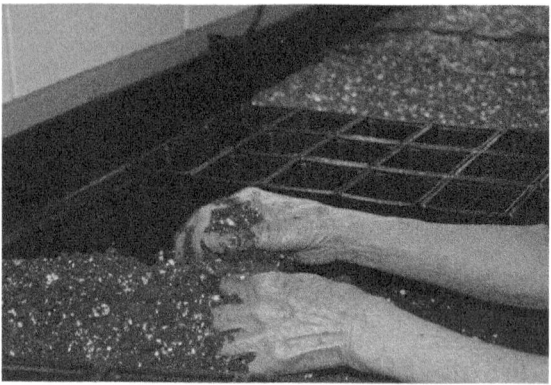

Image 9.5 Gardening as therapy

and recovery services to survivors of torture, sexual violence, substance abuse, depression, and mental illness. Connecting Cultures collaborates closely with AALV—supporting the youth group, providing its own parenting classes (including for infants and young mothers)—as well as working with physical therapy and other services to help refugees.

As I end this concluding chapter of the last section of this book, I must note that no intervention in uprooted and often broken lives may seem quick enough, full enough, and effective enough. But this sense of inadequacy is no reason for not trying. I have been heartened by the efforts made by refugee agencies, advocates, and most of all by refugees themselves to improve their conditions and their outcomes. One precondition for pragmatic planning and response is to identify crucial areas of need, and in this section I have selected three themes—transportation, food, and aging—for study as ones that illustrate the challenges that refugees in Vermont continue to face in their everyday lives as well as in the long-term course of their settlement in the US as integrated, contributing and valued members of American society. The account I present suggests that Vermont's response has been both humane and productive, its range of programs and support mechanisms showing the creativity and breadth of interventions crafted to try and address refugee needs in Vermont.

References

Beiser, Morton, and Feng Hou. 2016. Mental health effects of premigration trauma and postmigration discrimination on refugee youth in Canada. *The Journal of Nervous and Mental Disease* 204 (6): 464–470.

Bose, Pablo S. 2015. New Vermonters and perspectives on Vermont Migration. *Northeastern Geographer* 7 (2015): 89–101.

Burlington School District. 2014. *Strategic plan for diversity and equity 2014–2017*. Office of Diversity, Equity and Community Partnership. Available from http://www.bsdvt.org/wp-content/uploads/2017/07/BSD-Diversity-Plan-2014-2017.pdf.

Chenoweth, Jeff, and Laura Burdick. 2001. The path to integration: Meeting the special needs of refugee elders in resettlement. *Refuge: Canada's Journal on Refugees* 20 (1): 20–29.

Di Marzo, Nicolò, and Shiba Chapagain. 2012. Why is the resettlement in a third-country the chosen solution by the Bhutanese refugees? A personal answer to a political problem. *The Interdisciplinary Journal of International Studies* 8 (2012): 96–112.

Dubus, Nicole. 2018. Arriving old: A qualitative study of elder refugee women's self-perceptions of the first year of resettlement. *Journal of Gerontological Social Work* 61 (4): 393–410.

Flaitz, Jeffra. 2006. *Understanding your refugee and immigrant students: An educational, cultural and linguistic guide*. Ann Arbor: University of Michigan Press.

Im, Hyojin, and Jonah Neff. 2020. Spiral loss of culture: Cultural trauma and bereavement of Bhutanese refugee elders. *Journal of Immigrant and Refugee Studies*. https://doi.org/10.1080/15562948.2020.1736362.

Johnson, Jennifer, Joyce Beard, and Dena Evans. 2018. Caring for refugee youth in the school setting. *NASN School Nurse* 32 (2): 122–128.

Johnson, Shanthi, Juanita Bacsu, Tom McIntosh, Bonnie Jeffery, and Nuelle Novik. 2019. Social isolation and loneliness among immigrant and refugee seniors in Canada: A scoping review. *International Journal of Migration, Health and Social Care* 15 (3): 177–190.

Juang, Linda, Jeffry Simpson, Richard Lee, Alexander Rothman, Peter Titzmann, Maja Schachner, Lars Korn, Dorothee Heinemeier, and Cornelia Betsch. 2018. Using attachment and relational perspectives to understand adaptation and resilience among immigrant and refugee youth. *American Psychologist* 73 (6): 797–811.

Kiang, Lisa, Melissa Witkow, and Taylor Thompson. 2016. Model minority stereotyping, perceived discrimination, and adjustment among adolescents from Asian American backgrounds. *Journal of Youth and Adolescence* 45 (7): 1366–1379.

Kingston, Lindsey N., and Kathryn R. Stam. 2017. Recovering from statelessness: Resettled Bhutanese-Nepali and Karen refugees reflect on the lack of legal nationality. *Journal of Human Rights* 16 (4): 389–406.

Lewis, Denise. 2009. Aging out of place: Cambodian refugee elders in the United States. *Family and Consumer Sciences Research Journal* 37 (3): 376–393.

Mallett, Christopher. 2016. The school-to-prison pipeline: A critical review of the punitive paradigm shift. *Child and Adolescent Social Work Journal* 33 (1): 15–24.

Ranard, Donald, and Margo Pfelger (eds.). 1995. *From the classroom to the community: A fifteen-year experiment in refugee education.* McHenry, IL: Center for Applied Linguistics and Delta Systems.

Reynolds, Johanna, and Jennifer Hyndman. 2015. A turn in Canadian refugee policy and practice. *Whitehead Journal of Diplomacy and International Relations* 16 (2): 41–55.

Rizal, Dhurba. 2004. The unknown refugee crisis: Expulsion of the ethnic Lhotsampa from Bhutan. *Asian Ethnicity* 5 (2): 151–177.

Rowe, Cassandra, Rose Watson-Ormond, Lacey English, Hillary Rubesin, Ashley Marshall, Kristin Linton, Andrew Amolegbe, Christine Agnew-Brune, and Eugenia Eng. 2016. Evaluating art therapy to heal the effects of trauma among refugee youth: The Burma art therapy program evaluation. *Health Promotion Practice* 18 (1): 26–33.

RPC. 2019. Admissions and arrivals. Available from http://www.wrapsnet.org/admissions-and-arrivals/.

Scharrer, Melanie, and Fred Coleman. 2019. Culturally driven mental health care in Hmong and Cambodian refugee populations. *The American Journal of Geriatric Psychiatry* 27 (3): S102–S103.

Schneider, Lynn. 2018. Access and aspirations: Syrian refugees' experiences of entering higher education in Germany. *Research in Comparative and International Education* 13 (3): 457–478.

Seibel, Kimberly. 2016. Bureaucratic birthdates: Chronometric old age as resource and liability in US refugee resettlement. *Refuge: Canada's Journal on Refugees* 32 (3): 8–17.

State of Vermont. 2018. *Racial disparities in the criminal and juvenile justice system.* Disparities in the Criminal and Juvenile Justice System Advisory

Panel. Available from http://ago.vermont.gov/wp-content/uploads/2018/07/
RD-Panel-Minutes-June-12-2018.pdf.

Subedi, Rajendra Prasad, and Mark Warren Rosenberg. 2016. High-skilled
immigrants—Low-skilled jobs: Challenging everyday health. *The Canadian
Geographer* 60 (1): 56–68.

Türegün, Adnan, Rupaleem Bhuyan, Nancy Mandell, and John Shields. 2018.
*State of the art in research on and services for immigrant women, youth and
seniors*. Toronto: CERIS.

Winterton, Rachel, and Alana Chambers. 2017. Developing sustainable social
programmes for rural ethnic seniors: Perspectives of community stakeholders. *Health and Social Care in the Community* 25 (3): 868–877.

10

Conclusion

When I began the research that this book is based on, the world of global migration and refugee resettlement was entirely different. In 2006, refugee numbers had swollen due to the Iraq War but resettlement numbers in countries of the Global North were only slowly recovering from the cuts following 9/11. By 2009, resettlement in countries like the US had risen and stabilized, but the approach to those seeking sanctuary—refugees, asylum seekers, and irregular migrants alike—was slowly but surely changing. In 2014, the Obama administration had introduced new initiatives like the Deferred Action on Childhood Arrivals (DACA) program, stabilized and expanded the US Refugee Admissions Program (USRAP), and the Temporary Protected Status Program (TPS), and focused immigration detention and deportation policies on violent criminals. But 2015 bore witness to a sea change in the perception and treatment of forced migrants, not only in the US but across the world. This was the first year that the growing number of forced migrants globally began to reach a broader public consciousness, first in light of the sheer number of people undertaking increasingly risky journeys across land and sea to reach supposedly safer shores, and later in the chaos and instability that the influx caused in countries near and

© The Author(s) 2020
P. S. Bose, *Refugees in New Destinations and Small Cities*,
https://doi.org/10.1007/978-981-15-6386-7_10

far. Between 2010 and 2020, the number of those displaced worldwide has more than doubled.

In 2015, the plight of those forced to flee their homes and livelihoods was met initially by increasing generosity in the countries of the global refugee regime (primarily in the Global North), with many moved to take action by the sight of iconic images as that of the drowned body of Syrian toddler Alan Kurdi and donate to refugee organizations and pledge support to those fleeing. But by November 2015, a spate of terrorist violence—often falsely associated with refugees—brought suspicion and a backlash against those fleeing. A rising tide of xenophobia and right-wing populism saw multiple political movements and elections that placed migrants, immigrants, and refugees at the center of political, economic, and cultural anxieties about demographic change, racial and ethnic relations, and questions regarding identity, nationalism, and borders. The Brexit vote, the US Presidential election, the influx of migrants and elections in France, Sweden, Germany, and many other places soon became referenda about global migration as much as they were about domestic and national politics.

In the US, the eventual election of Donald Trump did not signal something new about xenophobia and anti-immigrant sentiment in the country; one might argue that such views are as old as the country itself. But at least in the contemporary moment, the ascension of the Trump administration has meant enormous changes in the existing policies and approaches to forced migration that the US federal government has adopted. For refugees, it has meant a halt to their arrival, a coarsening of the discourse surrounding their daily lives, and further separation and alienation from families, friends, and communities elsewhere. In 2020, as the world slowly shudders still in the grip of the worst global pandemic in a century, refugee movements too come to a halt, as borders reappear and are hardened, countries attempt to retreat into themselves and close themselves off to the foreign born, and even the UNHCR and IOM stop refugee travel.

But what have the lives of refugees been before as well as during this particular moment? More than 3 million refugees have arrived in the US since the 1970s. In more recent decades, many of them have been settled in smaller cities and sites outside traditional metropolitan regions like

New York, San Francisco, and Chicago that have long been the hallmarks of immigrant destinations. What do the lives of these people and their children look like? What has resettlement meant for them? And what has it meant for the communities that have received them? To explore such questions more deeply I have looked in this book at the local scale, at the state of Vermont and at a number of refugee communities and cities across it. Vermont is a small state and one of the whitest in the US, known for its natural beauty, agricultural heritage and its seemingly liberal sensibilities exemplified by its 'celebrities' like Bernie Sanders. What does it mean to be a refugee from Vietnam, Bosnia, Bhutan or Iraq to be settled in a place like this and to try and build a life here?

In *Refugees in the Green Mountain State: Immigration and Resettlement in Vermont*, I have explored this question from the perspective of both the refugee communities who have been resettled and of the various groups that have received them—service providers, civic officials, and local residents among them. The conceptual frameworks of my discussions are drawn from multiple scholarly traditions primarily in the social sciences—geography, sociology, anthropology, political science and history among them. My own lens in this book is primarily spatial— how has the influx of new people changed the landscape—of farming, of neighborhoods, of schools, of businesses, of the state and its historically semi-rural and decentralized character?

As such, this book adds to a growing list of studies that attempt to engage with these profound changes that affect global migration policies and practices and at the same time play out at the local level. Many such titles focus on legal frameworks and obligations (Singh Juss 2019; Freedman 2015; Nayak 2015; McAdam 2012) and the composition of different refugee communities (Hugo et al. 2018) while others look at the growth in immigration detention and securitization (Loyd and Mountz 2018; Fiske 2016). Some scholars have focused on the ways that refugees have been integrated (or not) into their new host communities, especially in Europe (Pries 2018; Asgary 2019) and North America (Poteet and Nourpanah 2016). In the US, such studies have focused on Southeast Asian refugees (Chan 2004; Hein 2006) as well as other groups (Bloemraad 2006; Haines 2012; Chambers 2017; Feuerherm and Ramanathan 2016). Relatively, few have looked specifically at the urban context of resettlement (Bauder 2019; Bagelman 2016). These books, however, represent a small fraction of the work on refugee resettlement and migration, which is often dominated by studies of legal obligation, human rights, and political discourse and dynamics. Where the literature has focused on the everyday lives of migrants, they have tended to focus on other forms of migration than refugees—undocumented immigrants in the US or transnational diasporas, for example.

In this book, I have taken a different approach, exploring the lives of refugees after their arrival in a specific location in the US, one that is marked not by long histories of immigrant settlement (as in traditional destinations like New York, Chicago, or San Francisco), but by its relatively recent emergence as a place undergoing significant demographic and cultural change. I have drawn in this book on extensive qualitative research with a range of informants—refugees, advocacy organizations, local and state officials, and various other stakeholder groups—in order to understand not only the politics and history of resettlement in Vermont, but the lived realities of daily existence as well.

In the first section of this book, I have explored the contexts of these newcomers to the state—what forced migration looks like across the globe today, how the refugee resettlement program in the US works, and how placements in the US have been organized since the inception of the USRAP. I have also detailed the history of migration into Vermont and what the attitude of the general population of the state has been toward the arrivals. In the second section, I have looked at the impact of refugee arrivals on three specific towns of three specific types—a small city (Burlington), a small suburban town (Winooski), and a rustbelt city that planned for an expansion but ultimately did not become a resettlement community (Rutland). All three are emblematic of resettlement sites across the US—small cities that have benefited from refugee resettlement (or hoped to) and that have been swept up in different ways by the ongoing and raging controversies regarding the welcome of immigrants. In the final section of the book, I have turned to the refugees themselves (though their voices are also present throughout) to try and understand what their embodied experiences of arrival in a new land have been. What I have learned—about the possibilities and obstacles that greater or more limited mobility affords them, how access to familiar tastes through ethnic grocery stores, restaurants and farming practices builds resilience and cultural ties, and how the particular processes of aging for young and older refugees have distinct trajectories—tell us much about the ways that refugees and Vermont are reshaping one another.

But the story I have told in these pages is not meant to be a parochial one. *Refugees in the Green Mountain State* details particular cases in Vermont, but the narratives I refer to here have echoes in many other places and contexts across the world. This book thus builds on the work of many other researchers and seeks to answer questions that are at the heart of debates regarding immigration across the country and in many parts of the globe. What are the economic impacts of new arrivals, how do refugees adjust to new lives, how do their children do in school, and how do the cities that receive them adjust to unfamiliar faces? These are important questions not only for researchers, but also for urban planners and civic leaders, for policymakers, and for residents in each of these communities, in different countries and different regions. Perhaps the most widely overarching question is, what is the future for those who have been forced out of their homes, their worlds?

I learned many lessons as a result of my research and have disseminated them not only through scholarly venues, but in collaboration with my community partners as widely as possible. My hope is to move as much as possible beyond the ideological and political dogmas that make intervention in the politics of immigration seem so hopeless at times. It is perhaps a naïve aspiration, but I hope that this work provides balanced and nuanced evidence for data-driven policymaking and information that helps to improve the lives of refugees, the communities that they are settled into, and the nation as a whole. In particular, I hope that there are lessons that others may take from the example of Vermont and its resettlement communities, lessons that are echoed in other places as well.

For example, it is clear from my work in Vermont that for smaller cities outside the traditional 'gateway' destinations (like New York, Chicago, or San Francisco) to which immigrants have always come, refugees represent an important source of new arrivals and civic renewal. In many of the cities I studied and visited—especially in rural regions, in so-called rustbelt areas, or places with aging populations—refugees are an important source of labor, skills, and diversity. For many towns grappling with declining tax bases and the loss of population (through aging or out-migration of youth, for example), refugees are often seen as a 'lifeline' to renewed growth. In this book, I have shown the most positive outcomes of this dynamic in the cases of Burlington and Winooski and a negative one in the case of Rutland.

It is also apparent that the outcomes for the refugees themselves can be a more mixed one. On the one hand, I found high levels of local support for most resettlement programs within the towns they are located, and indeed at the state level as in the case of Vermont. On the other hand, some of these communities have little experience with immigrant integration and thus have not always able to deliver necessary services. And as the last three chapters have shown, obstacles to full participation and integration for refugees in their new homes is often hampered by a lack of opportunity, by culture clashes, by the challenges of new systems, and by racism and poverty. In particular, the mismatch between refugee skills (including advanced skills in fields of healthcare and engineering) and initial job placements (especially in low-wage manufacturing, agriculture, and domestic labor) is a potential waste of human capital.

If refugee resettlement is to continue to place newcomers into newer destinations (and this is of course a challenge hard even to imagine in the context of the US and the world in 2020), more resources must be dedicated to long-term integration rather than short-term adjustment, as is the current model. Successful immigration outcomes need to be viewed and planned for in the five-to-ten year rather than one-to-two-year range. The private sponsorship model utilized to great success by the Canadian government for resettling a large number of Syrian refugees in 2016–2017 should be explored as a way of building a robust and deep network of local allies and supports for newcomers. Additionally, for smaller communities there should be more investment by federal and state governments in education and housing opportunities. Employment services and healthcare access are already important aspects of resettlement programs but along with education and housing, access to adequate transportation is a key determinant of successful outcomes.

Finally, we found refugee newcomers in Vermont to be especially enthusiastic and civic-minded; as some of the results from my Photovoice project in Burlington and Winooski highlight, refugees have strong opinions and suggestions for how the neighborhoods in which they live can be improved. These new arrivals evince high levels of engagement—volunteering for community events, participating in recreational activities, getting involved with their children's education, studying English diligently, and showing an eagerness to vote once eligible. Refugee resettlement in Vermont—and in the rest of the country—should not be feared. Instead, it should be and indeed can be seen as an ideal program for welcoming active and vibrant new residents and to help revitalize the many places in many parts of the world that urgently need an infusion of fresh faces, new ideas, and new energy.

References

Asgary, Ali (ed.). 2019. *Resettlement challenges for displaced populations and refugees*. Cham: Springer.

Bagelman, Jennifer. 2016. *Sanctuary city: A suspended state*. New York: Palgrave Macmillan.

Bauder, Harald (ed.). 2019. *Sanctuary cities and urban struggles: Rescaling migration, citizenship and rights*. Oxford: Oxford University Press.

Bloemraad, Irene. 2006. *Becoming a citizen: Incorporating immigrants and refugees in the United States and Canada*. Berkeley: University of California Press.

Chambers, Stefanie. 2017. *Somalis in the Twin Cities and Columbus: Immigrant incorporation in new destinations*. Philadelphia: Temple University Press.

Chan, Sucheng. 2004. *Survivors: Cambodian Refugees in the United States*. Urbana and Chicago: University of Illinois.

Feuerherm, Emily, and Vaidehi Ramanathan (eds.). 2016. *Refugee resettlement in the United States: Language, policy, pedagogy*. Bristol: Channel View Publications.

Fiske, Lucy. 2016. *Human rights, refugee protest and immigration detention*. Cheltenham: Edward Elgar.

Freedman, Jane. 2015. *Gendering the international asylum and refugee debate*, 2nd ed. New York: Palgrave Macmillan.

Haines, David. 2012. *Safe haven? A history of refugees in America*. Sterling, VA: Kumarian Press.

Hein, Jeremy. 2006. *Ethnic origins: The adaptation of Cambodian and Hmong refugees in four American cities*. New York: Russell Sage Foundation.

Hugo, Graeme, Mohammad Jalal Abbasi-Shavazi, and Ellen Percy Kraly. 2018. *Demography of refugee and forced migration*. Cham: Springer.

Loyd, Jenna, and Alison Mountz. 2018. *Boats, borders and bases: Race, the Cold War and the rise of migration detention in the United States*. Oakland: University of California Press.

Mcadam, Jane. 2012. *Climate change, forced migration, and international law*. Oxford: Oxford University Press.

Nayak, Meghana. 2015. *Who is worthy of protection? Gender-based asylum and US immigration politics*. Oxford: Oxford University Press.

Poteet, Morgan, and Shiva Nourpanah (eds.). 2016. *After the flight: The dynamics of refugee settlement and integration*. Newcastle-upon-Tyne: Cambridge Scholars Publishing.

Pries, Ludger. 2018. *Refugees, civil society and the state: European experiences and global challenges*. Cheltenham: Edward Elgar.

Singh Juss, Satvinder (ed.). 2019. *Research handbook on international refugee law*. Cheltenham: Edward Elgar.

Index

Voluntary Agency (VOLAG) 39–43

CPI Antony Rowe
Eastbourne, UK
September 23, 2020